IRELAND SINCE 1800
Conflict and Conformity

K. Theodore Hoppen

Longman
London and New York

LONGMAN GROUP UK LIMITED
Longman House, Burnt Mill, Harlow,
Essex CM20 2JE, England
and Associated Companies throughout the world

Published in the United States of America
by Longman Inc., New York

© Longman Group UK Limited 1989

First published 1989

BRITISH LIBRARY CATALOGUING IN PUBLICATION DATA
Hoppen, K. Theodore, *1941–*
    Ireland since 1800 : conflict and
    conformity. —— (Studies in modern
    history).
    1. Ireland – 1800–
    I. Title   II. Series
    941.5081
ISBN 0-582-03938-X CSD
ISBN 0-582-00473-X PPR

LIBRARY OF CONGRESS CATALOGING-IN-PUBLICATION DATA
Hoppen, K. Theodore, 1941–
    Ireland since 1800 : conflict and conformity/
    K. Theodore Hoppen.
       p.   cm. —— (Studies in modern history)
    Bibliography: p.
    Includes index.
    ISBN 0–582–03938–X
    ISBN 0–582–00473–X (pbk.)
    1. Ireland—History—19th century.
    2. Ireland—History—20th century.
    I. Title.   II. Series: Studies
    in modern history (Longman (Firm))
    DA950.H685 1989
    941.508—dc19   88–21874
                                                             CIP
Set in Linotron 202 10/12 Baskerville

Produced by Longman Singapore Publishers (Pte) Ltd.
Printed in Singapore

Contents

v

List of Tables

For

Leo and Anne van Brussel

Preface

This book is presented as an examination of the main aspects of Irish history since 1800. Had unlimited space been available I could have dealt with a greater range of topics and done so in more detail. Comparative brevity, if properly used, has, however, the advantage of forcing one to look more directly for the bones beneath the skin. I can only hope that some at least of my anatomizing will prove interesting to the reader.

Clearly any study of this kind depends heavily upon the work of others. The Irish past has, in recent years, attracted much talented writing from scholars in all parts of the world. If I have plundered the resulting treasure store with the unstoppable enthusiasm of a kleptomaniac, any other course would have been both self-defeating and absurd. I hope that the references given in the text will be allowed to act as repeated recognitions, however inadequate, of what is owed to my fellow labourers in the Hibernian fields.

A few individuals have, however, done so much that their names must be recorded here. As always Angus Macintyre's generous support provided encouragement when it was most needed. James Donnelly too proved a tower of strength. David Cannadine was a splendidly reassuring general editor. A blissful year as Benjamin Duke fellow at the National Humanities Center in North Carolina, though spent largely on another project, gave me time to think about historical matters in general. I owe much to Charles Blitzer and Kent Mullikin for smoothing my path and also to conversations with other fellows of 'the class of '85–6'. Of course none of these should be regarded as partners in any interpretative or other crimes which may still, despite their best efforts, continue to lurk in the pages that follow.

The love and scholarly sympathy of my wife, Alison, were, once again, given in unending measure, while our children – Martha, Katherine, and Theo – proved themselves to be reliable orchestrators of those 'displacement activities' for which all writers secretly crave. The dedication of this book to my uncle and aunt acknowledges a debt of gratitude and love which I can never hope to repay.

K. T. H.

True, I agree that, in its way, 'two and
two make four' is an excellent notion;
yet, to give everything its due,
the formula 'twice two makes five'
is not without its attractions.

Fyodor Dostoyevsky,
Notes from Underground (1864)

Boundaries of provinces
County boundaries
Northern Ireland

0   50 mls
0   50 km

DONEGAL

Derry

LONDONDERRY

ANTRIM

Ballymena

TYRONE

Omagh

Belfast

ULSTER

FERMANAGH

Enniskillen

Armagh

Downpatrick

DOWN

ARMAGH

Sligo

SLIGO

LEITRIM

Monaghan

MONAGHAN

MAYO

Carrick
on Shannon

Cavan

CAVAN

Dundalk

Castlebar

ROSCOMMON

Longford

LOUTH

Roscommon

LONGFORD

MEATH

CONNACHT

Mullingar

WESTMEATH

DUBLIN

GALWAY

Galway

OFFALY
(King's
County)

LEINSTER

Dublin

Naas

CLARE

Ennis

Nenagh

LAOIS
(QUEEN'S
COUNTY)

KILDARE

Wicklow

WICKLOW

Carlow

Limerick

TIPPERARY

Kilkenny

CARLOW

WEXFORD

LIMERICK

KILKENNY

Tralee

Clonmel

Wexford

KERRY

MUNSTER

CORK

WATERFORD

Waterford

Dungarvan

WATERFORD

Cork

Introduction

The interpretation of Irish history constitutes so remarkable a battlefield in large part because modern Ireland, 'like Dracula's Transylvania', has long been 'much troubled by the undead' (Stewart 1977: 15). Since at least the seventeenth century almost every group with an axe to grind has thought it imperative to control the past in order to provide support for contemporary arguments and ideologies. Indeed, historical allusions still do such sterling duty in sharpening antagonisms that sometimes it seems as if time itself has lost the power to separate the centuries. No local reader in 1980 of Ian Paisley's *Protestant Telegraph* could, for example, have harboured any doubts as to either the meaning or the source of the staccato headline: 'The Pope's Order, Murder Queen Elizabeth' (Hickey 1984: 67).[1]

By the time of the Act of Union in 1800 polemical writers on both the Catholic and the Protestant side agreed on only one thing: that the purpose of history was to teach political lessons (McCartney 1957: 352). If, however, the approach, with its emphasis upon history as a repository of 'sacred truth' (Hill 1988: 128–9), was similar, the stories that it produced were often very different indeed. The controversy over Catholic Emancipation in the 1820s generated one version of Irish history from supporters of reform, quite another from those on the opposite side. Soon the past was being used simply as a mirror to reflect the changing (or frequently the changeless) preconceptions of a wide variety of contemporary gladiators: nationalist and unionist, liberal and conservative, constitutional and revolutionary.

For Catholics there was one kind of St Patrick, for Protestants another. Both groups claimed to be the legitimate successors of an

1

early Celtic church whose nature was constantly adjusted to suit nineteenth- or twentieth-century circumstances (Hill 1988: 120). The Young Irelanders of the 1840s, with their intellectual debt to German romanticism, added image to argument and adopted a historical iconography of lasting power and force: harps, shamrocks, sunbursts, and pictures of 'revolutionary' patriarchs such as Brian Boru, Owen Roe O'Neill, and Patrick Sarsfield (Sheehy 1980: 37–9). While the membership cards of Daniel O'Connell's political associations had at first been 'as bare of sentiment as the price list of a commercial traveller', under the influence of the Young Irelanders 'new cards were issued which . . . blossomed into poetry and history' (Gavan Duffy 1884: 80).

At the time such things were, of course, by no means confined to Ireland. English historians waged bitter war concerning the relative merits of Normans and Anglo-Saxons. German scholars sought to assuage longings for political unity by creating a historical unity of the mind. Yet in Ireland a quasi-colonial situation combined with certain deep changes produced by the collapse of the Irish language and of Gaelic cultural norms allowed this kind of romanticism to render itself particularly indispensable to nationalist ideologies of almost every kind.

Before the Great Famine of the late 1840s the ballads sold in sheets and sung at markets and fairs, while including much conventional praise for heroes like O'Connell, often expressed a Gaelic savagery which owed everything to an urgent overwhelming desire for immediate violent revenge upon landlords, agents, parsons, police, and other contemporary representatives of economic and political power. Within two decades, as English increased its linguistic grip, much of this had vanished, driven out by more 'literate' and overtly nationalist songs derived from Young Ireland models (Murphy 1979a; Hoppen 1984: 424–9). Indeed, by the 1880s it was being noted that a new kind of literature which had, in the 1840s, been published primarily to create a novel political consciousness, was now being produced as a commercial speculation – a certain sign of its increasing popularity in home, library, railway bookstall, and emigrant ship alike (Pope Hennessy 1884).

Much of this – the ballads, the histories of A. M. Sullivan, the *Memoirs* of Wolfe Tone, John Mitchel's *Jail Journal* – was 'historical' in mode and, by introducing an overt, rather than merely a latent, nationalism into the ideological arena, ensured that history would henceforth become the first port of call for all those with a political point to make. By the beginning of the present century both nationalists and unionists had each constructed a self-contained theatre of the past in which to play out current aspirations against backdrops painted to represent the triumphs of former times. History, indeed, had been rendered so infinitely malleable that it could be pressed into almost any shape at all. Protestants 'used' it to confirm their own schizophrenic desire to be British and Irish at the same time. Catholics saw no contradiction in emphasizing one version of the past when it suited them to count 'non-Catholics' their fellow countrymen and quite another when engaged in making Irish nationalism into 'an expression of the felt needs, social and psychological, of the Irish Catholic body, including the apparent need to challenge other Christians on the island in various ways' (Comerford 1985: 30; Boyce 1982).

With the establishment in the early 1920s of both the Free State and a devolved polity in Northern Ireland the respective 'historical myths' of nationalism and Ulster unionism became at once institutionalized and strengthened by the realization of successful revolution in one part of Ireland and successful reaction in the other. And any subsequent weakening of the electric charge then generated has in turn been reversed by the violent events which have taken place over the last twenty years. So much so, that 'nowhere else in the European, North American or antipodean democracies does the writing of twentieth-century [or, indeed, earlier] history demand so constant a confrontation with mythologies designed to legitimise violence as a political weapon in a bid to overthrow the state' (Fanning 1986a: 142).

As a result, the explosion of scholarly research which has been so marked a feature of recent decades has had virtually no effect at all upon political attitudes, whether in Ireland, Kilburn, Boston, 'Fleet Street', Downing Street, or Whitehall. Curiously enough this is not because the findings of academic historians have always been *necessarily* hostile to nationalist (or unionist) beliefs as such. Indeed, it could be argued that an increased emphasis upon the complexity of the past is entirely compatible with a richer, fuller, and more authentic nationalism capable of articulating reality rather than illusion.

What, therefore, seems to have happened is that the inevitable subtleties of scholarship have, in themselves, made adjustment virtually impossible. The 'depressing lesson is probably that "history" as conceived by scholars is a different concept to "history" as understood at large, where "myth" is probably the best, if over-used, anthropological term' (Foster 1983: 192). In other words, though popular political attitudes have often been expressed in a manner which seems to be 'historical', this is so only in the superficial sense that references to past events are involved. For many people it is, indeed, the approach adopted by the writers of the early nineteenth century which still holds sway and, by virtue of having done so for almost two hundred years, gives continued energy to sectarian attitudes of unyielding resonance and power.

Such things have made the writing of modern Irish history rather like negotiating a minefield. Yet the enterprise must continue, for any other course would amount, quite simply, to an unforgivable *trahison des clercs*.

The approach of the present book is plain enough: to interpret the most significant specialist work of recent years without becoming entrapped in merely historiographical analysis, to avoid that academic self-congratulation which has occasionally reared its unattractive head, and to present a point of view that is neither perverse nor banal. The chapters have been designed so as to allow a coherent discussion of the three key aspects of the subject – the political, the social (and economic), and the religious – without, however, making it impossible to retain a sense of the importance of chronology and time. If the order in which the chapters appear is different in the second section from that in the others, this is not the result of any preoccupation with the primacy of economic structures in general, but because agrarianism and the land question provided the motor for political action during the later nineteenth century in a manner not true in Ireland of the periods immediately before or since.

The book has both explicit and implicit themes. The latter, as indicated in the title, chiefly concern the fluctuating relationship between two key phenomena of Irish political and cultural life over the last two centuries and more, namely, conflict and conformity. On the one hand, conflict of all kinds – among neighbours, within families, between social groups, between nationalists and unionists, between rulers and ruled – forms a kind of rolling base to much of what happened in the years since 1800. Yet, on the other, its course was paralleled by a marked growth of conformity in many important departments of experience such as religion and cultural behaviour in the broadest sense. By the beginning of the present century Ireland had become both a more 'modern' and a more conformist place. The churches exercised a more obvious impact upon the nature of accepted norms. A conscious sense of decorum pervaded society at large. Even conflict itself followed a narrower and more disciplined choreography than in pre-Famine times. Indeed, it was precisely this refashioning of conflict by conformity which helped to make possible those new manifestations of politics and ideology associated with the revolutionaries of 1916 and after.

Explicit themes congregate around the notion that, in all periods since 1800, there has existed a very wide gap indeed between rhetoric and reality. Men and women did not, it is clear, behave politically as mere pawns in some great game played out by O'Connell or Parnell or Carson or Pearse. Nor did they simply constitute anonymous elements in a drama whose course and conclusion were predestined by economic forces, by the imperatives of nationalism, or even by God himself. They had and have still an individual dignity of their own as well as particular desires, immediate perspectives, pragmatic hopes. And because of this it was not always the stated programmes of leaders which in fact brought about such mobilizations as took place.

The more one looks behind surface appearances the less simple do things become. Rural society did not consist exclusively of heroic farmers battling against a united set of landed demon kings. Agrarian movements were often riven by bitter internal disputes. Neither Catholic nor Protestant ecclesiastics were ever united as to political action or ideology. At times, indeed, only liberal doses of rhetoric could paper over the cracks which again and again opened up within the Repeal movement, the Home Rule movement, the Land War, the Plan of Campaign, the Ulster Unionist Party, the Ranch War of 1906–9, the struggle for independence after 1916, and the various groups involved in political life after the Anglo-Irish Treaty of 1921. To talk, therefore, about the 'Irish people' can be profoundly misleading. The Land War, to take just one example, involved, not an undifferentiated 'people', but individuals who saw themselves primarily as members of family groups and local communities and next perhaps as large graziers, middling farmers, small tenants, cottiers, landless labourers, shopkeepers, moneylenders, professional men, landlords of all sorts, agents, parish priests, curates – the list could be extended almost for ever.

Given that such is the case it is a matter of particular concern that no work of this kind, dealing as it does with almost two hundred years, can even begin to give adequate recognition to the many-sidedness of historical experience. Above all, I regret not having been able to present more of the flavour of lived lives – an aspect of history too readily dismissed as mere antiquarian shapelessness. In this respect creative literature of all kinds is

5

especially valuable for the insights it can sometimes furnish into the everyday worlds of relaxation, amusement, humour, grief, and bereavement, for we are all born and we all die even though we do not all shout for party leaders or exercise much power over other people. Thus the short stories of William Carleton and the novels of Maria Edgeworth and Gerald Griffin reveal much about certain aspects of Irish experience in the half-century before the Famine that is missing in blue books, polemical pamphlets, or collections of official documents.[2] And the same is true for later periods also, where, to pick just one work at random, David Thomson's autobiographical *Woodbrook* of 1974 displays the unravelled fibres of gentry life in the 1930s in a peculiarly convincing way.

Historians, however, should not be surprised at the ragged incompleteness which is all that their versions of the past can achieve. Nor is it to be wondered at that in Ireland's complicated story two and two so often seem to add up to five or sometimes even to six. Perhaps, in the end, one can only hope that some at least will be encouraged by what they read here to move on towards an engagement with those deeper truths about Ireland and the Irish which no mere historian can even begin to express.

NOTES

1. The headline was occasioned by the three-hundredth anniversary of Pope Gregory XIII's granting of a plenary indulgence to all who would take up arms against Queen Elizabeth I.
2. Especially Carleton's *Traits and Stories of the Irish Peasant;ry* (1830–3), Edgeworth's *Castle Rackrent* (1800), and Griffin's *The Collegians* (1829).

PART ONE

Limbering Up: From Union to Famine

CHAPTER 1
Politics

O'Connell: Innovation and Ambiguity

The nature of political life in early-nineteenth-century Ireland derived its particular flavour from the fact that conflict between those defending and those challenging the *status quo* was beginning to be conducted in a new way. But if this represented an innovation then the simultaneous survival of older forms of action and discourse meant that the ensuing reality was neither simple nor unambiguous. Almost every interest was engaged upon an attempt to rescue something from the wreckage of the 1798 rebellion and the consequent Act of Union of 1800, for these together constituted that remarkable equation – a defeat for almost everyone and a victory for almost nobody at all.

I

The political and economic ascendancy of the landed classes had reached its peak about the middle of the eighteenth century (Cullen 1985: 94), but from then onwards was increasingly challenged by a growing urban and trading middle class (which included many successful Catholic merchants). Simultaneously a widening rural unrest manifested itself through the activities of agrarian secret societies – first specifically and then generically known as Whiteboyism – which, though not aimed at landed proprietors alone, helped to destabilize the existing political culture in at first minor and then more serious ways. Furthermore, the various measures of Catholic relief passed by the exclusively Protestant Irish parliament in 1778, 1782, 1792, and 1793, which broadly

9

allowed Catholics to hold land in the normal way and eventually granted them the vote, were actually imposed by the British government, so that articulate Catholics began more and more to see London rather than Dublin as the source of reform and political amelioration. But revolutionary events in North America and France encouraged those of more radical tendencies to look to new shifts and expedients.

The Society of United Irishmen established in 1791 as the chief focus for such aspirations was and remained an eclectic organization. Increasingly revolutionary – and as a consequence losing a good deal of moderate support – it contained representatives of the three major religious traditions in Ireland: Roman Catholic, Church of Ireland (Anglican), and Presbyterian. While much of its remembered rhetoric tended to stress the unity of all Irishmen, the various elements within it sustained distinctive and not always reconcilable ambitions, so that, for example, many Protestant United Irishmen looked to the establishment of an Irish republic in which they would play the dominant role regardless of the insistent fact that four-fifths of their fellow-countrymen were Roman Catholics. Even those who thought like Theobald Wolfe Tone, the young Protestant lawyer who in 1792 became assistant secretary to the Catholic Committee (a body seeking greater political rights for the genteel sections of the Catholic community), were by no means innocent of such aspirations. But what Tone and others had come to realize was that effective revolution was impossible without mass support. It was, therefore, in part at least a sense of *Realpolitik* which persuaded them to overcome their aversion of the Catholic 'lower orders' – 'the Irish properly so called' in Tone's revealing phrase (Boyce 1982: 128) – and seek to connect their own movement with the gathering discontents of that great threatening backdrop to the febrile debates of the revolutionary intellectuals – the Irish countryside.

The Whiteboy-type unrest which had existed since the early 1760s in the South of Ireland (Donnelly 1977-8; 1978; 1983a) was, however, almost entirely concerned with specific local issues: rents, the availability of potato ground for labourers, tithes, evictions, even the dues levied by the Catholic clergy upon their parishioners. Though obviously a disruptive force it fired its ammunition in too many directions at once and was generally strongest in those parts of Munster and Leinster where the United Irishmen were few and far between. However, in the mid-1780s there appeared a somewhat different movement in that frontier area of southern

Ulster where, almost uniquely, Catholics and Protestants both constituted significant elements within the population. Here efforts by the gentry in Armagh to mobilize poorer Protestants by giving them weapons intermeshed with economic discontent among local weavers and sectarian disputes over land to produce an explosion of widespread unrest (Miller 1983). Protestant organizations such as the Peep-of-Day Boys and Catholic groups like the Defenders effectively combined elements of Whiteboyism with distinctly sectarian attitudes. In addition, while the Defenders undoubtedly articulated notions of political revolution well before their association with the United Irishmen began around 1795, they did so in a traditionally Catholic manner which derived its inspiration from memories of earlier land confiscations rather than from Paine, France, or the new America. Above all, they generally aspired to Catholic dominance (rather than mere equality), while the United Irishmen tended to envisage a republic in which Catholics would – for a time at least – continue to play an inferior role.

Although, therefore, the simultaneous development at all social levels of a bitter Protestant reaction, notably in the shape of the Orange Order founded in 1795, helped to push Defenders and United Irishmen together, the unresolved tensions of that alliance and a vigorous military response by the government ensured the failure of the revolutionary enterprise. It is in any case important not to exaggerate the clarity of purpose of those involved. Many rank-and-file Defenders knew little of republics and cared less. Some merely wanted arms, others were motivated by the possibility of exciting activity for its own sake – a strand of attraction generated by almost all contemporary political or quasi-political organizations. Indeed, the fluidity of the whole business is revealed in the way in which members of even such antagonistic bodies as the Orange Order and the United Irishmen could sometimes happily switch from one to the other, as occurred so dramatically in various parts of the country during and after the year 1796 (Curtin 1985: 492).

As it happened, government arrests and internal contradictions combined to ensure that the rebellion which broke out in May 1798 'was not a United Irish one . . . but a protective popular uprising which a spent United Irish leadership failed to harness' (Elliott 1982: 166). Indeed, in a very real sense, the whole business is best described, not as a single rising at all but more as a series of separate incidents based upon a kaleidoscope of local issues and imperatives. Whether this had always been the likely outcome remains a matter of debate. Certainly the problems involved in

11

achieving any kind of all-Ireland mobilization were substantial from the very start and grew ever more so during the two years before 1798. While those with some kind of interest in rebellion were numerous enough, their disaffections consisted of materials not easily coordinated and reconciled. The United Irish societies of Dublin and Belfast developed along very different lines. The former, essentially a propagandist debating club whose members' dramatic references to contemporary France disguised a firm adherence to the constitutional theories of Locke in preference to the democratic arguments of Thomas Paine, proved quite unable to establish daughter societies elsewhere in the South. By contrast, the Belfast society, made up largely of Presbyterian merchants and linen drapers, stood at the centre of a network of similar bodies spread throughout the eastern and central parts of Ulster (Dickson 1987: 182-7). Again, the Catholic Defenders of Armagh and the surrounding areas – though temporarily integrated into the United Irish structure during 1795 and 1796 – depended upon sectarianism for much of their motivation and coherence and were thus significantly distinct from the more single-mindedly agrarian secret societies of the rural South.

What however, in the end, torpedoed the chances of success was the way in which government repression succeeded in delaying things until the optimum moment for action had irretrievably passed away. In addition, the bad weather which prevented General Hoche's substantial French expedition from landing at Bantry Bay in December 1796 was undoubtedly a heavy blow, while the death shortly thereafter of Hoche himself (the leader of the pro-Irish party in Paris) deprived Tone of his main supporter in revolutionary France. With the help of an augmented militia and the mobilization in October 1796 of an overwhelmingly Protestant yeomanry the government was able to undermine the organizational coherence of the United Irish system in North and South alike. By late 1797 most of its leaders had either been arrested or had fled abroad. Among their followers the long months of delay had seriously damaged morale just at the time when military counter-measures, now more overtly Orange than ever, were heightening religious tensions as the yeomanry briskly burned down Catholic chapels in southern Ulster and raised the sectarian temperature all round (Dickson 1987: 190-1).

Ominously the centres of revolt in May and June 1798 were located in Wexford and parts of south-eastern Ulster – both of them regions containing substantial numbers of Protestants *and* Catholics

(Cullen 1981: 210-33). However, the revolutionary contacts between the two areas proved virtually non-existent. Indeed, the rebellion(s) of 1798, though initially planned to demonstrate an essential unity among Irishmen of every belief and station in life, ended up by revealing the exact opposite. Neither the savage peasant populism that marked the Wexford rising nor the biblical millenarianism that, in the event, encouraged some northern Presbyterians to take part owed much to the United Irishmen. The hoped-for French help arrived too late, though General Humbert's tiny thousand-strong army which landed in County Mayo in August showed what might have been achieved with larger forces more carefully despatched. The government received a severe fright, but emerged triumphant in the end. Tone was captured and committed suicide in prison having proved unable to ride the tiger he had so desperately attempted to mount.

While possibly as many as 50,000 men 'turned out' during 1798 – something of undoubted significance – they left their homes to fight for causes so different and contradictory that their actions almost certainly widened rather than narrowed the existing divisions of Irish society, above all those between Protestant and Catholic and between North and South. And the savage reprisals which followed rubbed yet further salt into the fissured wounds thus so dramatically deepened and displayed. In the longer term the effects of all this were of profound importance for Irish politics. The secular republicanism of Tone, though not entirely destroyed, was to survive largely through the muffled and garbled filter produced by the sectarian concerns of the Defender tradition. As a result Irish republicanism became an extremely eclectic phenomenon from which almost all groups could pick what they wanted and reject what they disliked. Humanitarian philosophy jostled with sectarian triumphalism. References to 'the common name of Irishman' were intermingled with religiously exclusive attitudes. Social grievances coexisted with ideas of national independence. But 'if there was something in it to appeal to everyone, there was also much in it to repel everyone' (Boyce 1982: 131). And it was towards the working-out of these ambiguities that the politics of the ensuing century were in part to be directed.

The immediate consequence of 1798 was the passing two years later of the Act of Union (McCartney 1987: 1-25). Although at first resisted by a superficially curious alliance of Orangemen (who feared it would expose their sectarian activities to a wider and less sympathetic imperial gaze), old-style Protestant 'patriots' (who still cherished notions of colonial nationalism), and office-holders (who were simply worried about their perquisites), Pitt's administration forced the relevant legislation through the Irish parliament by combining the carrot of patronage with the stick of fear. Catholics on the whole supported the measure because the government promised that emancipation (specifically the right of Catholics to sit in the new United Kingdom parliament) would soon follow. But before long these positions were dramatically reversed as the Protestant ascendancy clung ever closer to Britain for support and the Catholics became restless when emancipation failed to materialize.

The details of the union were simple enough. With the Dublin parliament abolished a hundred Irish MPs, twenty-eight Irish peers, and four Church of Ireland bishops would sit at Westminster. Provisions were made for the eventual merging of the two financial systems and for the creation of a free-trade area between the two countries. The British parliament accepted it all with devastating casualness. Indeed, crucial decisions concerning the continuation of a separate Irish administration under a lord lieutenant and chief secretary were only reached, like some unimportant addendum, after the event. But if in the midst of war with France the union had a somewhat jerry-built air, soon all concerned began to realize that the Protestant ascendancy was no longer in business on its own account but had been taken over by a larger international corporation, which, though itself 'Protestant', had different and more complex priorities at heart.

II

Politically the two decades following the union are often dismissed as something of an incomprehensible hiatus during which 'things' in some mysterious way 'took time to adjust'. This is to see politics in too narrow a light. Not only did manifestations of Whiteboyism continue to agitate the southern countryside, especially at times of severe economic distress such as the period 1813-17, but the Defender tradition also survived, if rather feebly, in the shape of what came to be known as the Ribbon societies. The fact that especially violent outbursts of rural discontent in the early 1820s also had strong millennial overtones shows how almost all such manifestations took their inspiration and attitudes from a common myth-kitty of beliefs, prejudices, and aspirations (Donnelly 1983b). And even if much of this embarrassed the more prosperous Catholics of the towns there can be little doubt that it too was yet one more element which helped to bring about a situation in which organized Catholic politics for the first time proved able to reach out and to orchestrate a genuine mass following.

Once emancipation failed to materialize directly after the union the Catholic issue inevitably became something of a running sore. In England support for the Catholic cause constituted perhaps the chief point of distinction between Whig and Tory. In Ireland a series of unsuccessful attempts to grapple with the matter made a wider politicization possible. Favourable motions were passed by the House of Commons in 1813 and 1821 but were accompanied by demands for some quid pro quo in the shape of a government veto over the appointment of Catholic bishops, state payment for the priesthood (which would, it was hoped, tie the clergy firmly to good order and moderation), and a substantial narrowing of the Irish electoral franchise. But the grudging manner in which solutions were offered allowed the leadership of formal Catholic politics to slip from the hands of aristocratic moderates and into those of the most important, dynamic, and creative figure to appear upon the nineteenth-century Irish political stage – Daniel O'Connell.

Born in 1775 of a minor gentry family in County Kerry which had, though Catholic and Irish-speaking, managed to retain some property, O'Connell was a barrister educated in France and London where he learned, respectively, a distrust of unrestrained blood-letting and a somewhat personal appreciation of Benthamite utilitarianism. One of the few prominent Catholics to oppose the union right from the start he always claimed its repeal to be the great priority of his life. A man of extraordinary ability and personal magnetism (for once the over-used term 'charisma' is appropriate) he was a master of that rarest of all political skills, the fruitful adoption and implementation of the powerful but half-formed ideas of others. By managing – at least fitfully – to attach fissiparous rural discontent to a system of formal national agitation he became one of the great innovators of Irish and indeed European politics. By combining within his own personality a jumble of different and seemingly contradictory attitudes – Gaelic traditionalism, popular understanding, Catholic nationalism, contemporary liberalism and utilitarianism – he brought to Irish life an influence at once powerful and unique (MacDonagh 1988).

Already by 1824 O'Connell had succeeded in transforming the small and exclusive Catholic Association established the previous year into something entirely novel: a broad movement with a real and effective presence throughout the whole of Catholic Ireland. The crucial breakthrough came with the setting up of a system for collecting a 'Catholic Rent' consisting of penny-a-month subscriptions from the poor paid outside Catholic chapels to priests who then transmitted the money to headquarters in Dublin. Not only did this raise substantial sums (£16,859 up to March 1825 alone and over £51,000 by February 1829), but, more importantly, it provided a means by which large numbers of people could feel themselves involved in a national campaign (O'Ferrall 1985: 67 and Appendix). In particular, the priesthood became politicized and was henceforth to constitute a much more formally important element in Irish politics as a whole.

Always keenly aware of knife-and-fork realities O'Connell tied the priests to his cause by supporting their educational work, allowing them to keep part of the cash, and by bitterly attacking the activities of new-style Protestant proselytizers now seeking converts among the rural poor. Soon the whole Catholic episcopate – not hitherto known for its political activism – was supporting the movement, while younger priests were more enthusiastic still. Yet, although this was a crucial and novel development, the priests themselves did not initiate the agitation. Nor (with a few exceptions) did they furnish its local leadership which remained in the hands of laymen – notably prosperous merchants in the larger provincial towns and lesser traders in the smaller places. Indeed, ecclesiastics consistently remained no more than one element within a 'total process of political change which affected the whole Catholic community' (O'Ferrall 1981b: 313).

III

Since 1793 Catholics in Ireland had 'enjoyed' the vote on the existing set of franchises. What this meant was that in the county constituencies all those with a forty-shilling electoral 'freehold' – *not* the same thing as ownership – had the vote while in most of the boroughs (which returned just over a third of the MPs) Catholics were still largely excluded because of certain technical and local considerations.[1] Landlords often granted the leases by which tenant farmers could enter the electoral registers in the belief that docile Catholics would prove more amenable than possibly independent Protestants. Though even before 1826 there had been instances of Catholic electors defying their superiors, this had never amounted to much (Jupp 1967). Most county constituencies had remained uncontested and Ireland had regularly returned a substantial majority of Tories to sit at Westminster (McDowell 1952: 49). The breakthrough occurred at County Waterford during the general election of 1826. Typically the first moves were the result of local initiative and O'Connell was slow to realize the importance of the new departure. Yet, placed as it was within the context of a wider Catholic campaign, the Waterford contest quickly displayed many of the characteristics soon to become the almost constant features of electioneering in Ireland: intimidation, clerical intervention on the 'popular' side, violence, the use of the military, and open sectarianism. And not only was the popular candidate returned, but in other constituencies similar dramatic victories were also obtained by those sympathetic to the emancipation cause. The impact was profound and the year 1826 marks a turning point in Irish political life.

After a short pause during which O'Connell held back in hopes of concessions from more moderate Tories like Canning the campaign entered an even higher pitch of activity in early 1828. Money flowed in as never before. On one January Sunday alone meetings were held in two-thirds of the country's 2500 Catholic parishes. Efforts were made to curb the distracting activities of agrarian secret societies and concentrate attention solely upon emancipation itself. As an Irish-speaking draper and churchwarden in County Kilkenny remarked in his diary 'It is on O'Connell's advice this renewal of friendship and this peace is being made among the children of the Gael: but the English do not like it; for they think it easier for them to beat people at variance than people in friendship; and this is true' (McGrath 1936–7: Part II, 27). Wellington's ministry became greatly alarmed and, indeed, it was not long before its chief members, the prime minister himself and Robert Peel, privately decided that damage control rather than outright opposition was now the only possible course. But Wellington handled matters badly and the government's difficulties escalated in the face of further electoral excitements.

Just as O'Connell had been brilliantly successful in slowly using other men's ideas over the Catholic Rent and the Waterford mobilization, so, when a by-election was called for County Clare, he at first cast about for some respectable Protestant candidate and only when none could be found did he agree to stand himself even though as a Catholic he was not in conscience able to take the oath then required of every MP. The Clare election of 1828 encapsulated in one compressed moment the multifarious nature of O'Connell's movement and personality. Priests canvassed and worked with extraordinary energy. Vast crowds gathered to cheer their hero. The hustings were aflame with green banners emblazoned with shamrocks, green handkerchiefs, green ribbons, green branches, green music too. With that smooth elision of the national and the sectional of which he was master O'Connell told the crowd 'Green is no party colour; it may, to be sure, be hateful in the eyes of our opponents, but that darling colour shall flourish when the blood stained orange shall fade and be trodden under foot'. He was triumphantly returned having sensibly taken the precaution of buttressing his popularity by the expenditure of at least £6245 on treating the voters and by employing hordes of so-called 'agents' to agitate his cause (O'Ferrall 1985: 194, 198).

After some complicated wrangling within the cabinet the government eventually announced its capitulation in February 1829, though it did successfully ensure that the county franchise be raised from forty shillings to ten pounds – thus effectively cutting the number of county voters from about 216,000 to no more than 37,000 (Hoppen 1984: 1). O'Connell's own attitude towards his departing electoral footsoldiers was, however, privately more ambiguous than his public statements tended to suggest, for, as he wrote in March 1829, the new ten-pound franchise might actually 'give more power to the Catholics' by concentrating it in more reliable and less demotically dangerous hands (O'Connell 1972–80: IV, 20).

IV

Thus were the ambiguities of the new politics rapidly revealed and made manifest. Certainly O'Connell had succeeded far more than the United Irishmen in aligning popular discontents to 'modern' issues and formal organization. Yet it would be wrong to think that he had somehow succeeded in confining such fissiparous materials entirely or permanently within a new political mould. He himself well realized that the mass of countrymen saw emancipation largely as a token of some great and imminent *bouleversement* throughout society in general. Contemporary ballads pictured the whole business as involving direct practical benefits: better wages, regular employment, lower rents, an end to evictions, abundant potato ground. Of course O'Connell never actually intended to encourage social revolution, yet the very tone of his orations, the constant harping upon a multitude of grievances, and the apocalyptic hyperbole of his language enabled him not only to tap the deeper recesses of popular (and especially Gaelic) consciousness but also to arouse expectations which, while immediately useful, were later to prove embarrassingly impossible to fulfil (Ó Tuathaigh 1975). And a sense of anticlimax followed quickly enough. 'I have', recalled a priest in 1832, 'often heard their conversations, when they say, "What good did Emancipation do for us: Are we better clothed or fed, or our children better clothed or fed?"' (Hoppen 1984: 379). A leader of the Whitefeet made his views starkly clear, 'Emancipation has done nothing for us. Mr. O'Connell and the rich Catholics go to Parliament. We die of starvation just the same' (Tocqueville 1958: 132).

Intertwined with such practical considerations was another major strand contained in O'Connell's language and within popular perceptions of that language, namely, the religious or more specifically the Catholic element. As early as 1826 he publicly identified the Catholics with 'the people, emphatically the people' and two years later declared the Clare election 'in reality, a religious ceremony, where honest men met to support upon the altar of their country the religion in which they believed' (O'Ferrall 1985: 144-5, 199-200). No wonder, therefore, that ballad writers reflected popular beliefs in picturing O'Connell as the culmination of millennial anti-Protestant prophecies, as, in very truth, a second Moses leading his people into the promised land of prosperity and domination (Zimmermann 1967: 34).

> The bondage of the Israelites our Saviour he did see,
> He then commanded Moses for to go and set them free,
> And in the same we did remain suffering for our own
> Till God he sent O'Connell, for to free the Church of Rome.

And O'Connell's chief oratorical lieutenant, Richard Sheil, drove the point home from the Clare hustings when he declared that 'We are masters of the passions of the people, and we have employed our dominion with terrible effect . . . Protestants awake to a sense of your condition' (Reynolds 1954: 159).

This development, though important, merely accentuated tendencies already evident before the union. But the appearance in Ireland of militant Protestant evangelicalism at about the same time added a new bitterness to religious and political relationships. With the exception of Wesley's eighteenth-century mission little attempt had hitherto been made to convert the Catholic masses to any version of the reformed faith. By the 1820s, however, the English evangelical revival was spilling across the sea and affecting both the Church of Ireland, which had always been theologically 'low', and the Presbyterians who had formerly replicated the contorted divisions of their Scottish counterparts into various species of moderates and fundamentalists. Though the impact upon both persuasions (which together accounted for about a fifth of the population) can be exaggerated, there is little doubt that the resulting increase in religious fervour briskly stirred an already bubbling pot (see Chapter 3).

The 'defeat' of 1829 and the Irish Reform Act of 1832 which reduced the influence of aristocratic patrons in the borough constituencies had the effect of releasing the forces of demotic urban Protestantism throughout the island. Working-class Protestants, not only in Belfast but also in southern towns like Dublin, Cork, Bandon, and Youghal, suddenly developed effective militant politics of their own (Barry and Hoppen 1978–9). While, therefore, prosperous Protestants retained a grasp upon positions of status, power, and responsibility, the rest began increasingly to depend upon a vested interest made up simply of 'the superiority of Protestantism itself' (Hill 1980: 64–5). They flocked into the Orange Order – to which by 1835 100,000 and probably more adult males belonged (Hoppen 1984: 320-1; Miller 1978a: 55) – and to revivalist political groups like those run in various towns by the charismatic clergyman, Rev. Tresham Dames Gregg, whose combination of violent anti-Catholicism, millenarian speculation, and sporadic radicalism constituted almost an exact reverse image of the popular Catholic agitation of the day.

O'Connell, in turn, was ignorant of Ulster in particular and Protestantism in general. Though a notable outburst in 1833 to the effect that Protestants 'are foreigners to us, since they are of a different religion' (*Hansard* 3rd Series: xv, 325) reflected no more than fleeting exasperation, his more eirenical comments were invariably as ill-informed as they were well-intentioned. He rarely visited the North and his most striking attempt in 1841 to pursue politics in Belfast was an ignominious and humiliating fiasco (Budge and O'Leary 1973: 50, 78). Long, therefore, before partition was ever considered, politicians on all sides seem, sometimes consciously sometimes not, to have behaved and talked as if a species of geographical and religious border was already firmly in place.

V

Almost immediately after the granting of emancipation O'Connell turned to his main political goal, the repeal of the Act of Union. Here he faced much greater difficulties because repeal could not easily be presented as the redress of some obvious civil wrong. For five years he campaigned in his old way. Although money was even more plentiful than before – £91,800 being raised between 1829 and 1834 (Macintyre 1965: 121) – there were no signs of any weakening in London. When in April 1834 O'Connell presented a repeal motion to the Commons he was overwhelmingly defeated (McDowell 1952: 159). It had, in addition, become more difficult to make effective use of rural discontent, which, by the early 1830s, was largely (though by no means entirely) concentrated upon the issue of tithes, that is the impost levied upon certain parts of agriculture by the established Church of Ireland (O'Donoghue 1965; 1966; 1972). Indeed, the ensuing 'Tithe War', though violent and energetic, revealed as much the divisions as the unity of the rural population, for tithes were of more concern to middling and larger farmers than to either smallholders or landless labourers.

With Catholics now able to take their seats at Westminster O'Connell set about the business of creating a parliamentary following. Here too he faced numerous obstacles. It was difficult to get reliable and able men to stand. Few were willing to accept their leader's dictation on points with which they disagreed. The existing party alignments of Whig-Liberals and Tory-Conservatives were not prepared to abandon the field, though the organizational differences between the former and the Repealers were often vague and indistinct. Of the 105 Irish members at Westminster after 1832 O'Connell rarely managed to return more than a third who in any case constituted a loose bloc rather than a disciplined party: 39 in 1832, 32 in 1835, 31 in 1837, and a disastrous 18 in 1841 (Walker 1978). In part this was the result of complex and confusing franchise arrangements by which many of those

21

supposedly 'entitled' to the vote were denied it while many of those who might have been thought excluded were allowed to enter their names upon the electoral registers.[1] As a result, elections reflected social and economic realities as through a glass darkly, if at all (Hoppen 1984: 1-33). Not only, therefore, did very few men have the vote (about 90,000 in 1832), but those who did were selected upon no ascertainable or rational grounds, so that it remained virtually impossible for O'Connell to identify any natural or reliable 'constituency' within the electorate as a whole.

In any case Irish electoral politics, like Irish politics in general, must not be perceived as entirely revolving around great national issues or debates. Partly because of the very nature of the electorate and partly because of fundamental traits in Irish political culture the concerns of voters often matched the preoccupations of agrarian secret societies in being local, immediate, and pragmatic. This does not mean that the people involved were apolitical, merely that the nature of their politics was often complex rather than simple, fissiparous rather than cohesive (Barry and Hoppen 1978–9). Only sheltered and innocent historians consistently deny that a concern for personal betterment, for the good of one's town, one's occupation, one's children, should be denied the dignified title of 'politics'. Yet in such a market place O'Connell was always at something of a disadvantage. The Irish Liberal Party – a loose amalgam of 'moderate' Protestants, a minority of landowners, some urban merchants and professional men, and certain prosperous Catholics – had much to offer at a time when Liberal governments held office almost continuously between 1830 and 1841 and again after 1846. And the Conservatives, who rapidly reorganized themselves after the defeats of 1829 and 1832, could draw on reservoirs of emotion more limited in extent but quite as powerful as those at O'Connell's disposal, while in addition enjoying the effective support of the bulk of landed proprietors. Given all this, it is O'Connell's comparative success and not his obvious failure to keep alive a constant mobilization which should cause surprise, even admiration. Throughout the 1830s he sustained an endless succession of organizations, maintained a highly visible parliamentary presence, made endless speeches, supported numerous reforms, and, despite bitter disputes with some of his supporters – notably in the Dublin trade union movement – successfully affirmed his position as the undoubted leader of popular and Catholic opinion.

The 1830s were, however, more notable for a number of crucial innovations in administration – all of them political in the broadest sense – than for any real movement in the direction of repeal. By 1835 the pragmatic side of O'Connell's character had persuaded him that half a loaf might well prove better than no bread at all. He concluded an informal alliance with Melbourne's Liberal government (the so-called Lichfield House compact) to the effect that repeal would be placed in cold storage in return for tangible concessions on a number of specific and important issues (Graham 1961). Reforms had, indeed, already been put in hand, and even though not all of them proved acceptable to O'Connell or his lay and clerical supporters, yet it was the 1830s which, in a very real sense, prepared the ground for Ireland's development as a modern political and administrative entity.

A national primary education system was set up under state auspices in 1831, which, while incorporating earlier private endeavours, undoubtedly helped to make Ireland literate in an altogether new and politically important manner – by 1881 three-quarters of all those aged between six and fifteen were, for example, able to read (Hoppen 1984: 457). As with almost everything else in Ireland the system was immediately subjected to a good deal of sectarian criticism and, as a result, soon lost its intended nondenominational character, being in effect transformed into a series of *de facto* religious fiefdoms supported by government grant. Nor did the reform of the Church of Ireland undertaken in 1833 involving as it did the suppression of ten bishoprics and the establishment of a central ecclesiastical commission, please many people. Episcopalian intransigents railed against any change, while O'Connell was disgruntled that none of the church's bloated revenues were, in the end, appropriated for other purposes (Macintyre 1965: 36-42).

With the arrival in Dublin in 1835 of a new under-secretary,[2] Thomas Drummond, matters took a more dynamic turn (Ó Tuathaigh 1977). Drummond, a bureaucrat rather than a politician (though he held radical views on certain matters), was not intimidated by vested interests and as early as 1836 privately described Irish landlords as 'cold-blooded and indifferent to the sufferings of their tenants' (McDowell 1952: 186). He kept the Liberal administration's side of the Lichfield House bargain by effectively opening large areas of official employment and patronage to Catholics and thus to a substantial extent satisfying the aspirations of those prosperous Catholics who had always seen jobs as the real reason for emancipation. Not that O'Connell was himself backward in this respect: the archives of ministers and officials are full of his letters recommending friends and relations for positions as clerks, magistrates, customs officers, and the like. But in addition Drummond embarked upon a programme of further legislative reform. In 1836 he reorganized the police as a single paramilitary force into which many Catholics were soon enrolled. Taken together with the increasing appointment of full-time stipendiary magistrates (who were more amenable to central direction than the mass of ordinary amateur justices of the peace) the new constabulary – already by 1837 nearly 8000-strong – proved a powerful arm of government and provided ministers and civil servants with much valuable local information as well as more effective means for maintaining law and order than had previously been available. Two years later an important act took the heat out of much of the discontent relating to tithes by reducing the amounts levied, converting the remainder into a rent charge collected from landlords (who could pass it on to most – but not all – tenants) and writing off the large arrears which had accumulated since 1834 (Macintyre 1965: 167-200).

More controversial was the new Irish poor law also introduced in 1838. Unlike England, Ireland had never had any official system of poor relief. A powerful royal commission appointed to enquire into the matter had reported in 1836 that the sheer ubiquity of poverty in Ireland made any solution along the lines of the new law passed for England in 1834 – that is, the building of workhouses and the virtual abolition of outdoor relief – quite unsuitable. This was not the answer that the Liberal government wanted. A few experts who knew nothing of Ireland were quickly consulted and the new English model imported in all the amplitude of its bureaucratic glory. O'Connell split his parliamentary party by rejecting the government's proposals, his opposition being based less upon humanitarian considerations than upon worries concerning expense and a belief (widely shared) that private charity would melt away in the face of governmental largesse. An extensive building programme was rapidly undertaken and over a hundred workhouses – which, together with the new schools, police barracks, and court houses soon came to constitute the chief physical monuments of Whig reform – were erected just in time to face and be overwhelmed by the catastrophe of the Great Famine in the late 1840s. More politically important in the long run was the establishment of partially-elected boards of poor-law guardians to administer the system. This for the first time injected an element of democracy into rural local government. And, because the boards were given more and more duties of a general nature over the next fifty years, they gradually replaced the unelected grand juries as the most important organs of rural administration, though the latter were not actually abolished until 1898. As such, the boards, composed of a mixture of ex-officio landed proprietors and elected guardians, were later to provide the proponents of popular politics with useful platforms for propaganda, power, and local mobilization (Feingold 1984).

The final Whig reform came in the shape of the Irish Municipal Corporations Act of 1840, a pale shadow of its English counterpart of 1835. Although this undoubtedly brought order to the jumbled chaos of Irish municipal affairs (which had hitherto been entirely in Protestant hands), it did so largely by abolition rather than reform. Only ten corporations were retained in the largest towns and while these were now opened to elective procedures, the adoption of a narrow franchise and high property qualifications for councillors ensured middle-class electorates and 'respectable' councils. Although most of the surviving corporations now came under Catholic control and O'Connell himself was elected lord mayor of Dublin in 1841, the results were mouse-like when compared with the mountainous parliamentary disputes which had brought them into being. In Cork, for example, not only was it the Liberal rather than the O'Connellite element which benefited most, but even the Tories proved altogether more successful in maintaining a strong (and in the 1840s a growing) minority presence than anyone had at first anticipated (Murphy 1976).

Drummond, with the help of Lord Mulgrave as viceroy and Lord Morpeth as chief secretary, had undoubtedly delivered a significant legislative package. Just as important was the change of tone adopted by the administration of which he was part, most notably in the case of his famous rebuke to the landed magistrates of Tipperary in 1838 that 'Property has its duties as well as its rights' and that 'to the neglect of those duties in times past is mainly to be ascribed that diseased state of society in which . . . crimes take their rise' (O'Brien 1889: 284). When combined with a more ecumenical use of patronage and the formal dissolution of the Orange Order in 1836 (though local lodges continued and a central body re-emerged within ten years) all this certainly constituted a significant shift in policy. But, at the same time, at least some of the legislation passed in the 1830s proved rebarbative to various sections of O'Connell's following and of course no progress at all was made on the issue of repeal. O'Connell, fearful that his popular support was beginning to melt away amidst the details of ameliorating reform, decided upon a slow and at first crab-like return to what for him remained the essential issue. Various preliminary organizations hinting at this were set up in 1838 and 1839, and in 1840 he established the body soon to be known – in characteristically O'Connellite vein – as the Loyal National Repeal Association. When in July of the following year the Tories were returned to power under Sir Robert Peel ('Orange Peel' as O'Connell called him) the period of pragmatic reformism seemed to have come to a definite end.

VI

It took a little time for the old machinery to grind into effective action, but soon O'Connell was once again addressing vast outdoor meetings, hinting heavily that violence might well ensue if his demands were not met, talking almost in the same breath about the unity of all Irishmen and the superiority of Catholicism as the authentic expression of national identity. Like many popular politicians O'Connell felt obliged to tell his audiences what they wanted to hear. His actual concept of repeal combined bursts of detailed precision – as when he drew up the exact structure of a new electoral system (Confidential Print in Peel Papers, British Lib. Add. MS 40540) – with large tracts of vague ambiguity. As was the case with many Protestants who did not know exactly what they meant by 'union' so O'Connell never really defined what he meant by 'repeal'. Aims of course had to be presented, but these were then so overlaid with garrulous inconsistency that – wisely perhaps – symbols ended up having to do the work of programmes (MacDonagh 1983a). O'Connell believed that 'there was a moral electricity in the continuous expression of public opinion concentrated upon a single point, perfectly irresistible in its efficacy' (O'Ferrall 1981a: 51-2) and in consequence turned his mass oratory into brilliant hammering essays in repetition – fierce, involving, but imprecise. With, however, no signs that Peel was prepared to concede, O'Connell was driven to keeping the momentum alive by increasingly unrealistic assertions culminating in his announcement that 1843 would finally be the 'repeal year' (McCaffrey 1966). When, however, the government proscribed the 'monster' meeting called for Clontarf (the place just north of Dublin where Brian Boru had in the early-eleventh century defeated the Vikings) in October 1843 and when O'Connell, fearful of violence, cancelled it, the whole campaign moved from unreal expectancy to disappointed confusion. Though agitation continued – and not without vigour – O'Connell began once again to hint that practical reforms might well prove an acceptable and realistic policy on all sides, and, indeed, it is significant that it was not until 1845, two years after the 'repeal year', that he produced anything which might remotely be designated a programme for land reform.

Various reasons have traditionally been given for the failure to obtain repeal. Only one counts for much, namely, the government's firm resistance backed almost universally by respectable political opinion in Britain. Admittedly, middle-class Catholics in Ireland were less enthusiastic than they had been over emancipation and hardly any Protestants could be found to support the campaign. But such things at most drove a few more nails into the coffin of Peel's intransigence. Again, it is sometimes suggested that the Catholic clergy was less committed and undoubtedly some bishops refused to join the Repeal Association. But the mass of the priests – and there were after all about 2400 of them and only twenty-eight bishops – were overwhelmingly active and enthusiastic, as a detailed government investigation in 1843 made clear (Kerr 1981). Indeed, the reciprocal relationship between O'Connell and the church helped to give repeal an even more confessional air than it already had. In his private dealings with ecclesiastics O'Connell went so far as to hail it as 'an event of the most magnificent importance to Catholicity', an importance so great he was 'prevented from presenting it in its true colours to the British people' lest they realize that it must end in the total disappearance of Protestantism from Ireland within ten years (O'Connell 1972–80: VII, 158). Whether he had willed it or not O'Connell had practically attached himself to the priorities of clerical politics just as much as the clerical politicians had tied themselves to his particular brand of nationalism. When, therefore, Peel – well aware of the important role played by the clergy in the matter – began in 1844–5 to adopt a policy of trying to divert more moderate ecclesiastical elements towards the quieter paths of accommodation and quiescence, O'Connell was virtually obliged to align the Repeal Association behind those bishops and priests most determined to play the sectarian card. Peel's policy, which focused particularly on concessions regarding the Catholic Church's ability to accept bequests, the establishment of a new university system less rebarbative to Catholics than the Elizabethan Protestant foundation of Trinity College Dublin, and increases in the government grant given to the seminary at Maynooth, represented in fact a Tory version of Drummondism. But, while not without beneficial practical results, its impact was greatly weakened by the anti-Catholic hysteria it evoked in England and by disputes in Ireland which rapidly shrouded the whole business in an atmosphere of sectionalism and distrust (Kerr 1982).

This was especially true of the university proposals designed to establish colleges in Belfast, Cork, and Galway, which, while formally nondenominational, would in fact prove acceptable to Catholics and Presbyterians alike. As such they almost inevitably brought to the surface tensions which had been latent within the repeal movement since the early 1840s when a group of younger men, predominantly intellectuals and journalists, had attached themselves to the cause. Most prominent among them were the Protestant poet, Thomas Davis, and the Catholics, Charles Gavan Duffy and John Blake Dillon, who were later joined by the Presbyterian republican, John Mitchel, and the Protestant landowner, William Smith O'Brien. The steady anglicization of Irish life had already produced something of a romantic backlash typified by Davis's stress upon an Irish cultural identity distinct and separate from that of England (Sheehy 1980: 29-39). Indeed, for Protestants like Davis, culture had become the main prop of nationalist commitment, and, as a result, the so-called 'Young Irelanders' – few of whom could actually understand the Irish language then still spoken by probably about half the population – saw the repeal struggle in a very different way from O'Connell whose pragmatic Catholic utilitarianism seemed to them at once sectarian, narrow, and drearily realistic (Davis 1987).

Through the pages of the *Nation,* established in 1842, they propagated their views, at first as loyal followers of the 'Liberator' (as O'Connell was now widely known), but increasingly as members of a separate movement with an ideology of its own. The *Nation's* first issue proclaimed its purpose as being to 'create and foster a public opinion in Ireland, and make it racy of the soil'. But, just as O'Connell's own political position was fraught with ambiguities, so too the Young Irelanders never succeeded in presenting a coherent and comprehensive programme or philosophy. Davis, who stressed the importance of racial distinctions between Ireland and England, strove, nonetheless, to deny such distinctions within Ireland itself, and was therefore obliged to insist that different and contradictory criteria should apply according to whether they did or did not suit his arguments. Unlike O'Connell he and other Young Irelanders developed a formal, though inchoate, theory of nationhood as something dependent on language, culture, and race. At the same time Davis's approach, despite protestations to the contrary, was essentially elitist. Though he never admitted it his cultural nationalism was, among much else, an effort to save Protestants from Catholic wrath and to retain for them a place of leadership within Irish politics as a whole (Boyce 1982: 154-64). However enthusiastically, therefore, the readers of the *Nation* responded to the poetic declarations of cultural identity put forward in its pages, O'Connell still retained the allegiance of the masses for whom Catholicity and redress continued to constitute the main ingredients of political life.

By 1845 the university question was causing severe rifts between O'Connell, who followed a section of the clergy in denouncing the 'Godless colleges', and the bulk of the Young Irelanders who took a different view. Though Davis's death in September produced a temporary truce, within a few months O'Connell had determined upon a test of his authority and in July 1846 engineered a brutal expulsion of the Young Irelanders from the Repeal Association on the – as yet very abstract – grounds that the latter would not totally, absolutely, and for all future ages abjure the use of violence. By then the Famine was already under way and political disputes began more and more to resemble a hermetic drama in which the participants and the issues remained almost entirely divorced from the realities of starvation and death. O'Connell himself died in May 1847. By the end of that year men like Mitchel were urging the peasants to arm themselves, something for which he in turn was expelled from the ranks of Young Ireland and, as a result, established his own, overtly republican, newspaper, the *United Irishman*. He and the hitherto obscure James Fintan Lalor (who had earlier corresponded amicably with none other than Sir Robert Peel on various aspects of the Irish Question) began to demand a social revolution and to call – in Lalor's oft-repeated phrase – for 'Ireland her own, and all therein, from the sod to the sky. The soil of Ireland for the people of Ireland, to have and to hold from God alone' (Fogarty 1918: 57). This of course went much further than O'Connell had ever been prepared to go, for even when the Liberator had at last in 1845 started to draw up an agrarian programme he had largely confined himself to proposals for taxing absentee landlords, changing the ejectment laws, and giving farmers legal compensation for improvements (Lee 1984: 71) – hardly the roughage of either social revolution or political iconoclasm.

What exactly the Young Irelanders intended at this time is impossible to establish. Events, however, were driven forward by a government nervously taking their threats perhaps more seriously than they themselves had so far done. The outbreak of the Paris revolution in February 1848 made the viceroy, Lord Clarendon, more anxious than ever. After public meetings at which Young Irelanders advocated physical force and after (quite unsuccessful) attempts to enlist French aid, Clarendon began to arrest the leaders and bring them to trial. In July Smith O'Brien led a tiny force of some one hundred men around the lanes of Tipperary in a 'rising' that was swiftly suppressed (Nowlan 1965: 211-13). The local towns, supposedly centres of Young Ireland opinion, ignored the revolutionaries and the countryside responded with an almost equal lack of zeal. By the end of the year O'Brien and the rest had been captured and tried. Showing unusual intelligence the authorities declined to execute anyone and instead transported the leaders to the convict lands of Australia.

Though practically ineffective Young Ireland had, nonetheless, grafted itself as ideal and model irremovably upon the increasingly complicated and many-branched tree of Irish nationalism. In no real sense had the 1848 rebellion been any kind of culmination of the work of 1798; yet it was soon to be seen as precisely that. Some of the younger rebels were later to be instrumental in setting up the Fenian movement, which, under their influence, began the task of stringing together an artificial but seductive necklace of violent nationalism in which 1798, Robert Emmet's attempted rising of 1803, and 1848 were to constitute the three first and crucial beads of revolt.

Henceforth Irish nationalism was to oscillate between the shifting attractions of two traditions – the O'Connellite and that produced by an uneasy amalgam of Young Ireland's romanticism and Wolfe Tone's republicanism – both of them individually full of contradictions and by their interactions productive of yet further ambiguities. All of the chief actors involved referred mantra-like to the 'people' in their exhortations and programmes, yet who precisely constituted the 'people' was invariably implied rather than specified. As the angle of vision differed so did the perception of the beholder. For Lalor the 'people' were essentially the farmers; for Davis they were Celtic rustics rather than deracinated townsmen; for O'Connell they were, above all else, Catholics. To bring these ingredients together into effective coordination was to prove a difficult, lengthy, and only fitfully successful enterprise. By the very rapidity of the mobilization he achieved O'Connell ensured that elements of nationalism, civil rights, and egalitarianism were to become firmly, if unusually, crystallized into 'a curious blend of conservative Catholicism and political radicalism' (Garvin 1981: 44). By their powerfully selective reading of Irish history the Young Irelanders, just as importantly, made certain that henceforth myth could always do sterling duty for reality. Yet neither succeeded in permanently overcoming the ingrained localism of political culture as a whole, so that, for the next century and more, Irish politics were to be shaped, not only by the complexities of nationalism and sectarianism, but by a continuing dialogue between the demands of nationwide campaigns and the more immediate realities of quotidian life.

NOTES

1. Briefly put, between 1793 and 1829 the Irish franchise in the counties was open to all those who 'possessed' a freehold worth forty shillings a year. But of course the great bulk of county voters did not actually 'own' any land at all, they merely held it by means of a lease 'for lives' which lasted until the last-named 'life' nominated in the lease (there were usually three) had died. Such leases – but not those which ran for a specific period however long – were accounted 'freeholds' for electoral purposes. Landlords could obviously grant and refuse them virtually at will. Until 1832 the boroughs functioned (as in England) under a variety of different franchises and in most of them Catholics remained effectively shut out. In 1829 the county franchise was raised to ten pounds which reduced the electorate from about 216,000 to about 37,000. In 1832 certain limited groups of leaseholders for years were given the county vote, while the borough franchises were now coordinated and votes given to all those who *occupied* property worth ten pounds a year. However, both in counties and boroughs, the enormous problems involved in the actual valuation of property made almost all franchises as much a matter of lottery as of exactitude. Voters also had to meet certain residential and tax requirements before they were admitted to the registers and the whole matter of registration was a complicated one. In 1832 there were about 60,000 county and 30,000 borough voters – a much smaller proportion of the population being enfranchised than in England and Wales.

2. The Act of Union had continued the system by which Ireland was administered by a lord lieutenant or viceroy (always a peer), a chief secretary (always a commoner, though some, like Lord Morpeth 1835–41 enjoyed 'courtesy' titles as the eldest sons of senior noblemen), and an under-secretary. As time went on the first of these became less of a figurehead and tended to reside for most of the year in the

Viceregal Lodge in Phoenix Park. The chief secretary was effectively the Irish minister in the Commons and as such spent most of the parliamentary session in London where he had a small office. The under-secretary minded the shop in Dublin Castle (the headquarters of the central administration) and was never a peer and rarely an MP. From 1853 the under-secretary became a 'non-political' official and was no longer replaced with each change of ministry. During the period 1800–1922 the relative power of the three offices varied according to their holders' ability, personality, and political weight. Normally the chief secretary was the most important, though between 1835 and 1840 Drummond as under-secretary enjoyed unprecedented prominence. Sometimes Irishmen were appointed (especially as under-secretary), though this was not the norm. A useful summary of what was involved was given in the early-twentieth century (O'Brien 1912: 25): 'The chief secretary, who is generally in the English cabinet, is really the captain of the ship . . . the lord lieutenant, who, as a rule is not in the English cabinet, wears the insignia of command, but only signs the log. The under-secretary is the man at the wheel.' In the whole of the nineteenth century there was not one Catholic viceroy, not one Catholic chief secretary, and all of two Catholic under-secretaries. (On the Irish administration in general, see McDowell 1964.)

CHAPTER 2
Society
Agrarian Crisis and Population Collapse

By the end of the first half of the nineteenth century Ireland had an even more agricultural economy than in 1800. Although some towns – notably Belfast – undoubtedly grew, the collapse of the domestic textile industry ensured that relatively more people were becoming dependent upon farming and its associated activities. In 1841, when statistics begin to emerge into reliability, less than 14 per cent of the population lived in towns of 2000 or more people and almost three-quarters of occupied males were engaged in farming (Hoppen 1984: 103, 436–7). Roughly comparable figures indicate that, by contrast, well under a quarter of the British labour force was similarly engaged (Deane and Cole 1967: 142), while only little over half the population of England and Wales lived outside settlements of 2500 people or more (Law 1967: 129–30). Ireland remained, therefore, overwhelmingly both a rural and an agrarian country. Its industrial sector was small and even the north-eastern region around Belfast did not develop significant heavy industries until the second half of the century. Economically Britain and Ireland drew further and further apart. Though in an important sense their economies became increasingly complementary, the outlooks and thought-patterns of their inhabitants and their leaders remained, in large measure, separate and distinct.

I

The grid upon which the early-nineteenth-century Irish experience was shaped consisted of networks of mutual interaction between

33

demographic, economic, social, political, and cultural change. The element which most struck contemporaries and has most often exercised historians was that of population growth, its speed, causes, and effects (Connell 1950). Scholarly interpretations have presented various explanations which resemble nothing so much as the Cheshire cat in their propensity for sudden appearance and equally sudden evaporation. That in 1841 the population was somewhere between 8.2 and 8.4 million (the census recorded 8,175,124) is now accepted and it would be reasonable to suggest that ninety years earlier it had been no more than about 2.5 million (Mokyr and Ó Gráda 1984: 473–88). The difference between these figures places Ireland at the top of the contemporary European demographic league, for it yields an annual growth rate *c.* 1750–*c.* 1845 of 1.3 per cent as opposed to 1.0 in England, 0.8 in Scotland, 0.7 in Sweden, and 0.4 in France. And, as it is fairly clear that in the 1820s and 1830s the growth rate fell to about 0.9/1.0 per cent and 0.5/0.75 per cent respectively – indeed some authorities suggest an even more drastic reduction (Carney 1975) – we are left with the astonishingly high percentage of 1.6 or thereabouts for the first seven decades beginning in the middle of the eighteenth century.

Many and ingenious have been the explanations offered for so remarkable an increase. Malthus of course had firm views as to both cause and inevitable result. But the first modern runner in the explanatory stakes appeared on the race card under the mighty name of 'potato'. By the mid-eighteenth century, it was argued, the potato was 'all but fully accepted' as the main diet for the mass of Irish people. It grew easily and plentifully and could support families upon less land than other crops. As a consequence, farmers happily divided holdings among their children who no longer had to wait until parents died before marrying and setting up families of their own. There is no evidence to suggest that illegitimacy rates were high or that contraception was widely practised (Connolly 1979). All other things being equal, therefore, significantly earlier marriage must inevitably have led to a population boom (Connell 1962).

There are, however, problems with such a view. Closer examination revealed that, certainly by the early-nineteenth century, the Irish did not in fact marry at unusually young ages (Drake 1963). Then it was argued that the ubiquity of the potato diet was a product rather than a cause of population increase (Cullen 1968). As a result, alternative side bets were placed on the possibility that population growth was primarily the outcome of falls in mortality rates themselves in turn produced by the fact that potatoes in due course provided a more available and nutritious food supply than had previously been the case. It was also pointed out that, with regard to many of the variables involved – age of marriage, nature of diet, mortality rates – the experiences of the poorer sections of the community probably differed significantly from those of the well-to-do (Lee 1968). Thus it is possible that landless labourers often – but not always (O'Neill 1984: 163–86) – married younger than did farmers with substantial holdings and there is evidence that by the 1830s at the latest the actual culture of marriage (dowries, arranged matches, and the like) differed substantially as between the various strata of rural society (Connolly 1985a). One of the few points of comparative certainty amidst this maelstrom of interpretative confusion is a general agreement that Ireland's high crude birth rate was caused largely by unusual marital fertility rather than by an unusually high propensity to marry as such (Mokyr and Ó Gráda 1984). But while the potato undoubtedly played a role within the overall process, its influence, though clear-cut, may not have been particularly large. Indeed, population growth would probably have occurred even in the absence of potatoes, though almost certainly at a somewhat slower rate (Mokyr 1981).

II

By 1800 a recognizably nineteenth-century Irish rural society was already in place, though the wealth, size, and experiences of its component parts were to change significantly during the succeeding hundred years. In very crude terms it was divided into three major groups: those who owned the soil (landlords), those who rented holdings (farmers), and those who merely worked the land (labourers). But such broad categories hide a myriad of subtle distinctions. Landlords, of whom there were at most 10,000, varied enormously in wealth and substance. A few large magnates possessed vast estates productive of almost equally vast rental incomes. Many others owned no more than a few hundred acres and found it difficult to keep up the appearances of a gentleman.

In the course of the eighteenth century it had become common for landlords to let substantial parts of their properties on long leases to so-called middlemen. These in turn subdivided the land into smaller parcels which were then let out to farmers at a higher amount. Landlords benefited by avoiding the costs of direct estate management and in effect allowed the middlemen to act as wholesalers. Although this system may well have pushed up the rents paid by those who actually farmed the soil, it would be wrong to see middlemen as entirely parasitic (Cullen 1981: 103–4; Dickson 1979). However, the agricultural boom produced by the French wars of 1793–1815 made landlords anxious to share in the advantage of rising prices. As long middleman leases at fixed rents clearly stood in their way, they began to take back land into their own hands as leases fell in and then to let it out directly themselves. Because, however, the agricultural crash which accompanied the end of the wars forced them to grant at least temporary reductions, their overall net rental incomes probably remained static between 1815 and the mid-1820s and then reached a level on the eve of the Great Famine only slightly higher in nominal terms than that which had prevailed thirty years before (Hoppen 1984: 110–11). But there were enormous differences between the experiences of the most efficient landlords and those who neglected their properties, for the disappearance of middlemen not only brought owners far more directly into economic contact with the farmer community but also placed a premium on professional and effective estate management (Donnelly 1975: 52–72; Maguire 1972; Proudfoot 1986). The efficient prospered and the extravagant sailed ever closer to the reefs of collapse: by 1844 1322 estates with a rental of £904,000 (possibly a tenth of the whole) were being managed by the courts, usually in preparation for sales to pay off creditors (Donnelly 1973: 18).

While proprietors constituted the economic apex of the rural pyramid its numerical base was supplied by those who actually worked the land. Here too important distinctions must be made. Almost innumerable shades of distinction were maintained by contemporaries, mostly economic, but sometimes relating as much to perceived status as to objective prosperity. Perhaps the most important was that between those with land or at least access to land and those without either, for it was the ability to benefit directly from the produce of the soil which marked out a crucial line of division between those enjoying some prospect of planning for the future and those who could live merely from one moment to the next. Farmers with substantial holdings clearly fell into the former category, and, while 'substantial' was subject to varying interpretations, the lower limit might convincingly be placed at somewhere between ten and twenty statute acres of land (though clearly the quality of the land in question was also an important variable). Then came the smaller farmers with between eight and fifteen acres who could manage well enough when prices and climate were favourable, but who had little in reserve when they were not. Below this level the nomenclature becomes complicated. Many of those with yet smaller holdings might still commonly also be regarded as 'farmers', but there was in addition a group known as cottiers who in most parts of Ireland rented cabins and small plots (usually of potato ground) on a more or less regular basis from *farmers* and paid for these in part at least by labour services. Even the so-called 'landless' labourers more often than not rented tinier patches still for potatoes in what was called the conacre system. Here there was little assurance of regularity and the patches in question were provided already manured by farmers again and in this case at 'high' rents which in the 1830s tended to fall somewhere between six and ten pounds an acre.

The great majority of such bargains for land, according to a contemporary, 'commence in extortion on one side and fraud on the other. One asks more than he knows he can get and the other offers more than he has any intention of paying.' In desperation many labourers promised rents they knew they might well be unable to pay while many farmers recouped a substantial proportion of the amounts they owed their own landlords by in effect acting as small landlords themselves and by charging rents far more exploitative than those levied by the actual owners of the soil. The Devon commissioners appointed to examine the land question in the early 1840s were told again and again how labourers were 'oppressed by farmers', made 'dependent as slaves', 'more wretched than the Fellahs of Egypt or the blacks of Cuba', how, indeed, 'every class in this country oppresses the class below it, until you come to the most wretched class. . . . There is no exaction practised by their superiors that they do not practise upon those below them' (Hoppen 1984: 94–5; Kennedy 1985a: 58). The labourers at the bottom of the heap also worked for wages – 6d to 10d a day was the norm (Connolly 1982: 19) – and while estimates vary considerably as to the annual extent of their actual employment it seems possible that in the mid-1830s they may well have worked in one way or another for as much as forty weeks in the year, though the Poor Inquiry commissioners of the time argued for a shorter period and therefore of course for lower overall incomes (Mokyr 1983: 215; Hoppen 1984: 98–9).

Table 2.1 reflects in round numbers the general state of things with regard to adult males, each of whom, it must be remembered, was usually required to support a considerable number of dependants as well as himself. What is immediately obvious is that the great bulk of the agricultural population was composed of cottiers and labourers and that probably no more than a quarter can be designated as farmers by any reasonable definition of that term (Hoppen 1984: 105; Fitzpatrick 1980a: 87–8; Connolly 1982: 15–23; Clark 1979: 114). Although only 7 per cent of holdings above two acres exceeded sixty acres in size (Bourke 1965), it was precisely the larger farmers who, together with the actual proprietors, controlled access to the bulk of Ireland's agricultural land (Donnelly 1985: 152; Solar 1983: 77).

Table 2.1 Adult males and rural social structure, *c.* 1841

	No.	per cent
Rich Farmers	50,000	2.9
(mean holdings 80 acres)		
'Snug' Farmers	100,000	5.9
(mean holdings 50 acres)		
Family Farmers	250,000	14.7
(mean holdings 20 acres and rarely		
employing outside labour)		
Cottiers	300,000	17.7
(mean holdings 5 acres)		
Labourers	1,000,000	58.8
(mean holdings 1 acre, though		
often without any land)		

(Source: Donnelly 1985: 152)

III

Because so much of this land was held in relatively large units Irish farming *as a whole* was a good deal less backward than has often been supposed. The sudden drop in prices which occurred about 1814/15 as a result of the ending of the French wars undoubtedly produced a good deal of anguish but then this was not something unique to Irish agriculture. Although the fall was especially severe for tillage crops (where war-time demand had greatly inflated prices), it was substantial over all sectors. By 1831–5 prices in general were only about two-thirds of 1812–15 levels, though they rose to about three-quarters over the next five years (Crotty 1966: 284). Nonetheless, the economically dominant farmers seem to have been able to continue along much the same lines as before and to have made full use of the rent abatements granted by landlords in difficult times. In any case, official inspectors who toured the countryside in 1840–1 in connection with possible franchise reforms concluded that *actual rents paid* were in general not much above the average level of the valuations which had been undertaken after 1838 because of the new poor law system, and that these valuations in turn were informally related to some concept of 'fair rent', or, in other words, to 'the rents of the proprietors in the district whose rents were lowest' (Hoppen 1984: 110). And the benefits of such a state of things to the substantial farmers were clearly greater than to those with smaller and more marginal holdings.

Suggestions that by the 1830s a significant shift away from tillage and towards livestock production was taking place (Crotty 1966: 42–6) cannot be sustained, nor had the subdivision of holdings reached anything like the epidemic proportions once claimed (Goldstrom 1981: 160–8). Although for large sections of the rural population a quasi-subsistence potato cultivation constituted the norm, Irish agriculture in general sustained a high level of commercialization, with, in the early 1840s, as much as two-thirds of total output being sold for cash. Productivity was roughly comparable with that of countries like France and seems low only in comparison with Britain which then led the world in this respect (Ó Gráda 1984: 152–3 and 1988: 47–67). Even in comparison with the much-lauded Scottish system, Irish agriculture performed remarkably well during the first half of the century (Solar 1983).

The benefits of all this were, however, very unevenly distributed. Most labourers and their families lived hard and materially deprived lives though within a culture capable of supplying fitful consolation and cheer in those matters of feeling and the spirit not easily calculable in economic terms. Substantial local potato famines in 1817, 1822, 1831, 1835–7, 1839, and 1842 caused distress and anxiety. And even if they resulted in comparatively few deaths they were yet another unknown which could help push men and women down the ladder of society from barely tolerable to quite intolerable conditions. Small farmers were haunted by such prospects for there were many who had gone before them into the depths. 'If once thrown out of our holdings we consider our station in life completely lost' a group of Cork farmers told O'Connell in 1846, 'and we know from the universal feeling in such cases that we never could raise our heads again in the community' (National Library of Ireland, O'Connell Papers MS 13649). More poignant still was the evidence given by a Mayoman to the Poor Inquiry Commission of 1835 (O'Neill 1973: 26):

> I have a wife and three children: I held 5 acres of land, but was unable to pay the rent and lost them four years ago; I then turned labourer and used to get employment for about three months of the year, mostly in the spring and harvest at 5d to 8d a day; my wife and children used to beg for themselves and me in summer and often in winter . . . I had to sell all my furniture consisting of a dresser and a pot for 7/- to support myself, – I sold them because we had nothing to eat. I was hoping for employment every day, and had no intention of begging until I spent the last of the price of them, I then determined to beg with my family, I had three halfpence leaving this place, it was the first time I begged myself and I did not beg until I got ten miles from home.

And such testimonies, recording as they do the actual experience of daily living, of struggle, degradation, gnawing anxiety, hunger, and shame, have a value and importance too often forgotten amidst the current excitements of statistical and econometric manipulation.

At times of local famine the numbers 'in distress' or 'absolutely destitute' could rise to remarkable heights: as many as a million in 1822 and 326,000 nine years later in Galway and Mayo alone (O'Neill 1973: 27). In 1841 two-fifths of the houses in Ireland were one-room mud cabins. The quality of clothing probably declined as home-made woollen garments were replaced by cheaper but less solid cottons (Ó Tuathaigh 1972: 148–9). Until the introduction of an Irish Poor Law in 1838 there was nothing to fall back upon in hardship save private or sporadic public charity, something which perhaps encouraged parents to have large families so that they might be able to rely upon the support of children in their own old age. And even if the workhouses built thereafter were stark and mechanical institutions, they at least provided a safety-net of last resort and may well, in any case, have been somewhat less intolerably run than has sometimes been supposed (O'Brien 1985; but see Mokyr 1983: 290–1).

Perhaps one of the most important negative influences upon the conditions of daily life for large sections of the population was the decline of the domestic textile industry. The general economic crises of 1819–20 and 1825–6 were reflections of severe recessions in England, but only in textiles, already prone to long-term weaknesses, were the effects much more than temporary. By the 1830s the woollen industry was in terminal decline, cotton was contracting rapidly, and linen (because of technical innovations in the spinning of yarn) was already moving substantially away from domestic and towards factory production (Cullen 1972: 106–8). Hitherto textile output had depended predominantly upon domestic producers and had provided employment for many small farmers and the like over large areas of the country: much of Ulster, north Leinster, north Connacht, and parts of Munster. But while in agriculture a rising production in the pre-Famine decades to a considerable extent helped to cushion a simultaneous fall in prices (though the benefits of this were unevenly distributed), the domestic textile sector soon reached a point at which any similar strategy was rendered impossible by the simple fact that no one can work for more than twenty-four hours a day. The proportion of the labour force substantially engaged in manufacturing *of any kind* fell dramatically during the 1820s and 1830s and only in Ulster were factories able to absorb a significant part of the slack (Ó Gráda 1980). In effect both domestic industry and potato cultivation represented responses to the growing pressure on land. With the former prop now knocked away, the latter was obliged to bear ever more of the weight. In this sense the background to the Famine was as much an industrial as an agrarian one.

Regional differences were becoming even more pronounced than before, in part because the decline in population growth after 1820 did not in fact relate directly, if at all, to local changes in the economy. Along the western seaboard, where the entire domestic textile industry had disintegrated by the 1830s and left a poor area poorer still, population levels continued to rise at higher than average rates. An important reason why this was so may lie in the different manner in which emigration – that palliative for unacceptable conditions – operated in the various parts of the country. Undoubtedly a massive outflow of people took place from Ireland in the thirty years after 1815 at a level which entirely dwarfed previous migrations. It is likely that no less (and probably rather more) than 1.5 million people left the country in these years, more than half of them for North America and most of the rest for Britain (Mokyr 1983: 230). But while the numbers leaving fluctuated considerably in response to economic circumstances at home – with peaks occurring in 1830–2, 1834, 1836–7, and 1841–2 during or just after failures in the potato crop (Fitzpatrick 1984: 27) – they came quite disproportionately from the northern midlands and south Ulster rather than, for example, from the West (Ó Gráda 1980).

Although, therefore, the socio-economic standing of those emigrating probably fell from the 1830s onwards, it remained the case that fewer of the poor in the poorest regions were leaving than of the poor (and the comparatively more prosperous) elsewhere (Adams 1932; Ó Gráda 1983). This was not because Mayo labourers were less able to afford the Atlantic fare than labourers from Westmeath but because less certain prospects abroad faced Irish-speaking peasants from the West and because the development of heavy *seasonal* migration from Connacht to Britain represented a kind of migratory compromise and reflected an unusually strong attachment to small farming culture as such. In other parts of Ireland a growing shift among middling farmers towards a system of impartible inheritance (by which only one son took over his father's farm as an undivided unit) provided a new stimulus for the other children to go abroad, while cottiers and labourers in many such areas found themselves increasingly cut off from access to land in a manner altogether more definite than in the West (Miller 1985: 218–20).

It is virtually impossible to make any convincingly accurate assessment of the real level of pre-Famine poverty or, indeed, to compare the actual situation in Ireland with those of other countries. Yet the materials to hand do permit some insights into relative movements over time. Certainly evidence given to the Poor Inquiry Commission of 1835 as to what well-informed respondents considered had been the trends in their own localities since 1815 strongly suggests that contemporaries perceived the lot of 'the poorer classes' to have worsened. At the same time the consumption patterns of certain 'luxury' consumer goods like tobacco, sugar, and tea imply that a modest (and unsteady) net improvement in living standards was taking place. The most convincing conclusion to draw from these and other findings is, however, not that – despite all contemporary opinion – things were universally getting better, but rather that stable or even rising levels of mean income were obscuring increasing inequality in standards of living and wealth (Ó Gráda 1988: 1–45). Middling and larger farmers prospered; the rest of rural society drifted unsteadily in the opposite direction (Kennedy 1985a: 36). If few actually died of starvation before 1845 this should be 'attributed not to absence of poverty, but to provision of relief by relatives, neighbours, or less frequently the state' (Fitzpatrick 1984: 28). Yet undoubtedly those

Irish farmers most involved in the market benefited from British industrialization which increased the demand for their products while it simultaneously killed off domestic textile production. But whatever improvements Ireland may have experienced the fact that these were slower in coming and smaller in extent than in Britain meant that the gap between the two parts of the United Kingdom was almost certainly growing. It is, in any case, no contradiction to say that, notwithstanding certain upswings in the Irish economy, 'Ireland's working class or people in the bottom half of the income distribution' were undoubtedly facing 'an increasingly harsh economic environment' (Mokyr and Ó Gráda 1986).

That Ireland was poor can perhaps, in a broad sense, be accepted. Why it was so or what precisely was the condition of the pre-Famine economy are more difficult questions. Rigorous, though controversial, statistical analysis has to some extent cut down a host of traditional explanations: overpopulation, undue dependence on the potato, tenant insecurity, and so forth (Mokyr 1983; but see Kennedy 1983a and 1984; also Solar 1984), with the curious outcome that we have in fact turned, historiographically-speaking, full circle. Once upon a time the reasons for all Ireland's ills were briskly laid at the feet of an oppressive landlord class, alien, lazy, expropriative, feckless, and irresponsible. Landlords, in this view, rarely visited their estates, merely collected rents, and evicted their tenants with abandoned relish (O'Hegarty 1952; Sullivan 1877; O'Connor 1886; O'Brien 1921; Hayden and Moonan 1921). Then appeared the revisionists who put forward very different views. Although much of their research was devoted to the latter half of the century the early years were illuminated by an at least refracted light. The ensuing picture – of more reasonable rents, fewer evictions, greater though patchy efficiency, sporadic benevolence even – was one in which landlords were seen almost as the victims of circumstances beyond individual control (Maguire 1972; Donnelly 1975; Vaughan 1977; 1980a; 1980b; 1984). But more recently we find again that if anyone was responsible for the 'dismal history of pre-Famine agriculture' it was the landlords after all, whose entrepreneurial failures, absenteeism, and incompetence deprived the economy of much-needed vigour and investment. Indeed, the leading 'neo-revisionist' has even gone so far as to argue that ultimately there is none other but that old inanimate entity 'history to blame: the creation of the landlord class from the British and Scottish adventurers and mercenaries, a class of parvenus and foreigners' (Mokyr 1983: 212).

Yet, in the end, such sweeping assertions depend as much upon faith as on evidence, for, presumably, the suggestion is that a different kind of landlord class – perhaps Catholic, Irish-speaking, indigenous – might have been able to orchestrate a dynamic economic revolution, something which, to put it mildly, is hardly capable of being either proved or disproved (Kennedy 1984). Of course landlords were often feckless and inefficient. Of course too the amounts they reinvested were generally low by British standards, though it could be argued that their rent policies may well – in a manner entirely unplanned – have left an investible surplus in the hands of tenants and thus made possible a 'more effective way of promoting agricultural investment' than would otherwise have been the case (Kennedy 1984). And although the original revisionists painted the social, economic, and political activities of the landed community in unduly roseate hues (Hoppen 1984: 116–70), we are still left with a more complex and ambiguous picture than was once the case.

IV

The most obvious, if generally opaque, reflection of the social and economic tensions of the pre-Famine countryside was furnished by its experience of violence, a phenomenon whose many-sidedness mirrors the ragged, cross-cutting, and often confused nature of contemporary relationships and aspirations. In particular, it highlights the existence of a continuum of suspicion and envy along which a place must be found for clashes between rich and poor, comfortable farmers and lesser farmers, farmers and labourers, landlords and tenants, Protestants and Catholics, between one kin group and another, between one locality and another, as also *within* families and *within* social categories. So varied and different could the driving force be that generalizations of any kind have a habit of exploding when pricked by the hard pin of particular cases and specific examples. One thing, however, should be kept in mind, namely, that, while rural Ireland was a comparatively violent place in the first half of the nineteenth century, most parts of the country were peaceable at any one time, the night sky was not constantly lit up by burning hayricks nor rent with the shrieks of victims being mutilated or put to death. Nor, indeed, was rural unrest a peculiarly

Irish prerogative. The South and East of England experienced severe disturbances in the years after Waterloo and continental peasants too were rarely slow to indulge in a wide repertoire of rustic protest, turbulence, and disorder.

Despite earlier manifestations of rural violence it was the so-called Whiteboy outbreaks of the early 1760s in Munster which established many of the characteristics later to become commonplace: oath-bound secret societies, intimidation of those perceived to be offenders against some kind of social and economic code, above all, an obsession with 'property' or at least 'occupation' rights, mainly, but by no means exclusively, in land (Donnelly 1978 and 1983a). By the end of the century two broadly separate, though often overlapping, traditions had become established. The first, that of the Whiteboys and in the 1780s the Rightboys (Donnelly 1977–8; Bric 1983) was active in Munster and contiguous parts of Leinster. Although its aims and composition were far from immutable it was in the main a movement of the landless and the land-poor and as such was particularly concerned with the availability and cost of conacre and the tithe on potatoes. Yet other issues also achieved sporadic emphasis. Thus the Whiteboyism of 1769–76 involved many farmers and their sons whose chief complaint concerned the tithe on corn at a time when commercial tillage was rapidly expanding in the South-East, while the Rightboys mobilized a vigorous protest against the dues levied upon parishioners by Catholic priests. The second main tradition grew out of the south Ulster/north Leinster 'frontier' area and because of this was far more overtly sectarian in tone, though here too the land question was of crucial importance especially when it interacted with the fluctuating fortunes of the domestic textile industry (Donnelly 1981; Miller 1983).

Inevitably any such typology grossly oversimplifies the shifting local realities of rural unrest, for the major outbreaks of the early-nineteenth century were shaped, not only by an established rhetoric and methodology of protest, but also by the changing imperatives of different places and different times. This at least was common to the Threshers in north-east Connacht in 1806–7, the Shanavests and Caravats of Munster in 1809–11, the east Leinster Carders of 1813–16, the so-called Ribbon protests in Clare and Westmeath in 1819–20, the Munster Rockites of 1819–23, the Leinster Whitefeet of 1830–4, and the Clare Terry Alts of 1831–2. Most outbreaks took place at times of distress and many were heavily focused upon the economic tensions between comfortable farmers and those lower down the scale of rural life. Yet the years immediately before 1815 were generally prosperous, though less so for labourers faced with higher food prices than for farmers. The most troubled districts were often – but not always, Clare being an obvious exception – areas of bigger farms with relatively high numbers of labourers slowly being squeezed out of their conacre holdings. Undoubtedly too the western counties were often less disturbed, in large part because their agriculture was a good deal less market orientated,[1] their land often too poor for anything other than potatoes, and because the distinction between farmers and labourers was there often indistinct and sometimes absent altogether (Lee 1980). Again, while it is probably true that agrarian activists were primarily angered by a local state of things which they regarded as unjust and 'exhibited very little in the way of nationalist or republican sentiment' (Beames 1983: 144; Connolly 1981: 170), yet the more politicized and partly urban Ribbon movement seems – at least fitfully – to have succeeded in attracting rural support for an inchoate programme of subversion along quasi-Defender and 'nationalist' lines (Garvin 1982; Beames 1982). Nor did those involved entirely avoid the more formal political platforms of the time, as when the Terry Alts openly backed a congenial candidate at the Clare election of 1831 and gathered in enormous numbers to dig up grasslands for potato ground tossing the sods into the air with the cry 'Hey for O'Connell, and hey for Clare' (Donnelly 1986).

More generally the relationship between the preoccupations of O'Connellite politics and of agrarian unrest seems to have fluctuated according to some complicated choreography of attraction and repulsion the details of which remain obstinately hidden and mysterious. Clearly at a time when, in the words of a contemporary, there were 'different districts of Ireland almost as unlike each other as any two countries in Europe' (Lewis 1836: 61) and when Young Ireland rebels on the run in 1848 could come across places where O'Connell was virtually unknown (Brown 1953: 434), it was extremely difficult for formal politics of any kind to penetrate at all evenly throughout the island as a whole. Not only that, but the very disposition of O'Connell's own political and social language was weighted heavily in favour of the 'respectable' farmers and against the aspirations of the rural proletariat (Hoppen 1984: 96). Even so, there were times, notably in the late 1820s and the early 1840s, when O'Connell seems, despite everything, to have succeeded in securing a remarkably wide social and geographical attachment to his cause.

Misunderstandings about pre-Famine agrarian unrest often derive from historians' over-zealous desire to see only long-term patterns and developments in the past – that great scholarly heresy of the modern age. But on the whole those actually involved at the time were poor and had little opportunity to do more than seize what passing chance could offer them. Small short-term gains were what they sought. A plot of potato ground, a lower conacre rent, higher wages for a month or two were all of them birds in the hand which counted for more than any number of plump partridges in the distant bushes of nationalism, revolution, or turning the world upside down. But because different groups perceived their situations differently so a multitude of contradictory motivations could coexist in practical if unlikely harmony. Thus one of the widest and fiercest of pre-Famine outbreaks, that of the Rockites in the early 1820s, was shot through with a vivid and intense millenarianism, which, based upon the so-called prophecies of 'Pastorini' (in fact originally the work of an eighteenth-century English Catholic bishop), predicted the total collapse of Protestantism for the year 1825. What millenarianism did for the Rockites was not to provide them with a programme but to help overcome internal social differences by giving their movement a strongly religious and anti-Protestant orientation (Donnelly 1983). The result was that ballad singers were able to press home a message combining apocalyptic triumphalism and physical betterment in almost equal proportions (Zimmermann 1967: 30).

> Now the year 21 is drawing by degrees,
> In the year 22 the Locusts will weep,
> But in the year 23 we'll begin to reap.
> Good people take courage, don't perish in fright,
> For notes will be nothing in the year 25;
> As I am O'Healy, we'll daily drink beer.

Because, therefore, the phenomenon of rural unrest was so many-sided, it is unrealistic to see either its personnel or its aims as constant and fixed. Those who insist that the chief targets of attack were improving landlords anxious to clear their estates and introduce a more efficient agriculture (Beames 1978) or prosperous farmers guilty of exploitation in the matter of conacre rents (Lee 1973a) or the poor and the weak, who, having transgressed some communal code, were easier to assault than those able to afford guns and ammunition (Lewis 1836: 194) all overlook too many contrary instances to elicit entire assent. After all, it did not take long for most sections of rural society to realize that agrarian unrest

47

offered something to almost everyone. Renegade 'gentlemen' are known to have been involved in the Rightboy movement (Bric 1983). The Tithe War of the 1830s attracted large numbers of well-to-do farmers into violent protest against an imposition almost universally unpopular but especially so among those who paid (absolutely if not relatively) the most (O'Donoghue 1965; 1966; 1972).

Nor should it be assumed that it was always a matter of the economically less favoured undertaking violence against those more prosperous than themselves. There are many examples of tension within rather than between social groups and certain official tabulations in the early 1840s suggest, for example, 'that disputes among labourers were the major occasion for homicide' (Fitzpatrick 1982: 40). Farmers, in their turn, were more than prepared to make pre-emptive strikes against recalcitrant labourers. Violence, indeed, was by no means invariably aimed in a socially upward direction but could instead often be part of that 'relentless but less familiar struggle of the oppressor against the insufficiently downtrodden' (Fitzpatrick 1982: 43; Lee 1980: 225). In the earlier years especially it was often a matter of *sauve-qui-peut* and in one well documented outbreak in east Munster between 1802 and 1811 rival groups of poor labourers and cottiers, on the one side, and comparatively comfortable farmers, on the other, engaged in a series of bitter, bloody, and mutually destructive battles (Roberts 1983). The former, who called themselves Caravats, were primarily a Whiteboy-type organization, while the latter went under the title of Shanavests and represented a combination of vigilantism, reactive middle-class counterviolence, and even something approaching a muffled species of nationalism. To most contemporaries it all seemed little more than yet another version of the so-called faction fights then common in many parts of rural Ireland in which kin and local groups attacked each other on fair and market days in what seems often to have been a manner entirely innocent of social or economic motivation. Yet in this one case at least it is evident that even such apparently random violence could, under the impress of particular circumstances, be transformed into something of a class war.

As it becomes evident that many of the tensions made visible by rural unrest were concerned with much more than the land question, however broadly interpreted, so the less clearly can neat arguments of social patterning be consistently sustained. Anything in short supply – illicit stills, beautiful girls, the best seats in chapel – created a temptation for rival claimants to enforce their demands violently and to do so, as often as not, through the mechanisms of neighbourhood and kinship rather than class (Fitzpatrick 1982). Nonetheless, within this wider turbulence it may still be possible to discover tentative pointers of a broadly social kind. Here the most interesting suggestion to date has come from J. S. Donnelly who argues that 'prosperity and depression influenced the social composition of agrarian rebellions in certain profound and differing ways' (Donnelly 1985: 154). Thus in prosperous times when prices were buoyant and land values rising unrest was largely the preserve of the landless and land-poor determined to restrain the inflation of conacre rents and to 'frustrate the land-acquisitive tendencies of large farmers and graziers'. However, when prices declined, there occurred a 'progressive widening in the social composition of the rebellious groups'; the poor remained active but were now only one element among many. Whether this analysis can be applied to all or even most outbreaks remains to be established. But the evidence from 1813–16, when, as prices dropped, a spreading social involvement took place in the Carder and Caravat disturbances of the time, suggests that it might well be found to have a more general, though probably not a universal, validity.

In broader terms still it is as yet far from clear how best to explain the wild fluctuations in unrest from one year to another. Some have put forward 'mobilization' theories in which collective action is seen as an assertion of power and solidarity by upwardly mobile groups: as wealth and numerical strength increase so the drive to mobilize in pursuit of further economic or political advance gathers pace. But such things depend upon comparatively long-term influences and can hardly explain precise variations over a few months or even years. The other favoured approach, the so-called 'breakdown' theory whereby violence is attributed to the fracture of some mutually tolerated relationship, has tended to be used so loosely that its explanatory power has dropped almost to vanishing point as 'virtually any disturbance of the *status quo ante*, whether for better or for worse', is regarded by its proponents as 'capable of generating collective action in rural Ireland' (Fitzpatrick 1985a: 102). Different economic, social, and kinship patterns, it seems, encouraged different kinds of unrest, and future answers will have to be found in a closer examination of changes – both in the short and long term – within and between these interconnected aspects of nineteenth-century Irish life.

The very fact, however, that there existed within rural society at least a tendency, even if a fluctuating one, towards sympathy with violence in general suggests that in the popular mind the perpetrators of outrages were not simply criminals and were in no deep sense separated from their local communities (Lewis 1836: 183). The aims most constantly kept in view were limited, socially conservative, and realistic, not jackpot demands of immediate riches for all. Yet, although claims have been made for the practical efficacy of rural unrest in halting the consolidation of farms and stopping evictions (Mokyr 1983: 124–44; Beames 1983: 205–11), the very frequency of eruptions designed to secure such ends suggests that success was usually ephemeral and short-lived though probably no less welcome for that. More important was the way in which a whole culture of violent action was being created, a culture which soon ceased to be confined to directly agrarian or economic matters and to embrace instead a wide range of actions and relationships, not least those which might best be described as 'political'. Thus, given the social ambience within which, for example, parliamentary and other voters found themselves, it is unsurprising that strategies designed to frighten landlords, bailiffs, farmers, and labourers should have been employed to frighten voters and candidates as well. Quite apart, therefore, from the survival of agrarian violence throughout the period, the continuing vigour of electoral intimidation shows how a tradition of rural outrage endured also in surrogate form, and how popular memories could give a sustained edge to the activities of political mobsters of all persuasions, whether Orange, Green, or merely Mainchance (Hoppen 1984: 356–7).

Perhaps the most telling contemporary image of this complicated rural chiaroscuro was captured by the novelists of the time. Just as John Banim's *The Nowlans* (1827) pictured the world of pushing strong farmers with insight and accuracy, so William Carleton, despite a tendency to swing violently from the overly romantic to the starkly realistic, held up a mirror to the intricacies of rural existence to such effect that, in his story 'The Fair of Emyvale' (1853), he fully anticipated those modern historians who have seen the post-Napoleonic price depreciation as perhaps the most important economic watershed of the time. Even Gerald Griffin, intent as he was on emphasizing for English readers the gentler aspects of Irish life, not only crammed the opening pages of his most famous novel, *The Collegians* (1829), with ominous symbols of death, but had no hesitation in using murder as the main metaphor for Irish society at the precise moment when O'Connell's emancipation campaign was about to enter the harbour of acceptance and respectability (Dunne 1986).

V

Nor did the experience of those who lived in the towns offer much in the way of positive contrast, for here too it is likely that any overall rise in living standards was so unevenly distributed as to leave the mass of unskilled labourers still poor and relatively no better off than before. Some industries, notably linen, did well enough, but in general and despite some recovery from the depths of depression after the early and mid-1820s, the story was one of decline (Cullen 1972: 107–8). Outside Dublin and Belfast towns tended to stagnate and insofar as their populations rose the increased numbers consisted largely of beggars and farm labourers looking for food and work. Although skilled wages compared well with those in England many artisan occupations declined as older crafts retreated in the face of manufactured and usually imported products (Daly 1981a: 100, 106). Yet this process was far from complete and urban affairs were economically dominated by wealthy local merchants and industrialists, who, depending on their religious affiliations, were the key orchestrators of either O'Connellite or Conservative politics, and numerically dominated by skilled artisans, many of whom had been given the vote by the Irish Reform Act of 1832. Retailing was still an infant (though a rapidly growing) sector and shopkeepers were not to replace artisans as the electoral shock troopers of the borough constituencies until the second half of the century (Hoppen 1984: 33–73).

Local power structures were often hermetically divided. In pre-Famine Cork (Pop. 1841 = 80,720), for example, the Catholic and Protestant mercantile elites, which were roughly equal in wealth, maintained separate clubs, charities, and political organizations, and came together only when commercial considerations such as rates or railway development demanded a combined response (O'Brien 1979). The effect of reforms in the parliamentary (1832) and municipal (1840) franchises was to allow the Catholic middle classes to reap the electoral rewards which their economic standing clearly entitled them to. And, just as people in rural Ireland expected great practical things from emancipation and repeal, so also did their cousins in the towns (Murphy 1981: 145–6).

> The tradesman and labourer that's now in poverty,
> Will sit in their parlour and sing melodiously.
> We'll have mutton, beef and bacon, with butter, eggs and veal,
> And religion will come again to welcome the Repeal.

As a result, the relationship between urban workers and nationalist (or even national) politics was punctuated by oscillating bouts of distrust and admiration. Especially in Dublin – still far and away the largest Irish town – the artisans actually proved more constant in the cause of repeal than did O'Connell whose *laissez-faire* denunciations of trade unions more than matched his condemnations of rural secret societies. Workers, O'Connell announced in 1838, 'were not entitled to wages out of capital; they were only entitled to them out of profits, and if their employers made no profits the wages must decrease' (*Hansard* 3rd Series: xl, 1086). And while such sentiments may have pleased his middle-class lieutenants they quickly enraged the Dublin artisans into demanding 'What advantage is it to the tradesmen of Ireland that thirteen hundred situations have been thrown open by emancipation? . . . Has it given a loaf of bread to any of the thousand starving families of the poor operatives of this city?' (D'Arcy 1970: 221).

Contemporary censuses do not make it possible to calculate the number of the unskilled in Irish towns. Yet statistical information concerning the low quality of housing (Daly 1981b: 252) and a massive weight of impressionistic evidence regarding the ubiquity of paupers in the streets (Hoppen 1979: 191) strongly suggest that a significant proportion of the urban population was no better (and possibly worse) off than the labourers and cottiers of the countryside. While the general deflation after 1815 reduced food prices, it was rarely an easy matter for those with only their physical strength to offer to take advantage of this in any steady or reliable way (O'Brien 1977). Not only was work often simply unobtainable, but illness, injury, and the death of a breadwinner could and often did sever the fragile threads connecting large numbers of families with the cash nexus of the time (Freeman 1977: 130–2). Whereas, however, agricultural labourers were, to say the least, prominent in rural unrest, the pre-Famine Ribbon movement, which, almost alone, maintained a significant urban base, had little success in attracting the unskilled of the towns into active membership (Beames 1982: 130–1; Garvin 1982: 151). Even before the Famine, therefore, Irish towns seem to have developed a political culture, which, in the almost invisible role it assigned to the poorest sections of society, foreshadowed a state of things that was not to become the norm in rural Ireland until well into the second half of the century.

Any account of unrest, and especially agrarian unrest, in pre-Famine Ireland must conclude, as it began, with a note of caution. At all times most of the country was probably comparatively quiet and it should be emphasized that when in 1837 some reasonably reliable statistics become available they suggest that the last years before 1845 were not, taking population into account, notably more disturbed than the supposedly tranquil decade of the 1850s (Hoppen 1984: 364–6). And while it may well be that the period 1837–44 witnessed a substantial lessening of activity when compared with what had gone before, it remains the case that any such suggestion, however plausible on general grounds, is unlikely ever to be supported by accurate data of a measurable kind.

VI

Although the Great Famine which broke out in the Autumn of 1845 has in this chapter made frequent premonitory appearances as if it was a goal towards which Irish society was inexorably moving this is not an accurate reflection of how early-nineteenth-century Irishmen and women themselves arranged the future furniture of their minds. Neither the jeremiads of the Malthusians nor the *local* food shortages of earlier times were then – or should now be – regarded as imperatively reliable predictions that dependency on a single source of food was bound to lead to disaster (Ó Gráda 1988: 122). While the Irish economy was certainly 'vulnerable', the disease which struck the potato crop in the late 1840s had never struck before and could not realistically have been anticipated (but see Mokyr 1983: 261–77). This, indeed, was part of the trouble and explains much about both the nature of the popular reaction and the manner in which the government responded to the catastrophe.

The chronology of the blight can be briefly stated. The fungus, for which there was then no cure, first struck in late-August 1845. But about a sixth of that year's crop was lifted in a healthy state and some parts of the country escaped altogether. However, in 1846 failure was total and in 1847, though the disease was less severe, little was planted as a despairing people had eaten their seed potatoes for food. The 1848 crop was a complete disaster. Although things thereafter improved it was not until 1850 that it became possible to regard the worst as being over and even then agricultural dislocation and large-scale emigration (which reached its peak in 1851) continued for some years more (Edwards and Williams 1956).

The Conservative government under Peel, which remained in power until June 1846, reacted with considerable promptitude. Local relief committees were encouraged and given substantial grants; public works were initiated (some 140,000 found employment during the 1845–6 season); and £100,000 was spent on buying Indian meal – a diet by no means unknown to the Irish poor before 1845 (Crawford 1981) – for storage in special depots and for future release should food prices rise to unusual heights (O'Neill 1956). *Sub specie aeternitatis* this was not a great deal, but, given the long-standing prejudice of governments towards Ireland, it was rather more than might have been expected. However, the arrival of Lord John Russell's Liberal administration in the Summer of 1846 signalled a retreat from the administratively forward positions Peel had established. Russell, his Chancellor of the Exchequer, Sir Charles Wood, and the permanent head of the Treasury, Sir Charles Trevelyan, were all of them convinced that Irish horror stories were invariably exaggerated, that governments should not interfere in the free workings of the market, and that Irish landlords – in their eyes a bloated and irresponsible breed – should be made to bear the costs of relief until the pips squeaked (Prest 1972: 234–45). It was not long, however, before this policy of disengagement crumbled in the face of overwhelming disaster. The numbers employed on relief projects rose to 720,000 in the Spring of 1847. It was clear that something more needed to be done (Ó Tuathaigh 1972: 203–21).

As a last resort the government, despite its declared adherence to non-interventionism, opened a network of soup kitchens: by August 1847 an incredible three million people were being fed daily and the central principle of the Irish poor law – that only indoor relief be granted – was being massively breached. In June 1847 the Poor Law Amendment Act authorized the giving of outdoor assistance even to the able-bodied and by the middle of 1848 about 800,000 persons were receiving food outside workhouses in addition to the substantial numbers being 'relieved' within their walls (O'Neill 1956). For some time leading British politicians had touted a sovereign remedy for Irish rural discontent, namely, the 'reduction' of cottiers and smallholders to the status of wage labourers (Hoppen 1984: 96). The new act, by denying relief to all those occupying more than a quarter of an acre of land, represented a decisive step towards the achievement of such a policy. That it was also a piece of (heartless) social engineering and might, therefore, convincingly be portrayed as outright interventionism does not, however, seem to have struck an administration otherwise so publicly anxious to declare its adherence to the principles of *laissez-faire*.

Although much admirable work was done by private charities and large sums raised from non-governmental sources in both Britain and Ireland, the experience of hunger and of the diseases which soon spread throughout the land (MacArthur 1956) was deep and terrible. The constabulary reported a massive increase in outrages but these were now overwhelmingly 'against property' rather than 'against the person' or 'the public peace' as starving cottiers and labourers desperately stole food or anything that could be sold for money with which to buy provisions (Hoppen 1984: 368). Only eye-witness accounts can capture, even feebly, the measure of the tragedy. 'Being aware', wrote a magistrate in December 1846 of a recent visit to Skibbereen in west Cork,

> that I should have to witness scenes of frightful hunger, I provided myself with as much bread as five men could carry, and on reaching the spot I was surprised to find the wretched hamlet apparently deserted. I entered some of the hovels to ascertain the cause, and the scenes which presented themselves were such as no tongue or pen can convey the slightest idea of. In the first, six famished and ghastly skeletons, to all appearances dead, were huddled in a corner on some filthy straw . . . their wretched legs hanging about, naked above the knees. I approached with horror, and found by a low moaning they were alive . . . in a few minutes I was surrounded by at least 200 such phantoms, such frightful spectres as no words can describe, either from famine or from fever. Their demoniac yells are still ringing in my ears, and their horrible images are fixed upon my brain (Woodham-Smith 1962: 162).

Some landlords did their best to help the poor in their areas, and even in a county like Derry where things were not as desperate as in many other places, one such proprietor recorded in January 1847 how

> the moment I open my hall door in the morning until dark, I have a crowd of women and children crying out for something to save them from starving. The men, except the old and infirm stay away, and show the greatest patience and resignation. . . . The only reply to my question of what do you want, is, I want something to eat . . . We are also visited by hordes of wandering poor who come from the mountains, or other districts less favoured by a resident gentry, and worst of all, Death is dealing severely and consigning many to an untimely tomb (Public Record Office of N. Ireland, Dawson Papers MS T2603/1).

Perhaps in their own way even more chilling, if that were possible, are the statistics. Here the best estimates suggest that the number of 'excess' deaths resulting from the Famine (that is deaths which would not otherwise have occurred) amounted at least to 1.1 million and may perhaps have even been rather greater than that. Somewhat surprisingly, although deaths were highest in the western counties, there does not seem to have been any significant correlation between excess mortality and the local extent of potato cultivation. More successful in explaining differences in the impact of the disaster are general economic variables such as income per capita, the level of literacy, housing quality, and the proportion of farms less than twenty acres in size (Mokyr 1983: 261–77). This suggests that, while the Famine undoubtedly affected labourers and cottiers most severely, it was only those farmers with holdings of more than twenty acres who managed to emerge relatively unscathed in some cases and in others stronger than ever before.

Whatever particular individuals may have done, substantial farmers in general do not seem to have greatly modified their traditional hostility towards those less fortunate than themselves. They continued to prosecute starving labourers discovered stealing food from the fields. They withheld conacre plots from those who could not pay in advance. They refused money wages to those for whom only cash could now ensure even the most minimal of diets (Donnelly 1975: 74–5, 87). More clearly than ever before rural society was divided by the Famine into haves and have-nots with the line of separation falling not between landlords and tenants but – in very broad terms – between those with at least twenty acres of land and those with either less or none at all. And it was, indeed, from the ranks of the latter that the bulk of the deaths and the bulk of the million or more who emigrated came. In this sense, therefore, did the Famine itself, the social engineering of the government, and the attitudes and behaviour of the larger farmers all combine to effect a settlement of that power struggle which had for almost a century constituted a dominant theme in rural life. Labourers did not of course disappear. Nor was the triumph of the middling and substantial farmers either total or immediate. But the social and economic landscape had undoubtedly been changed in ways at once significant and profound (Daly 1986).

Other European countries also experienced the potato blight of the late 1840s. But, even making every allowance for their generally lesser dependence upon the crop, it remains the case that it was above all their more extensive industrialization which allowed them 'to save their labouring poor from the fate of the Irish'. Thus, for example, in Belgium, the Netherlands, and Scotland alternative and stronger sectors of the economy were able to pull the starving peasants through the worst stages of distress. In this sense, therefore, the Irish experience serves – notwithstanding all the well-known costs of industrialization – as a grim reminder of what its absence could entail (Mokyr 1983: 276). And although the government's response was extremely inefficient, grudging, and limited (Ó Gráda 1988: 110–18), perhaps only an authoritarian state committed to the welfare of the poor at all costs could have *achieved* a great deal more. The problem after all lay not only in a general failure of food supply but in the inability of the poor potato eaters to *buy* food. Dramatic acts – which were never remotely probable – such as the compulsory slaughter of livestock or the banning of grain exports would almost certainly have faced the government with even fiercer class conflict because (as is too often forgotten) 'the chief beneficiaries of the unrestrained workings of market forces were not landlords, but Irish farmers and merchants' who showed little inclination to swap places with the poor (Kennedy 1985a: 29–30).

In any case, given the difficulties of communication, of an undeveloped retailing and distribution network, of an inadequate bureaucracy, the scale of the relief operations at their height does not compare unfavourably with the manner in which the 'developed' late-twentieth-century world has proved itself able or willing to handle similar disasters. Nor is it likely, given the class interests involved, that any Dublin-based government would have done much better at the time. Indeed, it is quite possible that a 'Repeal' administration might well have proved less rather than more effective. Yet, when all is said and done, there can be little doubt that the experience of the Famine did help to bring about that shift in attitudes and ideology which have subsequently made it possible to 'compare the public parsimony of the 1840s with the sums lavished on Ireland only a few decades later for the relief of what were minor crises by comparison' (Ó Gráda 1988: 117).

It has in recent years become something of a revisionist orthodoxy to deny that the Famine represented the most significant social and economic watershed of nineteenth-century Ireland. Efforts have been made to substitute instead the depression following the ending of the French wars in 1815, which, it is claimed, set Irish agriculture on the road from tillage to pasture and therefore established a firm agenda for the future in both specifically agrarian and more general terms (Crotty 1966: 1–65; Cullen 1972: 134; Winstanley 1984: 8). But while such claims were once at least historiographically invigorating they have always seemed strained and have more recently been subjected to intense and on the whole convincing attack (Goldstrom 1981). The fact that the population in 1851 was 6.5 million as compared with about 8.3 million in 1841, the fact that the labourer and small farmer communities shrank substantially in the 1840s and thereafter continued to do so – even if subdivision had not been as common before 1845 as was once thought (Bourke 1965) – the fact that the future now definitely lay on the side of pasture instead of tillage, the fact that the culture of the most Gaelic areas was soon to experience terminal decline are all of them interconnected phenomena of the very greatest significance. Of course aspects of these and other developments (such as the nature of marriage and inheritance) were already visible before 1845. But it was the Great Famine, which, by concentrating their fully-armed emergence into a few terrible years, saw to it that, in many crucial respects, Irish society experienced change not so much by slow and steady evolution as by something akin to a Big Bang.

Rural unrest did not disappear but became less socially opaque in that the preoccupations of those with little or no land were now steadily but remorselessly shunted to the margins of prominence. For the small band of intellectual revolutionaries the disaster furnished a unique polemical resource, though the masses of the poor most closely maimed seem to have viewed it as a scourge sent from God for sins unknown and unknowable. Thus it was John Mitchel's savage comment in *The Last Conquest of Ireland (Perhaps)* of 1860 that 'The Almighty, indeed, sent the potato blight, but the English created the Famine' which was soon to seize the imagination of those thousands who had emigrated and who, divorced from the changing realities of life in Ireland itself, could thereafter the more readily sustain a retrospective anger within the fixed and unyielding cement of revolutionary zeal (O'Farrell 1982–3). At home things took a less single-minded path. There the revolutionaries remained a minority and as such were, more often than not, overwhelmed by the localist priorities of political life, priorities which had developed well before 1845, had successfully maintained themselves during the Famine itself (Lee 1980: 228), and were to bloom into full luxuriance in the decades to come.

NOTE

1. Although this was broadly true, there is little evidence to support the view proposed by Lynch and Vaizey (1960) that pre-Famine Ireland maintained a 'dual' system in which a monetary economy along the east coast was sharply distinguished from a subsistence economy in the more western areas. While there remains a germ of truth in this idea it would be more accurate to see any such distinctions as following social rather than topographical lines, though of course class distribution was not devoid of spatial characteristics.

CHAPTER 3
Religion

The Birthpangs of Modernity

Although no one could ever have denied that Catholics constituted by far the largest denominational group in Ireland the reliable statistics produced in 1834 by the Commissioners of Public Instruction to the effect that 80.9 per cent of the population was Catholic, 10.7 per cent members of the episcopalian Church of Ireland and 8.1 per cent of various Presbyterian bodies confirmed the most optimistic claims of one side and the most extreme fears of the other (Connolly 1985b: 3). However much Protestants of all sorts could still stress their superior wealth, education, and position, the great numerical fact now at last precisely revealed could not be overlooked. Its reverberations throughout the spheres of political and social activity were profound and the sharper edge it gave to the concepts of sectarian majority and minority furnished one of the central realities of modern Irish life.

I

The commissioners published their findings at a time of transition during which all the major denominations were experiencing profound change. Already by the end of the eighteenth century the institutional life of Catholicism had emerged from the troubles and rigours imposed by the Penal Laws which had involved both an only-partially effective attempt to constrain religious practice and a more heartfelt effort to deprive Catholics of landed and political influence (Wall 1961). A bench of some twenty-six bishops provided increasingly active leadership. Communications with Rome were

60

frequent and brisk. Though caution was still the order of the day as regards episcopal relations with the government, a new confidence and self-assurance were slowly establishing themselves within the corridors of clerical power. Yet the problems facing the bishops were immense, the chief being that of numbers. At its simplest, the church had to run very fast merely to catch up with the growing size of the Catholic population. Despite the establishment in 1795 of St Patrick's College Maynooth as the chief Irish seminary and despite the granting of funds towards its work from a government anxious to prevent ordinands being trained in what was now a revolutionary France, the supply of priests, though increasing, was unable to match the demand. Thus, although the number of parochial clergy rose from 1614 in 1800 to 2159 in 1835 the average number of Catholics to each priest also rose from 2676 in the former year to 2991 in the latter. And matters were made worse by the fact that such averages concealed an extremely uneven distribution (Table 3.1) between the four ecclesiastical provinces – each with an archbishop at its head – into which the church was divided (Hoppen 1984: 172–3).

Table 3.1 Number of Catholics for each parochial clergyman, 1835

Armagh Province	2805
Cashel Province	3227
Dublin Province	2451
Tuam Province	3659

Quite apart, however, from the problem of numbers – and the parochial clergy was as yet augmented by only modest bands of regular priests and female religious (Clear 1987) – was that posed by the maintenance of clerical discipline and good order. Although socially and economically priests stood well above the bulk of the laity they were also still very much the products of a community in which factional disputes, kin rivalries, and class tensions counted for much. Fierce battles not infrequently took place between rival candidates for vacant bishoprics and parishes, many of them conducted in the full light of the public gaze (Connolly 1981). A minority of bishops still reminded their flocks of unhappier times when, for example, Archbishop Blake of Armagh had been suspended for non-residence in the 1770s and Bishop Butler of Cork had in the

1780s turned Protestant and married man on succeeding to the barony of Dunboyne. Thus Dominick Bellew, Bishop of Killala until 1812, was a careerist whose activities would have done credit to any Anglican hunter of sinecures and pluralities, while Daniel Delany, who held the sees of Kildare and Leighlin from 1787 to 1814, was accorded the tongue-in-cheek accolade of having been 'somewhat dilatory in performing the various arduous duties of episcopal life. Passionately fond of the society of intellectual and sincere friends he often forgot, in the charm of their presence, to execute some long-advertised visitation' (Connolly 1982: 64–70). Those bishops who tried hard to introduce stricter standards of behaviour among their subordinates were frequently met with strong opposition, public abuse, and stonewalling tactics at once effective and prolonged. Letters poured into the Congregation of the Propaganda (the Vatican department then responsible for Irish affairs) from priests accusing each other and the bishops of simony, causing scandal, drunkenness, factiousness, and even sexual irregularities (Larkin 1962).

If this did little to enhance the public standing of the priesthood the nature of the connections between clergy and people cannot easily be broken down into neat compartments of approval and disapprobation. While aspects of the relationship caused tension and dispute there was no general expectation in the pre-Famine countryside – though things in the towns were already rather different – that priests should strictly confine themselves to a purely specialist role and, in effect, constitute themselves into an entirely separate caste. But such a model was precisely the one which a reforming episcopate was attempting – however haltingly and at times confusingly – to introduce. As a result, the early-nineteenth century is best seen as a transitionary period during which opposing forces were pulling the church in different and often contradictory directions.

Administratively and in terms of ecclesiastical plant it was a time of reorganization and reform. Substantial progress was made in the business of education at all levels. New diocesan colleges enlarged the provision of seminary training. By the early 1820s nuns and teaching brothers provided seventy schools for the middling classes, while 352 free day schools and 9352 pay schools with 394,732 pupils catered for a wider market. The introduction of the National System by the Whig administration in 1831, despite all suggestions to the contrary, greatly increased clerical control, for many of the 'new' national schools were merely old pay schools now subsidized by the government with funding channelled largely through the hands of the local priest (Daly 1979; Murphy and Ó Súilleabháin 1971). Perhaps the most impressive of the church's achievements before 1850 was its enormous investment and progress in building work. Something like £5 million was spent in the first half of the century on constructing new or extending existing cathedrals, churches, convents, and seminaries. Under Archbishop Murray (1823–52) the Dublin diocese acquired £1.2 million worth of property, of which £700,000 represented expenditure on no less than ninety-seven churches (Larkin 1967: 856–7; Meagher 1853: 146). Throughout the country the old thatched chapels of penal times were replaced by slated buildings capable of accommodating significantly more worshippers (Kennedy 1970). Newspaper accounts of many of the churches built at the time indicate (even allowing for the inflations of local pride) substantial investment: 'Handsome Gothic', 'lately erected beautiful and commodious', '£2000 to date', 'magnificent', and so forth. Large and expensive cathedral projects were inaugurated in Carlow, Dublin, Belfast, Killarney, Ballina, Tuam, Ennis, Longford, Armagh, and Kilkenny. Indeed, the actual number of Catholic churches in Ireland did not thereafter require further increase – in part because of post-Famine population decline but in part also because of the dramatic building programme undertaken in the fifty years after the Union (Hoppen 1984: 206–8; Keenan 1983: 115–25).

What had once been occasional and informal meetings of the hierarchy became more frequent and after 1820 took place each year on a regular basis (Cannon 1979). Serious but only partly effective efforts were made to reduce clerical involvement in farming activities (something which inevitably led to disputes and accusations of avarice) and to transform the priesthood from what had almost at times amounted to a part-time occupation into a full-time one (Hoppen 1984: 178). A majority of bishops introduced new Roman devotions into their dioceses of a kind at once more formal, more controlled, and – in the ultramontane[1] sense – more modern than those emanating from existing manifestations of popular piety. Confraternities of lay people were founded to pray for the souls in purgatory, catechism classes established, and sodalities of the Sacred Heart set up. Charitable societies began to work among the poor, devotions to the Blessed Virgin achieved a greater prominence, and public liturgies became increasingly splendid, impressive, and Roman in tone. In short, the church was being gradually absorbed into a wider international Catholicism in which uniformity, spectacle, and obedience to the papacy counted for more than had previously been the case (Kerr 1982: 1–67; Cunningham 1960; Egan 1960).

Yet, as in the matter of clerical manpower, the effects of all this were both uneven and uncoordinated. The greatest impact was made in the eastern parts of the country and especially in the metropolitan diocese of Dublin where Archbishop Murray combined spiritual and liturgical dynamism with a somewhat guarded and cautious attitude to Roman triumphalism. Curiously enough, at the precise moment when the more active bishops were busily attempting a Roman *Gleichschaltung* of popular devotion and liturgical practice the Vatican lessened its own direct influence over episcopal appointments in Ireland – a reminder that historical change rarely follows neat or uniform patterns of development. Whereas previously there had simply been no 'system' and 'interested parties' had deluged Propaganda with canvassing letters and other arm-twisting activities on behalf of friends and relations – something which had led to violent public rows over appointments to the sees of Waterford in 1817, Achonry and Derry in 1818, Limerick and Cashel in 1822–3, and Armagh in 1828 – in 1829 a procedure was established by which the parish priests of a diocese were required to draw up (in order) a list of three candidates which the other bishops of the province would then transmit to Propaganda with their own comments attached. And while Rome was not obliged to appoint *any* of the names proposed, in practice it so rarely took matters into its own hands that between 1829 and 1849 only three out of twenty-seven bishops were appointed without having first found a place upon the *terna* or list initially drawn up by the parish priests. The effect of this was to produce a more cautious and local episcopate. Fewer men were appointed to dioceses other than their own and parish priests, like the barons of Runnymede, naturally preferred to select colleagues who would 'understand' clerical failings rather than outsiders who might wield the axe of discipline with too energetic an arm (Whyte 1962; Cunningham 1960).

II

Not all church reform was a matter for the clergy alone. In many respects the priests as a body, however disunited over questions of discipline, shared a broad identity of outlook as regards the nature of their functions within the community as a whole. And here too it was a time of transition as the church mounted a powerful assault upon the popular religiosity of Catholic Ireland. Until well into the nineteenth century this was made up of an amalgam of elements: orthodox Catholic beliefs, versions of such beliefs filtered through a folk comprehension of the supernatural and its interpenetrations with everyday life, and beliefs and practices only remotely connected with the recognized canons of Tridentine, let alone neo-ultramontane, Catholicism (Connolly 1983a). Aspects of the semi-formal rural celebration of seasons, of seedtime and harvest, had remained almost entirely divorced from Christian influences. Nor had the vigorous realm of fairies, of magical cures, popular healers, the evil eye, changelings, and curses yet yielded to the onward march of national religion and reformed manners (Connolly 1985b: 49–54; Jenkins 1977; Kennedy 1979a). Such popular supernaturalism, indeed, 'provided an explanation for what would otherwise have appeared as a meaningless pattern of good and bad fortune, while at the same time enabling people to feel that they exercised some control over that pattern' (Connolly 1982: 119). It found a physical manifestation not only in private and often secret practices hidden from clerical eyes but also, most notably, in the very public celebrations which, in early-nineteenth-century Ireland, still accompanied those rites of passage associated with individual, communal, and seasonal change. Coming to terms with death, for example, involved more than attendance at requiem mass or the provision of the sacrament of extreme unction; these, therefore, were still regularly augmented by energetic wakes notable not only for their often alcoholic abandon but for curious 'games' of a remarkably sexual, suggestive, and seemingly blasphemous kind. At such wakes priests were openly mocked and parodies of the Passion enacted, while sometimes naked, sometimes transvestite, people performed actions, which, in the opinion of a shocked outsider (who thought the whole business best 'confided to the guardianship of a dead language'), proved 'beyond doubt' that they were 'a relic of Pagan rites' (Prim 1853: 333–4). However that may have been, it seems rather that the participants, far from indulging in any deeply-felt critique of Christianity, regarded such events as simply inhabiting a sphere of understanding in which different rules and attitudes might quite properly be taken to apply.

More visible still were those many celebrations of the feastdays of local patron saints – the so-called 'pattern' days – in which elements of formal Christianity were almost indistinguishably amalgamated with a belief in the efficacy of holy wells or sacred mountains, with, indeed, a species of topographical supernaturalism (Hogan 1873; MacNeill 1962). Here the church was not excluded, but rather in danger of being overwhelmed and tainted by a combination of demonstrative religiosity and secular merriment in the shape of drinking, eating, singing, dancing, and courting. Above all, the pattern revealed that species of close intermingling of the sacred and the profane which was so marked a feature of pre-Famine religious practice and which at once diluted and muddied the clear waters of ecclesiastical authority.

Whatever the reactions of individual priests – and some at least were prepared to take a tolerant view – significant efforts were made during the half-century before the Famine either to suppress such practices or to reform them in the direction of contemporary theological respectability and modernity. Pioneering Gaelic scholars like John O'Donovan in 1837 bemoaned that 'the priests, I am sorry to see and to say, [are] inclining very much to Protestant notions, and putting an end to all . . . venerable old customs' (Connolly 1982: 112–13). 'The tone of society', recorded William Wilde (father of Oscar) in 1849, 'is becoming more and more *"Protestant"* every year; the literature is a Protestant one, and even the priests are becoming more Protestant in their conversations and manners. They have condemned all the holy wells and resorts of pilgrimage' (Wilde 1852: 17).

Just, therefore, as the various denominations were becoming more and more hostile to one another, so all of them began more and more to share one new thing in common: respectability, or 'Protestantism' as Wilde called it. Priests realigned the traditional Celtic Lughnasa festival of the beginning of harvest into a celebration of the feastday of the Virgin's Assumption on 15 August. They inveighed against 'pagan' practices and removed objects of traditional devotion – sacred trees, hallowed rocks, and the like. By mid-century some of the greatest patterns were in chronic decay: Slieve Donard, Church Mountain in Wicklow, Mount Brandon in Kerry (MacNeill 1962). Even the fairies took fright: 'their last great assembly was in the year 1839, when violent disputes arose among prominent fairy leaders, and the night following a large portion of the fairy host quitted the Green Isle, never to return' (Wood-Martin 1902: ii, 4).

Priests could not, however, simply crack the whip of modernization and without further ado drive the laity towards the uplands of orthodox respectability, for their very influence derived from a responsiveness to popular feelings as much as from the abstract possession of authority as such. 'Any religion which broke away from the people', a Mayo priest told Alexis de Tocqueville in 1835, 'would move away from its source and lose its main support. It is necessary to go with the people, Sir. There lies strength, and in order to remain united with the people, there is no sacrifice which one should regret imposing on oneself' (Tocqueville 1958: 172). And even if such humility was sometimes far from the minds of reforming prelates, save as a species of sentimentalism, the reality it encompassed necessarily exercised some measure of restraint upon the implementation of modernizing change and transformation. Priests, indeed, were themselves often happiest in that atmosphere of relaxed conviviality which was part and parcel of those traditional attitudes to religion they otherwise abhorred. They enjoyed dining pleasantly with their more prosperous parishioners (McGrath 1936–7). They liked the practice of hearing confession and saying mass in private houses – the so-called 'stations' – even when their superiors denounced the extravagant eating, drinking, and talking which tended to mark such occasions (Connolly 1982: 67). Accorded peculiar psychic and 'magical' powers by members of their flocks (though curiously such powers were thought especially strong in the case of defrocked or 'spoiled' priests) they were not always able to restrain themselves from cursing those who opposed them or from threatening to turn recalcitrants into 'goats', 'puck-haunes', or, less specifically, into 'amphibious animals'. Thus, Father Hickey, riding along the Waterford shore and shouting at voters on board a ship chartered by Tory candidates 'my curse and the curse of God upon you all . . . Mark you, I will raise such a storm around the vessel as will keep her at sea for six weeks', can hardly be considered entirely an untypical figure (Hoppen 1984: 212–13).

What it all amounted to was that in a society where the sacred and the profane, the orthodox and the magical, the modern and the traditional were so closely intermingled and where the supernatural was a matter of everyday concern and propitiation, there could be no immediate and total response to official Catholic reformism however powerfully presented and however insistently urged. The whole atmosphere of pre-Famine Catholicism was one of ambiguity. Church buildings were, not only for reasons of necessity, happily used for a wide variety of secular purposes. Priests adopted a comparatively relaxed approach in front of their congregations, which in turn expressed 'their sympathy with the preacher, as the Methodists in England do, by a deep and audible breathing' (Bicheno 1830: 173). On the one hand, therefore, we have a clergy increasingly anxious to drive the church towards what might be seen as modern practices – something in which priests were at one with many landlords, most government officials, and (in the words of a contemporary) with 'the schoolmaster and the railroad engineer' (Wilde 1852: 16). On the other, we have a society which, outside the major towns, often remained attached to practices of suggestive peculiarity and, in doing so, greatly retarded the impact of the reformist campaign.

It was, indeed, precisely in those districts of Ireland (notably the towns and the eastern counties) where modern formal religion had made the greatest impact that obedience to the outward practices of ultramontane Catholicism was most readily accorded by the people. David Miller has analysed the data for Sunday mass attendance collected by the Commissioners of Public Instruction in 1834 and has shown that, while in many towns the turn-out was virtually universal, in the English-speaking rural areas it was often no more than about a half and in the Irish-speaking countryside of the West it could often fall much lower still (Miller 1975). Though his findings have been criticized and upward revisions suggested (Corish 1985: 167), their overall integrity can hardly be doubted and they receive support from other evidence concerning the comparative unwillingness of many rural Catholics to perform much more than the minimum canonical requirements with regard to confession and the reception of communion (Connolly 1985b: 48–9).

Yet this should not be taken to imply any failure among the masses to identify themselves firmly as members of the Catholic community. Rather, their Catholicism was still deeply embedded in a network of attitudes which had not yet been entirely narrowed into that orthodoxy which was to establish itself more fully in the later decades of the century. If anything it was the very breadth and plasticity – perhaps one could even say the very *catholicity* – of their world view which allowed people to see no absolute contradiction between popular supernaturalism and attachment to an institution which increasingly sought to direct belief and behaviour into channels at once more exclusive and refined. But already before the Famine, as Miller's findings suggest, the church was proving itself especially successful in its mission of constrictive modernization among the 'respectable' sections of Irish society: the urban middle classes and the prosperous farmers. Just as the latter were already adopting the stem family system in the early-nineteenth century and handing on their holdings by impartible inheritance, so too were they the pioneering lay heralds of reformed Catholicism. That 'devotional revolution' in Ireland which Emmet Larkin originally postulated as occurring after the Famine (Larkin 1972) was in fact a much longer process and had by 1850 already been adopted, not only by many churchmen, but by the middle and upper-class sections of the laity. By contrast, traditional supernaturalism retained its grasp most strongly among the labourers, cottiers, and small farmers of the countryside. It was *their* demographic collapse during the Famine and the greater prominence of middling and strong farmers as also of urban society as a whole which brought with it the eventual demise of that mental and spiritual world which they had together guarded and sustained (Hynes 1978).

Such class distinctions in religious behaviour were not unconnected with the social background of the clergy itself. Although Protestants often referred disparagingly to 'peasant' priests and claimed that Maynooth was producing men of lesser refinement than had the continental seminaries it replaced, this was a profoundly erroneous view and showed little understanding of the gradations of contemporary Irish society. All the available evidence makes it clear that the cost of a clerical training alone excluded the mass of the rural poor from any aspirations to ordination. A return drawn up in 1808 by the Maynooth trustees revealed the comparatively narrow range from which the college recruited: over 77 per cent of the students had fathers who were graziers or (almost certainly reasonably substantial) farmers while another 15 per cent came from mercantile or retailing families (Connolly 1982: 35–43). As some contemporary students themselves put it, the mass of their fellows were the products of the 'middling order . . . the agricultural . . . or the commercial order', they were 'the sons of persons in business and trade . . . of the comfortable, middle, and humble farmers in the country' (Hoppen 1984: 175). Certainly 'humble' farmers, however defined, constituted the lowest stratum from which aspiring priests could emerge in any numbers, while the bishops were, if anything, somewhat more socially exclusive still (Keenan 1983: 64–5; Hoppen 1984: 176).

The mass of the clergy's closest and most direct family relationships were, therefore, drawn from a distinct minority of the rural population. Furthermore, many priests were themselves engaged in farming so that the connections between clergy and farmers operated at a direct as well as an inherited level of experience. As a result, open and effective clerical action on behalf of labourers was rare – and notable for its rarity. Priests proved anxious to divert labourer and cottier unrest into the paths of more formal O'Connellite politics. They criticized those demanding better wages and urged labourers 'to obey the law, if not, your cause will not prosper'. In 1829 the reforming Bishop Doyle of Kildare and Leighlin gave labourers a lecture on the tribulations of their masters: 'Consider the rents . . . look to the tithes . . . calculate the county cesses, the vestry cesses, the charges to maintain your own clergy and places of worship, and ask yourselves when the farmer has paid all these rents, tithes, taxes, and charges . . . what remains to him?' (Hoppen 1984: 179–80).

At the same time the increasing prosperity of the priesthood gave rise to tensions between people and pastors as a clergy entirely dependent upon 'voluntary' offerings sought to improve its own standard of living. Although all averages necessarily disguise a multitude of differing experiences it would seem to have been the case that the cash incomes of parish priests rose from about £65 in 1800 to something near three times that amount on the eve of the Famine, by which time the majority of bishops were receiving sums ranging from about £500 to as high as £1000 a year (Connolly 1982: 47–53; Keenan 1983: 63–4; Hoppen 1984: 224–32). For many clerics, though by no means all, parochial houses were also becoming more substantial, churches more splendid, vestments more ornate. The curates, who represented the most rapidly expanding group among the clergy, were of course much less prosperous, but even they experienced a modest improvement and could at least look forward with some confidence to eventual promotion to a parish of their own.

In a society whose agricultural labourers probably earned less than fifteen pounds a year such increments obviously depended in large measure not simply upon population growth but upon a willingness to pay on the part of wealthier farmers and the urban middle classes who thus, once again, identified themselves in a peculiarly compelling manner with the aspirations of their spiritual leaders. Although the pennies of the poor might cumulatively produce significant amounts, only the well-to-do could easily afford those larger fees for weddings and funerals which constituted the bulk of ecclesiastical incomes. Even if popular opposition and protest against what many thought excessive clerical demands were probably less intense than in earlier periods – though the efforts of men like the Cahir priest who in 1834 was observed allowing entrance to mass only to worshippers able to hand over a halfpenny coin can hardly have helped to reduce ill-feeling (Inglis 1838: 71–2) – protests were common and especially so from those who rightly felt the burden to be most severe (Murphy 1965).

III

In many ways the experiences of both Episcopalians and Presbyterians paralleled those of the Roman Catholics. Here too a distinctly new and more modern thrust led to increasingly narrow definitions of orthodoxy and thus further contributed to the by now mutually satisfying divisions of Irish life and culture as a whole. Of crucial importance in this respect was the impact of the evangelical revival first heralded by the appearance of Charles Wesley and the Methodists (Hempton 1980 and 1986) and then by a growing militancy amongst existing denominations. As Protestants launched themselves into a far more *conscious* sense of separateness from the Church of Rome, so, slowly at first and then more rapidly, they began to lay less stress upon their own internal divisions and to seek shelter beneath the umbrella of pan-Protestant feeling and identity.

The early-nineteenth-century Church of Ireland presented a strangely mixed aspect in which quiescent erastianism found itself in more and more uneasy juxtaposition with evangelical enthusiasm. Its structures were ossified and ill-suited to changing circumstances (Akenson 1971). Its bench of bishops included manifestly unworthy men like Jocelyn of Clogher who in 1822 was deprived of his see for having been discovered in a London public house in what a contemporary newspaper, with inflammatory blandness, described as 'a situation with a private in the Foot Guards, to which we will not more minutely allude' (Connolly 1985b: 8). Though an established church it ministered to only a tenth of the population while extracting tithes and cess from the people as a whole. Eventually the Whig government's Church Temporalities Act of 1833 reduced the number of bishops, reorganized the parochial structure, and vested the monies saved in a Board of Ecclesiastical Commissioners. Already by then, however, a minority of energetic clergymen had themselves experienced evangelical conversion – something largely the result of concurrent developments in Britain

– and begun to embark upon a campaign devoted to raising religious awareness both within and outside their own church. Bishop Power le Poer Trench of Waterford was 'converted' in 1816 and on his appointment to the archbishopric of Tuam in 1819 took the lead in supporting those societies recently or soon to be set up which had as their aim the wider conversion of Irish Catholics to the side of evangelical truth. Archbishop Magee of Dublin, in a notably fierce sermon of 1822, announced a more general approval for the cause, while the appointment in 1842 of evangelicals like James O'Brien (whose father had himself abandoned Catholicism for the establishment) to Ossory and Robert Daly to Cashel gave the movement an active and visible presence at the level of episcopal influence.

Although the evangelicals always remained a minority within the Church of Ireland – indeed they seem to have had little success in, for example, effecting greater attendance at divine service (d'Alton 1978: 73) – they proved themselves a highly public and in certain important senses a highly influential group. In curious counterpoint to popular Catholic attitudes they too exhibited intense interest in millenarian speculation (Bowen 1978: 67). They attracted support, not only from a small but active number of landowners who busily appointed 'moral agents' to superintend the spiritual welfare of their tenantry (Hoppen 1984: 123–4), but also from a parade of demotic clergymen like Rev. Tresham Dames Gregg who proved highly successful in arousing the sectarian temperatures of Protestant working-class communities in towns like Belfast, Dublin, Cork, Bandon, and Youghal (Hill 1980). Indeed, the development, in the South as well as the North, of a popular Protestant political consciousness – usually but not irremovably attached to the Conservative party – marked one of the first fruits of evangelical fervour precisely during those years when Protestants were experiencing 'defeats' in the shape of Catholic Emancipation, the First Reform Act, and the opening of municipal corporations to men of all denominations (d'Alton 1980: 159–99; Hoppen 1984: 309–15; Barry and Hoppen 1978–9).

While many Church of Ireland bishops remained indifferent to such developments and a handful – notably the Englishman, Richard Whately, archbishop of Dublin from 1831 to 1863 (Akenson 1981) – openly opposed them, the close temporal coincidence of evangelical revival and renascent Catholicism contributed substantially to a growing atmosphere of denominational distrust. Catholic priests reacted with unsurprising hostility to the attempted conversion of their flocks. Accusations that evangelicals bribed the peasantry to 'come over' by offering material as well as spiritual rewards flew across the contemporary countryside. Though most were exaggerated there was enough truth in them to poison the remaining wells of cooperation and understanding (Bowen 1970 and 1978). Especially notorious were the occasional apostasies of individual priests who moved from Rome to Canterbury (and sometimes even to Geneva) amidst much polemical agitation and publicity. Among the most famous were the Crotty brothers of King's County who became, respectively, a Church of Ireland parson and a Presbyterian minister after having in the 1830s first attempted to organize a dissident group of Catholics at Parsonstown in defiance of the Bishop of Killaloe, and not altogether without initial success. More dramatic still was the departure of an able and intelligent Cork priest, Father David Croly, who marked his apostasy with a fascinating pamphlet in 1834 denouncing his erstwhile clerical colleagues as avaricious, lax, and more interested in field sports than the saving of souls (Bowen 1978: 143–56). But in truth such cases were more notable for their drama than their frequency and even the Priests Protection Society (founded in 1844 to provide financial and moral support for disaffected Catholic clergymen) claimed to have helped no more than fourteen priests and twenty-four 'reformed Romanist students intended for the priesthood' in its first seven years of operation (Hoppen 1984: 196).

The effect of all this was to set sectarian antagonisms into the concrete of permanence. Admittedly the relics of an earlier cordiality were still evident, but more as fading and increasingly ineffective memories than as signposts to the future. The days when the Catholic Archbishop Slattery of Cashel (1833–57) was able as a young man to study at Protestant Trinity College Dublin, when the Dominican Bishop French of Kilmacduagh (1824–52) could be the son of Protestant parents, or when Archbishop Crolly of Armagh (1835–49) had as a boy been educated in a school run jointly by a Catholic and a Presbyterian were passing rapidly away (Kerr 1982: 8–27). Individuals could still work in harmony: Ryan and the saintly Jebb did so as Catholic and Church of Ireland bishops of Limerick in the 1820s and 1830s, as did Murray and Whately in Dublin, while Crolly enjoyed at least a courteous relationship with Henry Montgomery the chief (and vituperative) leader of 'enlightened' Presbyterianism. But developments such as the post-1837 cessation by the *Irish Catholic Directory* of its historical listing of bishops of the established church and the swift decay of the relaxed habit that sons of inter-church marriages followed their father's and daughters their mother's faith publicly marked the abandonment of decent civilities on all sides (Bowen 1983a: 293; Kerr 1982: 58). As the churches 'reformed' themselves so polemics intensified, public debates between rival theological gladiators flourished, and men of unflinching steel like Archbishop MacHale of Tuam (1834–81) on the Catholic side and Bishop Daly of Cashel (1842–72) on the other busily marked out the boundaries of their respective empires with new fortifications of intolerance.

The picture is completed by the contemporary history of the Presbyterian community almost all the members of which lived in the northern province of Ulster where they constituted over a quarter of the population – in Counties Antrim and Down as much as a half. In the eighteenth century they had split and resplit to match the contortions of their Scottish counterparts. Though the great majority adhered to the Synod of Ulster, even that body was informally divided between supporters of the 'new light' or theologically 'liberal' (though that term is sometimes of doubtful value here) view and those of a more fundamentalist or 'old light' persuasion. While in the 1790s both tendencies had proved themselves 'loyal', both had also furnished ministers and members who had 'come out' during the rebellion of 1798, 'new lighters' for reasons of all-purpose radicalism and 'old lighters' because they believed the rising to herald that anti-Catholic millenarian climacteric they so earnestly desired. But just as Catholic millenarianism was eventually pushed to the edges of popular experience, so, even earlier, did the growing evangelical revival reshape Presbyterian fundamentalism into a conversionist creed in which 'magic' and the supernatural were confined to individual rather than collective consciousness (Miller 1978b). In part this was a reaction to the spread of industry in north-east Ulster, in part a reflection of changes in the nature of Protestantism throughout the United Kingdom as a whole. And it was precisely the same tendencies which also eroded the self-confidence of the 'new light' party until its staunchest adherents were effectively marginalized while the rest became less and less distinguishable from their more evangelical fellows.

Although traditionally Presbyterians had in a strictly limited sense shared certain sympathies with Irish Catholics – for both saw themselves excluded by Anglicanism from the citadels of power – increases in the government grant towards ministers' salaries and a growing feeling that, at bottom, Calvinists had more in common with other Protestants than with Papists helped to undermine what was left of any sense of joint deprivation. Under the dynamic leadership of Rev. Henry Cooke, a master of invective and like so many Irish evangelicals the possessor of a strong populist streak, the Synod of Ulster moved slowly, and not without opposition, against the theological liberals who eventually seceded in 1829 to form the Remonstrant Synod under Cooke's rival Henry Montgomery. The split was made easier because the precise issue in dispute concerned the unwillingness of the Remonstrants formally to subscribe to the Westminster Confession of Faith of 1643 seen by Cooke as the touchstone of orthodoxy but by his opponents as a merely human formulation to which it was improper to demand assent. By 1840 the Synod of Ulster had so far purged itself of the 'new light' as to be able to reunite with a smaller body of conservative seceders who had originally broken away a hundred years before and with them to adopt the grander and wider title of the Presbyterian Church in Ireland.

Under Cooke's influence parallels began to develop between theological and political conservatism and although these were never absolute they undoubtedly contributed to a gradual coming together of a majority of Presbyterian and Anglican Protestants in firm political opposition to the increasingly Catholic forces of Irish nationalism (Holmes 1982). At a large Conservative gathering held at Hillsborough County Down in 1834 Cooke announced 'banns of marriage' between the Church of Ireland and Presbyterianism and henceforth he was to devote his considerable energies to bringing about a practical consummation of the match (Holmes 1981: 115–16). Political Protestantism mobilized itself forcefully in the Orange Order, which, though theoretically dissolved in 1836 under pressure from the Whig government, maintained a lively underground existence and re-emerged formally in 1845 to resume its task of popular resistance to Catholic and nationalist demands (Senior 1966; Dewar, Brown and Long 1967). Electoral contests, especially in religiously-mixed towns, adopted a more and more sectarian character. The era of fierce urban rioting was inaugurated in 1832 as working-class Protestants and Catholics – often with open encouragement from their more genteel co-religionists – took to the streets at the first Belfast election held after the Reform Act of that year (Baker 1973). As electoral politics became increasingly demotic so too, under the impress of economic and religious change, did they become more fiercely violent and more

75

capable of involving local communities as a whole (Hoppen 1984: 278–332, 388–408). With territorial imperatives now shaping the ways in which different religious groups regarded one another so the supporters of both orange and green began to march (or, as they usually put it, 'walk') through the streets in order to establish their citadels, taunt their opponents, and raise the temperature all round (Budge and O'Leary 1973: 41–100; Stewart 1977).

The internal disputes among Presbyterians were marked by a linguistic excess which even the most strident Catholic champions might have envied (Holmes 1981: 83). Anglican evangelicals too, like Rev. Alexander Dallas, had nothing to learn in the mobilization of unlimited abuse (Bowen 1978: 208–56). By the 1840s significant elements within Irish Protestantism – not excluding the Methodists (Hempton 1980) – were ready to take a full part in the violent campaigns being orchestrated from Exeter Hall in London (the temple of evangelicalism) against Sir Robert Peel's attempts to conciliate Catholic opinion by increasing the government grant to Maynooth, changing the law of charitable bequests, and reforming university education in Ireland (Kerr 1982; Norman 1967; Cahill 1957). Their task was made easier by the divisions among Catholic bishops and politicians over all but the first of these matters with the result that Peel's efforts attracted instant bombardment from both sides of the religious divide.

Although it would be an exaggeration to say that already by 1850 none dared cross those political boundaries which were increasingly being aligned to match religious differences, it cannot be doubted that cross-frontier traffic was on the decline. It is, for example, significant that it was the wealthier urban Presbyterians who longest remained prepared to vote for Liberal candidates while their poorer Protestant fellow-townsmen led a mass move in the opposite direction and in doing so injected a populist aspect into Conservatism which was later often to be at loggerheads with an aristocratic and professional leadership determined to channel enthusiasm into more formal and acceptable campaigns (Hoppen 1984: 307–32).

From the 1830s onwards Irish Protestants adopted a defensive imagery. Increasingly aware of being in a minority position in the country as a whole they still consoled themselves with the pride of possessing not only the truth in religion but a disproportionate share of the wealth, land, and productive capacity of the country – sure signs of divine approval (d'Alton 1980: 200). But while the evangelical revival and the intensification of Catholic nationalism were each confined to a single community both also shaped the manner in which these communities regarded one another and did so in quite different ways. Thus, while nationalists proved able to conceive of a sort of secular salvation for the other side without compassing its religious conversion (even though the lessons of experience increasingly belied such hopes), most Protestants entirely discarded any apocalyptic expectations of being able to convince Catholic nationalists of the errors of their ways. Irish nationalism, in other words, continued to be capable of reaffirming itself 'not only as it was – a sectarian nationality – but also as it "ought" to be – an Irish nation transcending the sectarian division of Irish society in this present age'. Protestants, by contrast, were merely left with a myth, which, once it was clear that Catholics, as individuals, would not be converted, was only able to reaffirm the nature of the Protestant community 'as it really was' – a group 'deeply divided from its neighbours' (Miller 1978a: 86).

IV

As the religious experience of all sorts of Irishmen and women became more 'modern', so priests, parsons, and ministers were increasingly seen by their flocks and increasingly saw themselves as the guardians of theologically formal and consciously sectarian attitudes. Not only were they all well on the way to achieving a virtual monopoly of spiritual power but in the process they were also energetically abandoning that multiplicity of roles which traditional belief had accorded them. As time went on only politics still offered them a potential empire beyond the strict realm of sacerdotalism itself; though, in the event, beggars turned out to be very enthusiastic choosers indeed as clergymen of all denominations showed impressive zeal in the pursuit of this new imperialism.

At first clerical involvement in politics was almost entirely a matter of support and organization. Under O'Connell Catholic priests, though important, were virtually always lieutenants rather than generals (O'Ferrall 1981b). But once Pandora's box had been opened and religion had become, in a new and important way, the prime item upon the political agenda then the future possibility of any purely secular agitation largely disappeared (O'Farrell 1971: 84). While a few bishops did return to their tents, the majority –

together with the overwhelming bulk of the priesthood – actively supported O'Connell as he pursued first 'justice' and then Repeal (MacDonagh 1975; Nowlan 1974). Having by 1815, despite pressure from Rome, decisively rejected proposals for state emoluments in return for a government veto over episcopal appointments, the Irish Catholic Church equally firmly resisted Roman promptings in the 1830s and 1840s that it should withdraw from politics (Broderick 1951). Various pastoral letters did indeed enjoin the priesthood to remain aloof and to prevent chapels being used for political meetings. But, however immediately sincere their compilers may have been, one is left with a sense that, for many bishops and priests, such documents were perceived as little more than scraps of empty rhetoric (Hoppen 1984: 234–6): and as such they and the various Roman rescripts recommending quiescence and disengagement 'passed rippleless across the Irish scene' (MacDonagh 1983b: 96). In short, the priests, by ceasing to fulfil the role of magician were inexorably being accorded (and indeed grasping) that of politician instead; and much the same, though in a rather different way, was happening to Protestant clergymen as well.

If the first half of the nineteenth century witnessed the gathering pace of religious modernization the process was nonetheless a slow one and certain ambiguities remained to be resolved in the years that followed. Thus, even an eminently 'modern' and deeply Victorian phenomenon like the temperance campaign so dramatically orchestrated in pre-Famine Ireland by the Capuchin friar, Theobald Mathew, carried with it intimations of a distinctly older kind. Father Mathew, like his many Protestant admirers, saw his mission as one of improvement and in that sense it was a simple matter for O'Connell to absorb the whole business into his own philosophy of utilitarian liberalism. But many in the vast crowds which flocked to hear the friar's exhortations and to obtain the temperance medals he distributed saw the affair in a very different light. For them Father Mathew was a traditional holy man who could make the lame walk and the diseased whole again. They jostled to touch the hem of his garment, they pressed his tokens upon their wounds, and some believed that those who wore his medals could not be shot by policemen or the military. While urban middle-class admirers and respectable farmers established water-drinking temperance associations (though like O'Connell many soon found it expedient to abandon their pledges for 'health reasons'), rural labourers and cottiers looked to Father Mathew for hope, for release, for something more than sobriety and the ethics of self-improvement (Kearney 1979; Malcolm 1980).

But if some ambiguities remained, the separation of the religious communities was undoubtedly becoming more intensely perceived on all sides. The rising political importance of Catholicism alone saw to that, though the tendency was reinforced by the failure to make non-denominational education work, a failure to which virtually all sides heartily contributed. As Catholics became politically and economically more prominent so they established an effective culture of their own in the spheres of commerce, leisure, and political organization. Not only were there, by the second quarter of the century, Catholic clubs and Protestant clubs, Orange libraries and Repeal reading rooms, but even breweries, hotels, and stage coaches often attracted customers on strictly denominational lines (Inglis 1838: 20–24; Thackeray 1879: 34). Although such divisions had long historical roots it was renascent Catholicism which made them more dramatic, striking, and effective than they had been for many years. It was, indeed, not so much the divisions in themselves but the changing perceptions they evoked which crucially emphasized and reinforced the sectarian nature of nineteenth-century Irish life as a whole.

Because the religious divide was also in large degree a geographical divide so the effective partition of Ireland between a Protestant North-East and a Catholic South was already becoming deeper and more significant, not only as to matters of belief and church affiliation but with regard to politics, social outlook, and economic behaviour also. In short, many of the developments characteristic of the post-Famine period were shaped and foreshadowed by that rendering down of religious ambiguities which had taken place in the previous fifty years. While, therefore, religious modernization in Ireland in one sense meant a programme of reform leading to a diminution of abuses and a narrowing of popular beliefs, in another it involved a sharpening of hostilities and the building of new and ever more impenetrable stockades.

NOTE

1. Ultramontanism was that tendency within Catholicism which stressed the central authority of the papacy, while its opposite – Gallicanism or Cisalpinism – emphasized the relative independence of local

episcopates from Rome and their possible subservience instead to
secular authority. By the early-nineteenth century these terms had
also acquired a devotional or liturgical meaning, with the lavish
ceremonials of Rome and the related fall-out of plaster-cast saints, blue
and gold madonnas, glittering halos and the like being described as
'ultramontane' to distinguish them from the plainer procedures and
iconography formerly common in Ireland and other parts of northern
Europe.

PART TWO

Winners and Losers: From Famine to Partition

CHAPTER 4
Society

Agricola Victor

The social and economic fabric of Irish life during the seven decades after the Famine continued to be dominated by the experiences of the agricultural community and the shifting relationships between its constituent parts. Though a somewhat decreasing proportion of occupied adult males was, as time went on, directly employed in farming (about three-fifths in 1881 as compared with seven-tenths forty years earlier), the rural areas outside towns of 2000 or more inhabitants remained as fully agrarian as they had ever been (Hoppen 1984: 103–4). At the same time, however, the countryside underwent a series of transformations which eventually helped to establish what amounted to a new social order. These changes did not all occur simultaneously and the different time-scales involved not only shaped the final result but provided an important backdrop to many of the political developments of the age.

I

The historiography of this interrelated set of metamorphoses is instructive in itself. Twenty years ago the story still turned almost exclusively around the struggle between exploited tenant farmers and predatory landlords. The latter were assumed to have deployed their extensive legal rights to the full by charging enormous rents and resorting to frequent evictions against those who stood in their way. In this analysis, therefore, Gladstone's Land Acts of 1870 and 1881 assumed overarching importance as the fulcrums of rural change, restricting as they seemed to do the ability of landlords to rule their estates with unfettered and autocratic power (Pomfret 1930; Palmer 1940).

Although already in the 1960s isolated criticisms of this approach had begun to emerge (Robinson 1962; Crotty 1966), a serious assault was not mounted until the following decade. On the one hand, a series of local and national studies made it clear that neither tenants nor landlords could be treated as homogeneous groups locked in a species of eternal conflict in which the rules of engagement were simply the product of what contemporary law might or might not allow (Donnelly 1975; Bew 1978; Clark 1979). On the other, a more direct examination of the rural economy suggested that landed proprietors, far from maximizing their rentals in the quarter-century after the Famine, in fact allowed these to fall substantially behind increases in agricultural prices, with the result that tenants as a group found themselves in the happy position of enjoying a substantial rise in gross farming profits between the early 1850s and the mid-1870s (Solow 1971; Vaughan 1977; 1980a; 1980b).

Not only did such revisionism turn the traditional interpretation on its head – with farmers now seen as the chief beneficiaries of a generally prosperous period of agricultural growth – but, almost as important, it had the effect of injecting a note of social complexity into the cardboard verities of former times. One of the most glaring defects of the older view was at last rectified, namely, the entire omission from the historical canon of the landless labourers who before the Famine had of course numerically dominated the social structure of rural Ireland but who had, by some mysterious if perhaps politically necessary sleight of hand, been simply written out of the script by late-nineteenth and early-twentieth century commentators. Their rediscovery modified any insistence that all that mattered after 1850 was the confrontation between farmers and landlords. Undoubtedly the Famine began a process by which the relative sizes of the two groups moved decisively in favour of those occupying land as against those merely working it. Yet, beginnings are not conclusions and the whole business took longer than has sometimes been supposed. Even the bare categories of 'farmer' and 'labourer' disguise as much as they reveal. Many labourers continued to rent land under conacre or as cottier tenants. And, although it has been argued that this sub-group experienced relative attrition during the 1850s and 1860s (Clark 1979: 114), a more plausible view suggests that 'occupation of land by labourers was in fact becoming more commonplace rather than less so' (Fitzpatrick 1980a: 77) – a development which may well have helped to induce an increasing rather than a diminishing sense of solidarity in the countryside at large. Again, the relevant census data make it difficult to disaggregate the broad category of 'agricultural labourers' into landless men *tout court* and those commonly labelled 'assisting relatives' who lived with their farmer kin, shared to an extent in the mores of the tenantry, but worked for money wages during the months of seedtime and harvest when labour was temporarily in short supply.

Yet no amount of qualification can overcome the undoubted fact that labourers, however defined, represented a diminishing group in the years between 1850 and the Great War, with the most rapid reduction taking place during the first three decades of that period. Thus, while in 1841 labourers and 'assisting relatives' had together constituted 73 per cent of the total occupied adult male 'farming' population of Ireland (the remainder being farmers as such), comparable percentages for later years show a marked decline: 1851 = 69.6, 1881 = 59.8, 1911 = 56.7 (Fitzpatrick 1980a: 88). More striking still is the fact that between 1841 and 1881 the proportion of farmers plus 'assisting relatives' rose from two-fifths to just over three-fifths, that is, to a majority of the farming population as a whole (Hoppen 1984: 105). What this meant was that the decades after the Famine constituted, above all, a time of growing demographic triumph on the part of farmers as opposed to labourers and that, as a result, tenants found it more and more possible to realign the 'land question' in such a way that only *their* aspirations were given attention and publicity. While, therefore, violence in all its forms continued to flourish in the quarter-century after 1850 more intensely than has often been appreciated and while its character continued to reflect a good deal of labourer–farmer antagonism (Hoppen 1984: 341–78), the balance of social presence and of political advantage began to tilt ever more decisively in favour of the latter. Nor did labourers experience any really *significant* improvement in their standard of living. Average nominal weekly wages certainly rose between the 1840s and 1860s and may have done so by as much as a half or more (from 4s 6d to 7s), but they remained pitifully low in comparison, for example, with those of English agricultural let alone industrial workers (Boyle 1983; Kennedy 1985a: 47).

Given that the Irish population fell by almost a half between 1841 and 1911 from about 8.2 million to less than 4.4 million, it is remarkable how very different were the demographic experiences of the farmers – who declined by just over a quarter – and the farm workers (including 'assisting relatives') – who were reduced by almost two-thirds. Indeed, after 1851 the number of farmers changed comparatively little and may even at first have increased somewhat before falling, by the start of the Great War, to a level not substantially lower than that of sixty years before. Although clearly the 'average' farmer was as mythical a being as the 'average' labourer, yet certain broad trends in the distribution of holdings and the relative movement of agricultural prices exercised an influence upon tenants as a whole. Many farms undoubtedly stayed small and especially so in the West of Ireland where demographic and economic trends remained for about twenty years frozen in the pattern of pre-Famine times. Overall, however, the size of holdings increased, so that, by the end of the century, those of more than thirty acres had come to constitute almost a third of all farms rather than a sixth as had been the case in 1841 (Hoppen 1984: 91). Despite, therefore, obvious and important regional differences, it cannot be doubted that it was the middling and upper ranks that were generally assuming a higher prominence. And because of changes introduced by the Irish Franchise Act of 1850 it was precisely this group which was coming to dominate the county electorate in an altogether new and important way. Thus, while the electorate of O'Connell's time had included many very poor farmers, this now ceased to be the case and only those occupying holdings with a rateable valuation of twelve pounds or more – usually men paying no less than fifteen pounds a year in rent – were entitled to vote in rural constituencies. Not only, therefore, was the electorate far more socially and economically homogeneous than before, but within its ranks farmers of a substantial kind had the overwhelming voice (Hoppen 1977a; 1977b; 1984: 105).

The agricultural world inhabited by such farmers was a rapidly changing one. Prices rose substantially but in an extremely uneven manner. The returns from grain became much less attractive than those from the animal and meat sectors: between 1851 and 1876, when wheat prices rose by 20 per cent and barley prices by 43 per cent, those for beef and butter recorded an increase of 87 per cent and for young store cattle of no less than 143 per cent – and this over a period when the least defective general price (or cost of living) index went up by hardly more than a quarter (Barrington 1927). For a few years the Crimean War of 1854–6 gave a temporary stimulus to the demand for grain. But thereafter Irish farmers reacted rationally to changes in the market place (Ó Gráda 1975a). The acreage under tillage began to move decisively downwards after the late 1850s while pasture acreage increased, so that the ratio between the two shifted significantly in favour of grass and animal production: from 1.90 in 1851 (i.e. 1 acre of tillage for every 1.9 acres of pasture) to 3.23 in 1880, and to no less than 4.16 thirty years after that (Huttman 1970). Not only did this have obvious implications for the employment prospects of labourers – pasture farming being more capital and less labour intensive than tillage – but it also involved a redistribution of relative prosperity among farmers themselves. As animal numbers grew (by the end of the century there were twice as many dry cattle and sheep as there had been fifty years earlier) so too did regional specialization (Kennedy 1981), with the result that some areas and some farmers did better than others. Although Ireland continued to be a country of relatively small (if growing) farms, yet it was also a country in which a great deal of land was in the hands of very substantial tenants indeed: by 1861, for example, 40 per cent was held in farms of 100 acres and more (Vaughan 1984: 4). And it was precisely these large farmers who increased their output and incomes most substantially during the latter half of the nineteenth century, though the smaller men were by no means entirely innocent of economic advance of a more modest kind (Vaughan 1980a: 88; Cuddy and Curtin 1983).

Landlords, for their part, emerged from the Famine in a strengthened rather than weakened condition. Bankruptcies and the numerous sales of bankrupt properties through the mechanisms established by the Encumbered Estates Act of 1849 augmented the Famine's role as a Darwinian selector of the fittest among the members of the proprietorial community. Much of the land sold (and almost a quarter of the total eventually changed hands) was bought by owners who had survived the Famine in good financial shape and were able to meet the future with optimism and confidence (Donnelly 1973: 49 and 1975: 131; Lane 1972–3 and 1981–2). In aggregate landlords were enormously wealthy, though, as with farmers, this wealth was most unevenly distributed. Twenty years after the Famine about 2000 of them, each with 2000 acres or more, owned two-thirds of the country's land surface. Indeed, half that surface belonged to less than 800 individuals (Vaughan 1980b: 176). Together they enjoyed a gross annual rental in the region of £10 million, and this at a time when total United Kingdom central expenditure on civil government amounted to £6.6 million and even the royal navy cost only £5.8 million a year (Vaughan 1980b: 187; Mitchell and Deane 1971: 397). Gross rental was not of course the same as net income. Not only did all landlords have to pay taxes and meet the costs of estate management (which rose with the increasing professionalism of the agents and bureaucratic procedures employed), but almost all were burdened in various degrees with mortgage interest payments and with the often extensive jointures assigned to younger sons, daughters, widows, even uncles and aunts. And while Irish landlords undoubtedly re-invested less in agricultural improvements than their English counterparts, few could avoid investment altogether and some ploughed substantial sums into improvements of various kinds (Ó Gráda 1975b; Robinson 1962). The result of all this was that usually only about half (and sometimes a lot less than half) of gross rental was actually available to allow landlords to maintain the style of life thought appropriate to their rank (Vaughan 1980b: 189–90). In good times there was usually little to worry about. But when depressions reduced the regularity of rent payments and obliged proprietors to grant temporary reductions the impact upon net incomes could often prove quite disproportionately severe (Curtis 1980).

Given that their tenants were essentially independent small producers Irish landlords were able to exercise power by means of a wide (but not limitless) variety of strategies. Thus, although, on the one hand, they could not resort to the very direct methods open to elites involved in wage-labour relations with their tenants, they did, on the other, possess greater potential control than those faced with producers enjoying ownership and paying no rents at all. In the Irish case landlords achieved dominance through the legal powers they enjoyed over their properties, through informal economic and social influence, through their control of local administration, justice, and electoral politics, and by being able to act as brokers between their tenants and the growing apparatus of the contemporary state.

None of these methods was, however, without its problems. Certainly *in law* proprietors enjoyed almost limitless rights. They could raise rents as they pleased. Because fewer and fewer tenants held by lease they could evict after only the shortest of delays. They could insist on good agricultural practices. They could demand deference and subservience. But in fact the simple exigencies of real life rendered such powers less complete than theory or over-eager equations between 'rights' and 'behaviour' have tended to suggest. Rents did not function in an economic void. Large-scale evictions could severely reduce revenue. The achievement of good farming demanded eternal vigilance. Evictions, in particular, exhibited an enormous gulf between legal potential and actual practice. Though most farmers held only 'from year to year' and though notices to quit were regularly showered about, the number of families put out of their holdings and not readmitted was, once the effects of the Famine had worn off, remarkably small – something in the region of 3 or 4 per cent of all tenants during the whole period from 1855 to 1880 (Solow 1971: 56–7; Hoppen 1984: 127–8). Nor was absenteeism especially widespread and in any case many of the most benevolent and well-run estates belonged to landlords who, because they owned land in a number of different counties or in Britain as well, were rarely able to reside on any one property for more than a few weeks or months at a time (Hoppen 1984: 109).

Nonetheless, tensions arose out of a clash between the farmers' insistence that they be granted certain things by law and the landlords' that these should remain no more than concessions. The Tenant League of the 1850s established the demands which were to remain the core of the farmers' case for the decades to come, namely, the so-called 3 Fs: fair rent, fixity of tenure, and free sale. The first was in many respects the linchpin of the whole business and, by being at once vague and indefinable, gave rise to endless disputes as one man's fairness was denounced as another's victimization. The second, despite much propaganda to the contrary, was effectively already in operation, as the low level of evictions makes clear. Free sale – the ability of tenants to 'sell' an 'interest' in their holdings upon peaceably giving these up to their successors – was a curious practice that often went under the names of 'tenant right' or the Ulster Custom though it was present to a lesser degree in many other parts of the country also. Its curiosity lay both in the many different ways it could be interpreted and in its implicit recognition that tenants somehow possessed property rights in land they did not own. It was thus very different from the contemporary English practice of mere compensation for unexpired improvements (though this too was often involved) – something English politicians were very slow to grasp. And though it was the incoming tenant who made the payment his ability to do so depended to a large extent upon landlords charging a rent lower than it might otherwise have been (Kennedy 1985a: 38–41; Vaughan 1984: 17–20, 25). In truth, most such customs were neither very old nor very precise and their history reveals above all the Irish tenants' undoubted success in inventing traditions and then rapidly encasing them in a thoroughly bogus yet energizing antiquity. At the same time, however, the agitation to enshrine them in law represented at first no outright attack upon the principle of landlordism as such.

II

Having demonstrated that the social and economic relationships of the post-Famine countryside were more ambiguous than was once supposed, the revisionists then sought to show that in the third quarter of the nineteenth century (for reasons they never explained) landlords actually allowed their overall rents to fall dramatically behind the increasing value of agricultural produce and thus, in effect, permitted the lion's share of a growing rural prosperity to fall into the hands – not of either proprietors or labourers – but of the tenants who farmed the land. However superficially odd this view may have seemed, the statistics marshalled in its support persuaded most students – not excluding the present writer (Hoppen 1984: 112–16) – that a convincing new insight had been born. Yet, on both empirical and a priori grounds, so drastic a revisionism has always had its problems. Why, in particular, should discontent have continued if extra cash was being shovelled into tenant coffers? Three possible explanations were put forward. In the first place, 'while the burden of rents as a whole was moderate, individual rents were often high and the whole system of levying rents was riddled with inconsistencies'. In the second, the 'very fact that rents lagged behind increases in the value of agricultural output gave tenants a vested interest in securing legislation which would prevent them from ever catching up'. In the third, it is possible that smaller farmers were simply 'unable to take advantage of rising livestock prices' (Vaughan 1977: 217). However, even if all of this was, indeed, true, an examination of the considerable prowess with which post-Famine landlords conducted their electoral affairs creates unease about the suggestion that the very same men who were proving successful in enforcing political control should also have been so prepared to forgo the more electric attractions of hard cash and money in the bank (Hoppen 1977a).

The whole argument depends crucially upon the accuracy of certain estimates concerning changes in the values of agricultural output, rent, and labour costs. And only very recently have three distinguished scholars begun to produce new figures which cast serious doubt upon the current view of post-Famine proprietors as genial all-the-year-round embodiments of Santa Claus himself.[1] The point is most clearly made if one compares the hitherto widely accepted data of W. E. Vaughan (1980b: 187) with revised output figures produced by Michael Turner (with which other recent calculations broadly agree), while retaining Vaughan's estimates regarding total rents and the cost of labour (though the latter might also not unreasonably be subject to a degree of adjustment – for which, see below). Three things should be remembered. First, all such exercises inevitably involve heroic assumptions. Second, by excluding the very difficult potato sector Vaughan (however understandably) injected secular distortions into his data. Third, 'gross farming profits' have in all cases been regarded as the residual remaining once rents and cost of labour have been deducted from the value of output as a whole. It will be seen that the adoption of new output estimates brings about a *bouleversement* of what had only recently become little short of universal orthodoxy. On the one hand, farmers enjoyed a far higher overall level of gross profits in 1852–4. But, on the other, it would now seem that, while labourers and landlords were able to notch up improvements *in current terms* of a fifth and a quarter respectively between the mid-1850s and mid-1870s, farmers as a group effectively stood still.

Table 4.1 Agricultural output (previous and new estimates), rents, cost of labour and gross farming profits, 1852–4 and 1872–4, in current terms. The amounts are in £ millions

Years	Output		Rents	Cost of Labour	Gross Farming Profits	
	Vaughan	Turner (new)			Vaughan	Turner (new)
1852–4	28.70	41.10	10.00	9.00	9.70	22.10
1872–4	40.50	45.00	12.00	11.35	17.15	21.65
% change	+41	+9	+20	+26	+77	−2

Now, although this is not the place to enter into enormous detail on the matter, it should be admitted that the picture suggested above represents perhaps somewhat too stark a revision. This is because, while Vaughan's rent estimates have been accorded widespread assent, it is quite probable that the dramatic fall in the number of agricultural labourers in the two decades immediately after the Famine may well have produced a rather lower wages bill in 1872–4 than he suggests – even if pay rates increased, as they undoubtedly did. But, while this would of course yield some shift *from* wages *to* gross profits, the amount was probably no more than about three-quarters of a million pounds.[2] The consequent changes in group allocations, though reducing the labour increase from 26 to 17 per cent, would, therefore, merely turn a farmers' profits *decrease* of 2 per cent into a rise of 1 per cent – hardly a move from stasis to cornucopian growth.

We are, therefore, left with a state of things in which, during the twenty-five years after the Famine, rents and the cost of labour increased by about a fifth while gross farming profits remained virtually unchanged. And even if one allows that many 'labourers' were assisting relatives who often worked regularly only during the seasons of intense agricultural activity – something which would have depressed labour costs and thus augmented profits – the overall trend now suggested of farmers as a group performing significantly less well than landlords remains broadly intact. Of course the choice of years for comparison also affects the results obtained. In this case the first period of 1852–4 includes two years (1853 and 1854) in which output was unusually high because of the demands of the Crimean War. But even if this has the undoubted effect of limiting the possibilities of future *growth* in farming profits, it has been retained in order to provide a parallel with Vaughan's original calculations. Thus, while such profits fell after 1855 and especially heavily during the agricultural depression of 1859–64 (Donnelly 1976), it remains the case that the farmer sector in rural Ireland not only experienced a decline in profits during the 1860s but had, by the 'prosperous' years of the early and mid-1870s, achieved little more than a return to the position it had enjoyed twenty years before.

Because such aggregates disguise the nature of individual experience it might be worthwhile, despite all the pitfalls involved, to attempt a rough calculation of mean per capita gross incomes for labourers and farmers, remembering always that averages also reflect but dimly the differing fortunes of large and small farmers, of those involved in livestock and those still wedded to tillage, of healthy regularly-employed workers and sick men hardly able to lift a spade. While wages are largely recoverable from contemporary records, estimates of average per capita gross farming profits rely heavily upon the number of farmers who at any one time were alive to divide up the residual agricultural cake once rents and labour costs have been removed.[3] And because money changes alone can be a very distorting measure if unrelated to movements in the overall cost of living, the estimates that follow (which should, it must be emphasized, be regarded with caution as no more than rough approximations) are given in both current and real terms.[4] At a time, therefore, when aggregate rents in real terms experienced a small increase of about 3 per cent and a nominal increase of a fifth, the average per capita gross annual profits of farmers *fell* in real terms by about a seventh and in nominal terms remained unchanged. For their part labourers, though they may well have succeeded in obtaining a significant proportionate increase in wages, were still paid absolutely so little that their standard of living had at best moved merely from the permanently to the intermittently intolerable and at worst (because of changes in consumption patterns) may hardly have improved much at all (Fitzpatrick 1980a: 80–82).

Table 4.2 Average gross annual per capita receipts of agricultural labourers and farmers, 1852–4 and 1872–4, in current and real terms (1852–4 = 100)

Years	Labourers		Farmers	
	current	real	current	real
1852–4	£10.7	£10.7	£56.6	£56.6
1872–4	£16.8	£14.4	£57.2	£48.9
% change	+57	+35	+1	−14

The success of the landlords in exercising political control over the post-Famine countryside and adopting an increasingly professional approach to property management (Donnelly 1975: 173–218) had, therefore, not merely a historical but also – in economic terms – a contemporary basis. With estates, as with farms, the period saw a move towards consolidation (Hoppen 1984: 106–7), with the result that economically and politically the landed community was able to present in the 1850s and 1860s a notably stronger front than before. Although some individuals were undoubtedly more successful than others, as a group landlords were not only absolutely wealthy but considerably more sure-footed in benefiting from such growth as took place in the real value of agricultural output than were the farmers to whom they let their land.

Given that this was so it is not surprising that Irish farmers were scarcely overjoyed with their experience of post-Famine life. And while it needed more than sudden economic decline to push unhappiness into open revolt – the depression of 1859–64 elicited comparatively little in the way of violent unrest (Donnelly 1976; Lee 1980) – the potentials for such a development were never far below the surface of events (Murray 1986b). What was required was the construction, even if only for a short time, of something approaching a universality of discontent coincident with the availability of effective political leadership and co-ordination. Although neither existed in the 1850s and 1860s, the new county electorate of 1850 was economically coherent and therefore capable, should it ever be given the kiss of life by a suitable combination of circumstances, of mobilizing in favour of both political and agrarian revolt. Gladstone's first Land Act of 1870, which granted legal recognition to the Ulster Custom, paradoxically also helped to create a more overt discontent, for disappointment at its feeble provisions was almost universal, while its unintended effect of increasing farmer indebtedness – the recognition of tenant right made it easier to borrow money (Hoppen 1984: 470) – undoubtedly rendered farmers more susceptible to any sudden decline in agricultural prices that might thereafter take place.

III

Up to this point it cannot be said that the post-Famine history of Irish farmers could justify the title given to the present chapter: 'Agricola Victor'. But now there occurred that series of events which, in all but the shortest of runs, helped to raise the very farmers who had formerly struggled merely to maintain their incomes to economic levels few could have foreseen. Of these developments the most beneficent – or so it turned out – was the agricultural depression of the late-1870s. By reacting to this seeming disaster as they did the farmers of Ireland ensured that, whereas it had been the landlords who had moved ahead during the previous quarter century, this state of things was now to be dramatically reversed.

Yet at first the world-wide depression, coinciding as it did with a series of disastrous seasons in Ireland, triggered a crash which abruptly snatched back from farmers their very recent return to the comparative prosperity of the mid-1850s. The background to the Land War of 1879–82 was not, therefore, a 'revolution of rising expectations' (Donnelly 1975: 250) but a state of deep anxiety that the economic roller-coaster was once again heading in a downward direction. The decline in cattle prices hit those small farmers of the West now increasingly locked into a commercial relationship with wealthier ranchers to whom they supplied young beasts for 'finishing'. Elsewhere a significantly reduced tillage output caused by bad weather was no longer being matched by a rise in prices, for these now responded as much to North American as to domestic levels of production (Clark 1979: 109–11, 225–32; Barrington 1927). Emigration too, which had continued to supply something of a safety-valve, was being tightly restrained by the American slump of 1874–9, so that an unusually large number of young men remained 'captive' at home – frustrated, discontented, and ready to vent their rage if given leadership and opportunity (Lee 1980: 231; Schrier 1958: 157). The effects of this were especially severe in Connacht and Donegal because of a simultaneous sharp decline in the availability of harvesting employment in Britain which in the 1860s had absorbed no less than 100,000 migratory workers each year (Ó Gráda 1973).

As the value of agricultural output fell from about £50.1 million in 1876 to £37.5 million in 1879 so farmers of almost all kinds found it difficult to repay their debts and so needed little encouragement from those who had given them credit – notably shopkeepers in the towns – to look to landlords for reductions in rent. Something, it seemed, would have to give. The question was whose that something would prove to be.

Although landlords had already suffered a series of electoral and psychological set-backs in the 1870s, they were still powerful, wealthy, and prepared to fight. What, however, rendered this new confluence of discontents so much more formidable than before was the existence of an effective political leadership on the tenant side. In this sense the 'new departures' of the 1870s (see Chapter 5), by bringing together forces which had long been divided and by providing the materials for both local organization and national authority, furnished the match with which the tinder might be set alight. When, therefore, violent discontent first erupted in Connacht in 1879 it was not simply allowed to burn itself out in sectional or parochial pyrotechnics but was harnessed to an agitation whose implications soon reverberated far beyond the West. And, as a result, the Land War and the Land League formally inaugurated in October 1879 by Davitt and Parnell were, despite their internal contradictions and jealousies, phenomena of comparative coherence in a century hitherto noted for a quite different state of affairs.

There was nothing very principled about all this. It just so happened that a strong leadership was unusually successful in keeping the various parts of the machine from flying apart until certain substantial concessions had been won. And if, in the event, these concessions proved to be neither universally applicable nor complete that, for some of the most powerful elements on the tenant side, was to constitute the chiefest of their charms. Both agrarian violence and evictions reached levels unknown since the Famine, though the temporal relationship between the two is not easy to untangle. The Land War was, indeed, marked, not only by a rise in all forms of outrage 'specially reported' by the Constabulary, but by a shift away from less and towards more serious crime and also by a dramatic growth in the proportion of outrages designated as 'agrarian' (Hoppen 1984: 367–8). While, however, all this was remarkable in itself, more noteworthy still was the manner in which the different sections of rural society were for a time prepared to support the agitation, if not always with a similar degree of zeal. If labourers, as has often been pointed out (Lee 1980; Orridge 1981; Boyle 1983), proved less eager than farmers, that, given the history of rural relations, was hardly surprising. The wonder is that labourers were prepared to participate at all, and participate they undoubtedly did (Bew 1978: 174–5). In the few cases where records have survived it is clear that League branches were able to attract a membership representative both in terms of the distribution of small, middling, and large farmers and of the relative presence of farmers and labourers in the surrounding districts (Hoppen 1984: 475–9). Although, therefore, it was the more prosperous farmers and their retailing allies in the country towns who often came to dominate the *leadership* of the League at the local level (Jordan 1987; Bew 1978; Clark 1979), for a time at least, such men proved to be the officers of an army remarkable for its ability to recruit from almost all sections of the rural community.

What is remarkable is that the whole thing held effectively together for as long as it did, a tribute both to the qualities of the national leadership and to the havering incompetence of the government. As, however, the agitation spread beyond Connacht, so the contradictory priorities of different types of farmer came forcefully into play once more. Thus, while the smaller men of the West (who would have found it difficult to make ends meet even if they had paid no rent at all) demanded more land and the break-up of cattle ranches in order to make this possible, those with bigger holdings aspired first and foremost to reductions in rent itself (Bew

1978: 88). And although it was Gladstone's reluctant delivery of a
Land Act in 1881 incorporating machinery designed to meet the
latter expectation which brought these differences into universal
collision, already by then the agitation in Connacht had begun to
disintegrate as long-felt tensions bubbled once more to the surface
of affairs (Jordan 1987). The act, indeed, was important above all
else as a device for controlling rent. Soon tenants flocked to take
advantage of its provisions and it was not long before the new
Land Court was – according to no very obvious criteria – awarding
significant reductions all round (Solow 1971: 161–3).

What in effect the act did was to make the proprietors pay for
the economic ravages of the time. As such it gave the victory to
the farmer community, but only in a fashion which exacerbated
the tensions which had long existed within that community as a
whole. In particular nothing was done to meet the demands of
small western farmers for more land, though some rather feeble
moves towards improving the lot of labourers as regards housing
and the like were inaugurated by the Labourers (Ireland) Act of
1883 (Boyle 1983: 332). Already during the Land War itself the
imperatives of the various groups had been reflected, not only in
an adherence to different goals, but in the adoption of different
strategies, with middling and large farmers prepared to execute
tactical withdrawals if the pressure upon them became too great
– yielding rent 'at the point of the bayonet' – rather than holding
out desperately to the end in favour of that redistribution of
holdings which alone could have yielded a tolerable living to
the poorer men of the West (Bew 1978). The implementation of
rent strikes, boycotting, agrarian crime, and even attacks on the
fox-hunting activities of the gentry, varied, therefore, from one
part of the country to another (Curtis 1987). The sectional nature
of the concessions delivered by the Land Act further deepened old
wounds so that the prohibition of the League by the government
in October 1881 represented no more than a coda to an already
fading harmony. The 'No Rent Manifesto' which followed had
little widespread effect and Parnell's new National League of
1882 proved a more narrowly political and centrally controlled
organization than its predecessor.

Of course the landlords were not at once driven from their
broad acres. The comparative failure of the 'Plan of Campaign'
of the late-1880s, in which tenants on particular estates embarked
upon a series of co-ordinated rent strikes (Geary 1986; Donnelly
1975: 308–76), showed how, if stiffened by the resolve of a chief

secretary as determined as Arthur Balfour, landlords could still win a number of battles. But they had been grievously wounded. Most of the arrears accumulated after 1877 were probably never made good and a set of statutes from 1881 onwards had the effect of depressing nominal rents – by about 10 per cent by 1886 and a massive 28 per cent by the early 1890s (Solow 1971: 176–8). Even on so well-run an estate as that of the Duke of Devonshire in Cork and Waterford 'both real and money income fell sharply in 1883–5 and again in 1886–7' (Proudfoot 1986: 44).

Indeed, so far had the balance of advantage shifted that the great majority of farmers at first responded unenthusiastically to the various purchase acts which, beginning in 1885, provided substantial state funding to those interested in buying their holdings. Very few bought under the earlier legislation and it was not until Wyndham's Act of 1903 made purchase so attractive – farmers could now acquire their holdings for terminable repayments significantly less than their already-reduced rents – that a really massive transfer of property began (Solow 1971: 187–93). Politics had effectively short-circuited economics *tout court*. Proprietors, squeezed by falling rents and a collapsing land market and faced with incumbrances which refused to decline in line with declining incomes (Curtis 1980), became increasingly anxious to escape. It was, however, to prove the last occasion on which southern landlords succeeded in drawing upon the credit of their English connections and loyalties. From then on the account was closed.

Up to the end of the century over 60,000 tenants purchased their holdings. After 1903 the floodgates opened. By 1920 nearly nine million acres had changed hands since Wyndham's Act and another two million were in process of being sold (Lyons 1971: 214). Only the relatively less encumbered landlords of the North-East were able to retain a position at all reminiscent of former times. Indeed, the 'solvency of Ulster's large landlords and the strength of the sectarian context in which they operated provide some explanations as to why Unionism proved an irresistible force in Ulster' (Curtis 1980: 367). That, however, the chief beneficiaries of the whole government-subsidized transaction should have proved to be the farmers of the period is one of those ironies with which history (and not least Irish history) so satisfyingly abounds.

IV

Because of the way in which the land agitation of the 1880s had been pursued it was of course the case that labourers and smaller farmers (especially in Connacht) benefited far less than tenants with middling or substantial holdings. That many rural aspirations remained unfulfilled became obvious when renewed western unrest broke out in the late-1890s (and was almost at once followed by the formation of William O'Brien's United Irish League) and again during the 'Ranch War' of 1906–9 (Jones 1983; Bew 1987). In both cases the chief targets were not so much landlords as the graziers renting large cattle runs in Connacht and northern Leinster who were seen as standing in the way of land redistribution. These episodes were, therefore, less universal than the Land War had been and their violence was on a lower and more restricted scale. Nor, indeed, was the United Irish League ever able to sustain a consistently intense commitment. Many graziers were also shopkeepers and as such proved especially successful in gaining important positions in local nationalist organizations (Higgins and Gibbons 1982), with the result that, once the League was adopted as the re-united Parliamentary Party's political machine in 1900, its capacity for single-minded devotion to the small farmers' cause was seriously undermined.

In general terms, however, the farmers of Ireland had at last entered into their economic kingdom. Many still remained 'poor' and some pulled more rapidly ahead than others. But overall there can be no doubt that the decades after the Land War witnessed a dramatic relative advance when compared with the quarter-century that had gone before. This becomes especially evident when real rather than current values are computed and even more so when per capita receipts are calculated in an attempt to reflect the patterning of demographic change over the period as a whole. Tables 4.3 and 4.4 extend the findings presented in Tables 4.1 and 4.2 and incorporate those slightly different estimates for cost of labour which have already been discussed.[5] The movements in real terms make it clear that, while in the 1850s and 1860s – when rents rose by a small amount – farmers probably experienced something of a decline and certainly failed to make progress, thereafter the story was a very different one. Labourers, indeed, continued to advance, but still from so low a base that their absolute standard of living can hardly be said to have attained great heights. Farmers, however, were able to combine their acquisition of land

Table 4.3 Agricultural output, rents, cost of labour and gross farming profits, 1852–4 to 1905–10, in current and real terms (1852–4 = 100) The amounts are £ millions

Years	Output		Rents		Cost of Labour*		Gross Farming Profits	
	current	real	current	real	current	real	current	real
1852–4	41.1	41.1	10.0	10.0	9.3	9.3	21.8	21.8
1872–4	45.0	38.5	12.0	10.3	10.6	9.1	22.4	19.1
1882–4	40.1	45.6	11.5	13.1	11.0	12.5	17.6	20.0
1905–10	45.5	55.1	8.0	9.7	10.6	12.8	26.9	32.6
% change 1872–4 to 1905–10	+1	+43	−33	−6	0	+41	+20	+71

* The differences between Tables 4.3 and 4.1 with regard to the estimates for cost of labour in 1852–4 and 1872–4 are explained in the text above. Those in Table 4.3 have been used in the calculations presented in Tables 4.2 and 4.4.

Table 4.4 Average gross annual per capita receipts of agricultural labourers and farmers, 1852–4 to 1905–10, in current and real terms (1852–4 = 100)

Years	Labourers		Farmers	
	current	real	current	real
1852–4	£10.7	£10.7	£56.6	£56.6
1872–4	£16.8	£14.4	£57.2	£48.9
1882–4	£19.3	£21.9	£46.1	£52.4
1905–10	£23.0	£27.9	£76.8	£93.0
% change 1872–4 to 1905–10	+37	+94	+34	+90

with a notable increase in economic standing. For Irish farmers as a group there was in truth no sustained 'Great Depression' in agriculture at all. To them went the triumph and the spoils; theirs the victory alone.

V

All the more, therefore, did it become the case that the culture of Irish society in general and of rural society in particular reflected above all the values of those many farmers who had proved successful in bettering their lot. It was a culture in which modernizing and 'archaic' elements were held together in a curious unity itself rendered stable by the safety-valve of continuing and heavy emigration. Although emigration rates varied (most obviously in response to economic changes in the receiving countries) and were especially high in the 1850s, 1860s, and 1880s, it is likely that altogether somewhere between 4.5 and 5 million people left Ireland in the period 1852–1910 – about a quarter for Britain and most of the rest for the United States (Ó Gráda 1975c). To put it another way, for the generation 'entering the employment market in about 1876, when the pace of post-Famine flight had already slackened, the probability of eventual emigration was still almost one-half' (Fitzpatrick 1980b: 126). And it was in large measure the widespread personal expectation of departure that helped to make the farmer's traditional preoccupation with property increasingly central to the Irish experience of marriage and family life (Fitzpatrick 1985b: 126). As farmers became demographically and economically more important, so increasingly did their disposition towards impartible inheritance (i.e. keeping the farm intact in the hands of a single heir) and a reluctance to subdivide holdings help to mark the second half of the nineteenth century as a period of steady growth in celibacy even though the actual age of marriage changed hardly at all. More and more did men without land find it difficult to get wives, so much so, that the percentage of men never married among the population aged 45–54 rose from 10 in 1841 to no less than 27 in 1911 (Fitzpatrick 1985b: 129). The system of the arranged 'match' – by which a sole (usually male) inheritor was paired off with a girl supplied with adequate cash in the form of a dowry – became more widespread and symbolized and reinforced the notion that marriage was above all a union of property. And as the other children were increasingly being compensated in terms of money, emigrant tickets, apprenticeships, and the like, so both the intensity and the length of quarrels over exclusion from land may well have been reduced (Fitzpatrick 1982: 62–5).

If a countryside peopled by celibates and by married couples producing large families cannot perhaps be regarded as having responded smartly to the drumbeats of modernity, yet in other respects Ireland was becoming both a more homogeneous and a more 'modern' society. Though the demographic idiosyncrasies of the West never entirely disappeared, they became notably less marked as time went on. Literacy levels rose everywhere, as did the numbers attending school. And it was this increasingly Anglicized and literate society which provided a growing audience for newspapers of all kinds and for a new national literature encompassing both the revolutionary and the constitutional traditions. Housing was improving, though much of it remained primitive. Banks were extending their branches throughout the countryside. More letters were being written and posted. Diet and dress became increasingly dependent on retail purchase, and, as a result, more standardized. Transport facilities grew and the number of passengers carried by rail rose substantially. And while there can be little doubt that Ireland remained a country in which even quite small distances could separate the consciousness of men, horizons had begun to broaden and geographical perceptions to change (Hoppen 1984: 461–4).

The gathering economic and political triumph of Irish farmers was matched by and related to a concurrent growth in the importance of retailing in general and shopkeepers in particular. Outside the few really large towns farmers and shopkeepers enjoyed an increasingly symbiotic relationship. Although their interests were rarely identical they were sufficiently close to make a certain degree of compromise and accommodation fruitful for both parties. As the volume of agricultural output that was marketed increased so 'shops expanded in number and in the range of goods they carried' (Cullen 1972: 142). Particularly in the smaller country towns retailers adopted a higher economic, social, and political profile than before. Their premises – pubs above all – were often the centres of local gossip. A network of kin relationships connected them ever more tightly to those who lived in the surrounding countryside. Because of this townsmen played a notable (if ancillary) role in the land agitation of the time (Clark 1971). By the 1890s, although in some of the remoter areas of the West the exploitative figure of the 'gombeenman' lording it over small farmers reduced to a state of debt-bondage was far from unknown, in most parts of rural Ireland competition militated against the creation of local monopolies and retail transactions generally involved benefits for customers and shopkeepers alike (Kennedy 1977 and 1979b). When the third Reform Act of 1884/5 abolished the great majority of Irish borough constituencies and 'threw' their voters into the surrounding county divisions shopkeepers were to some extent deprived of an urban focus for their activities and in consequence were more inclined than ever to use their crucial location at the centre of various economic and kin networks to involve themselves closely in the political concerns of the agrarian world.

As farmers in general became more prosperous so once again they resumed the free-wheeling jealousies of former times: those who had done only moderately well looked enviously at those who had done very well indeed. By allying themselves with the more successful elements traders were able to achieve a presence in Irish political life – and a representation in parliament, on the new local authorities introduced in 1898, and on other elected bodies – out of all proportion to their numbers (Kennedy 1983b). With their allies among the clergy (for priests in general also came from well-to-do farming and trading backgrounds) they succeeded in capturing nationalist politics for their own particular objectives and ambitions. In return for acting as political surrogates for the economically-dominant sections of the farmer community they were rewarded with powerful assistance in their efforts to circumscribe the growth of the co-operative movement which they had early identified as a potential threat (Kennedy 1978a). Admittedly this was made the easier because the pioneers of co-operation in late-nineteenth and early-twentieth century Ireland were many of them Protestants and unionists (if unionists of a 'constructive' variety). Nationalism could, therefore, be wheeled out to do perfect duty for self-interest, as when proposals to establish a co-operative creamery in the County Limerick town of Rathkeale on non-party lines were greeted with the ringing declaration that Rathkeale 'is a nationalist town – nationalist to the backbone – and every pound of butter made in this creamery must be made on nationalist principles, or it shan't be made at all' (West 1986: 30). As a result the original idea of men like Sir Horace Plunkett to introduce co-operatives into the retail sector had to be entirely abandoned and even in dairying the spread of the movement was rather less than it might otherwise have been (Ó Gráda 1977).

What in the end is perhaps most remarkable is how a particular kind of farmer culture was able, despite the splits and tensions between various sections of the agrarian and retailing worlds, to align nationalist politics in the broadest sense (and religious outlook and belief as well) to its own particular view of life. If very occasionally the new men of substance could still be mobilized behind a programme for change, this should not disguise the fact that their more constant role had become that of a thirsty sponge soaking up as quickly as possible any radical floods which might from time to time threaten the prosperity and power they had now at last achieved.

VI

One of the most obvious reasons why all this should have been so, lay in the fact that Ireland remained an overwhelmingly rural country not only in demographic but perhaps even more so in mental terms. Indeed, a strong ruralism was shared by landlords, priests, romantic nationalists, and men of letters, and constituted a unifying thread amidst the many splinterings of Irish life. 'I am not fond', noted the novelist Martin Ross in 1912, 'of anything about towns' (Curtis 1970: 60) – a view which was easily extendable across the sea to England, the baleful contemporary headquarters of those intertwined horrors: megalopolis and unbelief. And while it would be misleading to suggest that the slowly growing band of Irish separatists had no place for industry in their vision of the future, yet the new Ireland of their dreams was – at the deepest level – always portrayed in terms of an idealized conception of 'traditional' rural values and attitudes of mind (Garvin 1986a and 1986b). Although, therefore, a growing proportion of the post-Famine population began to live in towns – 17 per cent in 1851, 33 per cent in 1911 – this exercised only a marginal impact upon the governing values of Irish society as a whole.

Few places experienced much industrial growth and Irish towns developed into administrative and marketing centres with, notably in Dublin and Cork, perhaps a certain amount of consumer-orientated light industry as a kind of optional extra. The character of most of them was determined above all by those physical manifestations of government, commerce, and gossip: the post office, the workhouse, the bank, the school, the shop, and the pub. While Irish industry in general was relatively prosperous in the 1850s and 1860s the growing availability of mass-produced goods and the collapse of the international industrial boom about 1874 combined to bring about a crisis foreshadowing that which was soon to engulf Irish agriculture. British manufacturers increased their exports to Ireland and drove craft producers such as blacksmiths, nailers, and shoemakers to the wall (Cullen 1972: 145–7). And even if this to some extent helped retailers (who sold the factory-made boots, clothing, nails, and so forth) the 1870s and 1880s were, nevertheless, decades of urban stagnation and decay. Townsmen, as a result, found ever more reasons for involving themselves in the depression-induced discontents of the farmers living around them. And while the industrial sector (like the agricultural) soon experienced a notable recovery, the growing concentration of industry in the North-East meant that few ripples of improvement ever managed to lap against urban shores elsewhere.

Outside Belfast the proportion of occupied workers engaged in manufacturing fell substantially. Even in Cork City it declined from 40 to 20 per cent between 1841 and 1901 and in Dublin from 33 to 20 per cent in the period 1841–1911 (Murphy 1981: 128; Daly 1982: 121–2). Only to some extent was compensation provided by an expansion of the transport and domestic service sectors, though even this, by encouraging a shift from skilled to unskilled employment, depressed earnings because the wage gap between those with and those without skills was far greater in Ireland than in Britain.

More and more was Belfast becoming a peculiar and special place. With in 1911 387,000 inhabitants it was the biggest city in Ireland. Although linen was then still the most important local industry in terms of output, exports, and employment, its recent growth had been slow and a shrinking world market for linen products rendered the future uncertain. What made Belfast so formidable was the rapid development of shipbuilding and engineering from the late-1880s onwards, though both had already begun to expand some thirty years before.

While national statistics for the first decade of the twentieth century actually suggest that Ireland was, in international terms, a comparatively 'industrialized' country (with about a third of the combined net output of agriculture and industry being supplied by the latter) and also one which exported almost half its total output of manufactures and processed food and drink, this was a profoundly misleading picture. In the first place, the bulk of production was concentrated upon only a handful of industries, notably linen, brewing, distilling, shipbuilding, and engineering; in the second, probably a third of net industrial output and two-thirds of exports originated in Belfast and its immediate hinterland alone (Cullen 1972: 156–62). It was not, in any case, 'really the process of industrialisation but Protestant control of that process that gave the political economy of the North-East its unique character' (Ollerenshaw 1985: 65–6). Few Catholics achieved positions of power. The influential Belfast Chamber of Commerce was at once Protestant and unionist. Industrialists became increasingly prominent in anti-Home Rule politics in the years leading up to the Great War. To a significant degree, therefore, can the unique economic development of the area be seen as having – long before 1921 – 'helped to pave the way for the partition of

Ireland and the creation of a Northern Ireland state' (Ollerenshaw 1985: 66). The situation at the top was mirrored at the bottom as Catholics (who actually constituted a shrinking proportion of Belfast's inhabitants after 1851) found themselves confined largely to low-paid work. At the same time, however, while the aristocracy of labour was overwhelmingly Protestant, numbers alone ensured that Protestant workers dominated virtually all levels and categories of employment.

Even if living conditions and especially housing were undoubtedly worse in Dublin than in Belfast (O'Brien 1982; Daly 1984a; Jones 1967), it is still hardly surprising that trade unionism and labour politics should have established their earliest substantial home in the North (Patterson 1985). But in both places labour found it difficult to make more than sporadic headway. In Belfast sectarianism, although capable of providing short-term boosts to agitation, was inimical to worker solidarity, while in Dublin local politics fell into the iron grip of those publicans, grocers, and tenement landlords who had achieved prominence in post-Parnell nationalism and were ready, willing, and able to trump the labour card with the Home Rule ace. As James Connolly said of one of their number: 'Scully is running in the interests of the United Irish League, and high rents, slum tenements, rotten staircases, stinking yards, high death-rates, low wages, Corporation jobbery and margarine wrapped in butter paper' (Daly 1984a: 218). Indeed, throughout both rural and urban Ireland many of the nationalists who came to dominate local government after the reforms of 1898 rapidly acquired a reputation for opportunism and graft as, in the words of Joseph Lee, they 'dutifully attended to the three Fs of popular politics – family, friends, and favours' (Lee 1985a: 84).

VII

The political somersaults of the second decade of the twentieth century left much of this remarkably unchanged. The Great War brought about a sudden jump in agricultural prices so that farmers enjoyed the most prosperous years of the Union just as British rule was coming to an end. Traders and manufacturers too shared in the martial boom. Urban and rural workers, however, limped well behind as wages failed to match rising prices because, with emigration virtually blocked, the supply of labour greatly exceeded demand (Cullen 1972: 171–2). In the period 1914–21, therefore, Ireland was not simply a country divided between nationalists (of all persuasions), on the one side, and unionists, on the other, but one in which the more ancient fault lines separating the bourgeoisie of town and country from the men of little and no property had lost neither their depth nor their importance. Looked at in this way Sinn Fein after 1916 was more a continuation of the Home Rule Party than any shining new invention or departure. Already at the South Longford by-election of May 1917 it received support from the local grazier interest against an anti-ranching Home Rule candidate. Elsewhere it happily attacked the Parliamentary Party from the opposite direction with calculated appeals to the unsatisfied yearnings of those with few acres or none at all (Bew 1987: 214–16). But, when it mattered most, Sinn Fein usually lined up behind those with a vested interest in stopping the wheels of reform from rolling onwards towards the break-up of large holdings and the redistribution of land (Bew 1988).

By issuing repeated calls for unity behind the separatist banner and occasional bursts of rhetoric hinting at social justice once separation had been achieved Sinn Fein also effectively short-circuited the attempts of the Labour movement to rewrite the political agenda of the time. Between 1918 and 1920, as the boom continued, the Irish Transport and General Workers' Union succeeded in attracting many agricultural labourers to its ranks (O'Connor 1980; Laffan 1985). At the same time the Ranch War of the previous decade experienced violent revival as small farmers in the West turned once more against graziers and took up cattle driving as the best way to make known their discontents. Indeed, many of the incidents commonly labelled as IRA engagements were in reality no more than land seizures thinly disguised (Fitzpatrick 1978: 119). But, just as the republican leaders – like the Home Rule leaders before them – successfully exploited the energy of Labour's rank-and-file without giving much in return, so, when in 1918 and 1920 cattle driving became especially intense, they swung decisively behind the entrenched interests of the rural middle class. In June 1920 a Dail proclamation insisted that 'energies must be directed towards the clearing out – not the occupier of this or that piece of land – but the foreign invader of our Country' (Laffan 1985: 205). Austin Stack, as Secretary for Home Affairs in the Dail's executive government, denounced cattle driving for diverting 'the attention of the people from the national struggle' and, in later years, Sean Moylan, a leader of the Cork IRA, was to glory in the energy with which he and others had 'cleaned up' the 'selfish' efforts of small farmers and labourers to 'cash in on the work of the IRA' (Fitzpatrick 1977: 175; Bew 1982: 86, 91). Just, therefore, as the Labour movement had been vampirized by the republicans so republicanism itself was 'tamed by the men of substance almost from the start' (Fitzpatrick 1977: 267, 235–80).

The collapse of the boom in 1921 further reinforced the economic and social conservatism of the new Free State. The power of the landlords might indeed have gone, but it was quickly and smoothly replaced by the more steely grip of those – in country and town – who had most obviously profited from the 'national struggle' – the Irish equivalents, if you like, of those hard-faced British businessmen described by Baldwin as having 'done well out of the war'. Although there were still difficulties ahead, the middling and larger farmers had good reason to congratulate themselves. After a shaky start during the third quarter of the nineteenth century they had improved their economic and social standing to an unprecedented degree.

With the partition of Ireland in 1921 and the exclusion of the bulk of industry from the territory of the Free State independence increased rather than diminished the influence and importance in the South of those elements which had done best during the last decades of British rule. Apart, however, from the (admittedly crucial) matter of independence itself, in political and social terms the effects of all this were far less than some had feared and many expected. Under the guise of insurrection Ireland had in fact awarded itself little more than a rearranged continuity. As Yeats, with his usual cruel insight, put it

> Parnell came down the road, he said to a cheering man;
> 'Ireland shall get her freedom and you still break stone'.

NOTES

1. I am extremely grateful to Cormac Ó Gráda of University College Dublin, Peter Solar of the Catholic University of Louvain, and Michael Turner of the University of Hull for allowing me to use their estimates of agricultural output in this period. Although these have not all yet been published in full, some are available in Ó Gráda 1984 and 1988 and in Turner 1987. While the scholars in question do not always precisely agree (and understandably so given the difficult assumptions involved), the broad measure of similarity is remarkable.

Certainly the same *trend* emerges from all their calculations and this differs markedly from that presented in Vaughan 1977; 1980a; 1980b; 1984 (and the output estimates in Solow 1971 would now also seem to require revision). In my own calculations I have generally used Turner's 'compromise' figures because he has actually produced (unpublished) *annual* output data for 1850–1914.

2. My total wage estimates are based upon a combination of census information on the number of labourers (see also Hoppen 1984: 105) and wage data (in Fitzpatrick 1980a; Bowley 1899 and 1900) making the same assumptions as Huttman (1970: 521) with regard to employment levels. My figures come to £9.3 million for 1852–4 (a slight increase on Vaughan's estimate) and £10.6 for 1872–4.

3. Clearly some 'gross farming profits' accrued to landlords from home farms etc., just as some 'wages' went to farmers for personally working their holdings.

4. The Sauerbeck-*Statist* price index (Mitchell and Deane 1971: 474–5) has been used because, with all its faults, it probably remains the most useful and has been widely accepted as such.

5. Based on the sources referred to in notes 1, 2, and 4. The estimates for cost of labour have been computed from the wage data already mentioned. The rent for 1882–4 has been adjusted to take account of post-1881 reductions and that for 1905–10 is an estimate made by Cormac Ó Gráda for 1908 (1988: 130).

CHAPTER 5
Politics

Nationalism and Localism

The very speed with which O'Connell's political machine wound down is evidence that, however impressive O'Connell's achievements had been, they had injected new potentials into political culture rather than fundamentally changed the nature of that culture as a whole. It is tempting to blame all of this upon the Famine. But, while that catastrophe proved an important solvent in the political as well as in the socio-economic sense, the events of the 1850s and 1860s showed that politics could still continue to be lively and embracing without necessarily being either national in flavour or nationalist in conception. It is undeniable that a greater variety of models was now available – in the shape especially of O'Connellite constitutionalism, on the one hand, and of Tone's violent and Davis's cultural nationalism, on the other – but mere availability could not of itself secure universal adoption or consistent assent. If, therefore, politics now contained a wider range of options than before and oscillated between these in new and interesting ways, it would, nonetheless, be a mistake to imagine that the only question that remains to be answered is why for long periods after 1850 little of national(ist) moment seemed to be occupying the centre of the popular stage. To approach things from such an angle involves making the political nation resemble nothing so much as an inherently triumphant Sleeping Beauty laid out upon the refrigerated slab of colonial oppression to await the inevitable kiss of some ardent prince, who, depending on one's point of view, had learnt the art of osculatory resuscitation from either the Liberator or the men of '98. Not only, however, does this trivialize the complexities of reality, but, by forcing events into a procrusteanism of hindsight, it elevates what was never more than one strand in political experience into the sole 'authentic' and 'normal' expression of popular feeling and aspiration.

I

The quarter century after the Famine was in fact a time in which a complicated *mélange* of developments sustained a species of politics in which the local, the immediate, and the everyday provided important contexts for interaction and involvement. In demographic and social terms the Famine helped to bring about the triumph of the farmers of the countryside. However, not only did labourers and cottiers, though undoubtedly now a lesser force, fail to disappear overnight, but the landed community was also able to emerge from the Famine financially and politically stronger than might have been expected (Hoppen 1977a). The weaker landlords had been forced to sell out (Lane 1972–3 and 1981–2), the bulk of their property being bought by those proprietors who had succeeded in weathering the storm (Donnelly 1975: 131). Because of this the Irish Franchise Act of 1850, which placed the electorate upon an altogether more rational basis than before and in so doing undoubtedly benefited the middling to larger farmers (Hoppen 1984: 17–33), did not immediately enable such men to have things entirely their own way. Not only were they faced by a renascent body of landowners far from prepared to flee the fields, but early attempts to establish campaigns entirely subservient to farmer interests continued to arouse opposition from the declining and voteless but still potent legions of the rural poor.

In formal terms the organization of Irish political life in the 1850s revolved around three related phenomena: the farmers' efforts to align things completely to their own preoccupations by means of the Tenant League, the continuation of Catholic politics in the shape of the Catholic Defence Association, and the reaction to such developments by a vigorous and revived Protestant Conservatism. Although all of these were authentically 'Irish' (not least the last), they were none of them nationalist in any real sense, and much the same was true of the Independent Irish Party which emerged as a parliamentary reflection of agrarian and Catholic aspirations only to collapse into ineffective confusion before the decade had come to an end (Whyte 1958).

The Tenant League appeared in 1850 to coordinate the

activities of local tenant societies set up since 1847 to agitate for what soon became the basic programme of farmer politics, namely, the 3 Fs, or fixity of tenure, fair rent, and free sale. Although a good deal of populist rhetoric was quickly poured over its work, the League consisted almost exclusively of well-off farmers whose sleight-of-hand in equating the 'people' with themselves alone was rivalled only by an inability to extend their agitation much beyond the geographical confines of agricultural prosperity (Hoppen 1984: 102, 480). In truth the League was an organization of those who not only believed themselves strong enough to be able to acquire further increments of strength but who also feared that they had something substantial to lose. Hence the brief involvement of certain Presbyterian farmers in Ulster afraid that the extra-legal Ulster Custom might soon be mown down by an increasingly confident landlord class. But though contemporary leaders like Gavan Duffy were later to canonize the business under the ecumenical title of 'The League of North and South' (Gavan Duffy 1886), the movement was predominantly a southern one 'with a few northern allies of doubtful reliability' (Whyte 1966: 8).

The Catholic Defence Association grew out of events in England rather than Ireland and was a response to the widespread anti-Catholicism evoked by Pope Pius IX's re-establishment of a full hierarchy for England and Wales in 1850 and the subsequent Ecclesiastical Titles Act of 1851 which attempted, with ludicrous emphasis on shadow rather than substance, to ban Catholic bishops from taking their titles from places in the United Kingdom (Machin 1977: 210–39). Not only did the Association's concerns mingle with those of the Tenant League, but together the two bodies constituted an alliance which at the general election of 1852 was able to secure the return of forty-eight MPs either already or soon to become pledged to a vaguely-defined policy of remaining aloof from British parties unless offered substantial agrarian and religious concessions (Whyte 1958: 83–109). Soon, however, this proved to be little more than a charade. Some of the noisiest Catholic partisans quickly deserted and took office in Aberdeen's coalition ministry of 1852–5 without having extracted concessions of any kind. Many of the other 'pledged' MPs drifted back to that orthodox Liberalism which, with Liberal governments in almost permanent power between 1846 and 1874, could alone promise them advancement and position. The hierarchy under the influence of Archbishop Cullen of Dublin was suspicious of a movement which to it seemed (however bizarrely) a reincarnation of Young Ireland and rapidly issued one of its periodic demands that the priesthood stay out of politics. By the middle of the decade the party had, indeed, virtually ceased to exist (Whyte 1958: 118–57).

Having seen off their secular rivals the bishops emerged to reap a disappointing harvest. Deprived of the discipline and leadership which O'Connell had provided, the clergy, though still powerful in constituency affairs, lacked both cohesion and impact. Groping about for a political programme the church alighted upon the twin issues of educational change (i.e. more sectarianism at state expense) and the disestablishment of the Church of Ireland, neither of them as yet capable of mobilizing much enthusiasm from the people at large. With the arrival on the political scene of Fenianism in the late 1850s it seemed more important than ever to orchestrate a form of constitutional politics at once capable of eliciting mass support and of inoculating the more restless sections of the laity against the new revolutionary disease (Whyte 1967a; Corish 1967). The National Association of 1864 was the outcome of such preoccupations and its programme of mild agrarian reform, educational concessions, and disestablishment reflected a compromise between clerical ideals and the world of practical reality (Norman 1965; Corish 1962). Although it attracted a number of Irish MPs such success as the Association achieved was as much the result of English as of Irish developments. On the one hand, its opportunistic alliance with the largely Nonconformist Liberation Society over disestablishment made it part of a wider United Kingdom campaign, on the other, Gladstone's eventual conviction that disestablishment and land reform were issues capable of cementing the cohesion of his parliamentary following broke the log jam more effectively than agitation alone would ever have been able to do (Steele 1974; Bell 1969; Vincent 1977).

Much of this was, however, little more than surface froth. In the counties landlords were proving themselves well able to contain the few brushfires which occasionally lit up the sky (Hoppen 1977a). Elsewhere the slow economic and demographic emergence of urban Ireland produced – in a manner paradoxical only to those intent on sustaining iron equations between urbanism and radicalism – a situation in which the local and fissiparous priorities of particular places counted for more than Independent Parties or National Associations. Like a pressure cooker from which the O'Connellite valve had been removed the borough constituencies flourished amidst a political culture in which local notables such as shopkeepers, priests, and property owners led what amounted to rival electoral armies based more upon occupational and kin relationships than upon ideological principles of any kind. As in contemporary England elections were a rational business largely in the sense that they reflected and re-arranged the relative positions of the political elements within each town (Vincent 1966: xv). Candidates were returned because they could provide jobs, enjoyed local reputations for largesse, or were able to bring numerous dependants to the poll. This was neither new nor unusual; nor was it a necessary outcome of the franchise arrangements of 1850 as a result of which only a sixth of all adult males enjoyed the vote (Hoppen 1985), for in the early 1880s a virtually identical franchise was to coexist happily with the return of 'radical' Parnellite candidates. Rather it was the result of the absence of countervailing forces, an absence which allowed certain ever-present normalities to flourish with unfettered luxuriance (Hoppen 1979).

The only national agency which proved capable of extracting real benefits from the situation was Irish Conservatism. Led by able men, producing far earlier than its English counterpart an effective electoral organization (the Central Conservative Society founded in 1853), dexterously tapping both Protestant fears and a degree of Catholic disenchantment with the Liberal Party, the Conservatives succeeded at the general election of 1859 in actually winning a majority of seats (55 out of 105) in what was an overwhelmingly Catholic country with a predominantly Catholic electorate (Hoppen 1970 and 1984: 278–332). Indeed, not until 1874 did the proportion of Conservative seats fall below a third. Perhaps, therefore, it would be at least as convincing to see the two post-Famine decades as ones of Conservative revival as to follow the path trodden by so many and concentrate – among constitutional movements – only upon the 'inadequacies' of the Tenant League, the Independent Party, or the National Association.

II

Beyond constitutionalism the flag of violence was kept flying, although only just and for years without much success, by the Irish Revolutionary (later Republican) Brotherhood set up in 1858 and by its counterpart in America, both of them eventually, though somewhat incorrectly, subsumed under the general title of the Fenian movement. Founded by some of the younger men who had taken part in the rising of 1848, the IRB was a secret society (and thus feared and condemned by the church), though, like most similar groups in Ireland, it was rapidly infiltrated by government spies. To describe it as a 'popular movement' (Garvin 1981: 59) is to credit its early days with more recognition than is warranted; indeed even its founder, James Stephens, had at first been struck by 'the apathy of the farmers [and] the pigheadedness of the *bourgeoisie*' (Ryan 1967: 80; Garvin 1986b). Although the IRB's size in the 1860s is impossible to assess accurately – its leaders were given to extravagant claims (Comerford 1985: 124–5) – the only groups from which it attracted significant numbers were urban artisans and shopworkers (Hoppen 1984: 361; Clark 1979: 203) and many of these were more interested in the opportunities for communal recreation offered by 'the Organization' (gymnastics, boxing, rambling, and the like) than in its amateurish attempts at military mobilization (Comerford 1981).

It would, however, be a mistake to concentrate entirely on the IRB's farcical secrecy or on its pathetic and easily quelled rising of 1867 (Ó Broin 1971), for, partly by accident partly through a willingness to compromise by *some* of its leaders, Fenianism was at times able to become a force of considerable, if sporadic, importance (Moody 1968). Its debate with the church on the role of the clergy in politics and on the whole relationship between the secular and spiritual arms, though shot through with self-deception on both sides, ensured – just as O'Connell had done – that naked clericalism would rarely be allowed to have the field entirely to itself. Its provision of dead patriots in the shape of the 'Manchester Martyrs' of 1867 and the simultaneous incarceration of many others called into being an Amnesty movement which for a time was to constitute the most widespread and powerful political phenomenon in Ireland. More important still, the willingness of some Fenians to water down their adherence to revolution and join the land agitation which grew out of agricultural depression in the late 1870s helped to produce an interlude during which agrarianism, constitutionalism, Catholicism, and modified republicanism were able to coalesce and thus briefly overcome the normal particularism of Irish politics as a whole.

Gladstone's success in disestablishing the Church of Ireland in 1869 and passing a symbolically important but practically innocuous Land Act in 1870 angered many Protestant Conservatives because too much, and many Catholic farmers because too little, had

115

been conceded. As a result a few Conservatives were prominent in establishing a Home Government Association in 1870, some because they genuinely believed in devolution but most because of an all-consuming desire to rid themselves of Anglo-Saxon Liberalism and of Gladstone in particular (McCaffrey 1962). Protestant political life was in a confused state. A recrudescence of that populism which had long marked its urban manifestations combined with discontents among Protestant farmers in Ulster (who, like their Catholic counterparts, were disappointed by the *inadequacies* of Gladstonian legislation) led to electoral victories by maverick candidates at Belfast and Carrickfergus in 1868 and Tyrone in 1874. But though the official leadership was greatly worried by such developments, both the populists and those landowners and intellectuals briefly tempted into dalliance with devolution were reluctant to follow the logic of their dissatisfactions and in most cases returned to the fold on realizing that there was little future in cutting themselves adrift from English attachment and support.

On the other side a combination of popular involvement in the Amnesty movement and a curious mixture of both rising expectations that Gladstone would make important concessions and anger when these proved unsurprisingly feeble produced something of a sea change in political discourse and practice. A series of significant southern by-elections between 1869 and 1873 showed that the mere reiteration of mild Liberal panaceas was no longer enough, that Fenian or crypto-Fenian candidates were now capable of attracting significant support, and that the landed community was showing incipient signs of losing its political nerve (Hoppen 1984: 166–70, 464–8). Towards the end of 1873 a Home Rule League was established under the Protestant lawyer, Isaac Butt, formerly a pillar of intransigent Conservatism but now convinced that the union required at least adjustment and perhaps even something more. At the general election of 1874 fifty-nine MPs were returned on Home Rule 'principles', though, as in the 1850s, many of them were at best fair-weather friends (Thornley 1964: 176–211). Nonetheless, the social background of non-Conservative members was slowly shifting from its traditional dependence upon landowners towards an increasing emphasis – which became more pronounced still in 1880 and 1885 – upon journalists, merchants, shopkeepers, and the like (Thornley 1964: 207; Hoppen 1984: 332–9).

Butt, however, was a gentleman both in his adherence to

parliamentary traditions and in a penchant for managing his own financial and amorous affairs with neither competence nor effectiveness (De Vere White 1946). With Disraeli in power between 1874 and 1880 he did little more than issue polite protests. What, however, changed everything was the agricultural depression which Ireland, in common with almost all of Europe, began to experience towards the end of the decade.

As early as 1870 certain Fenians had started to realize that sea-green attachment to violence held out little prospect of imminent success. Among them were members of the Supreme Council of the IRB which itself in 1873 adopted an amended constitution allowing it to 'support every movement calculated to advance the cause of Irish independence consistently with the preservation of its own integrity' (Moody 1981: 123). This was the first of several 'new departures' by which the forces of revolutionary and constitutional nationalism (including the former's financially important American wing) entered into an effective, though often tense, marriage of convenience. In 1874 the Ulster merchant, Joseph Biggar, Home Rule MP for Cavan, was allowed to join the Brotherhood and later take a seat on the Supreme Council. At Westminster Biggar inaugurated the policy of 'obstruction' by which, much to Butt's discomfort, he made every effort to hold up proceedings on all sorts of matters in protest against parliament's refusal to grapple with Home Rule. After the Meath by-election of April 1875 he was joined by a recruit greater than himself, the Protestant Wicklow landlord, Charles Stewart Parnell, whose background, abilities, and cunning were eventually to make him the most formidable Irish politician since O'Connell (Foster 1976).

At the same time other significant forces in Irish life were also exhibiting disenchantment with the Liberal honeymoon of the late 1860s. The Catholic hierarchy, delighted by disestablishment, was far from delighted by Gladstone's inability to deliver university reform in 1873 and repelled by his lurch towards anti-Catholicism in his pamphlet outburst of 1874 against the Vatican Council's recent promulgation of the dogma of papal infallibility. Gladstone, indeed, believed he had done all that was necessary for Ireland – perhaps rather more than all. If the Land Act of 1870 satisfied almost no one else it certainly satisfied its author, and the resulting complacency 'about his handiwork dominated his approach to Irish affairs in 1870–81'. When in 1877 Gladstone briefly visited Ireland for the first and last time he emerged from the country houses of the aristocrats with whom he stayed to announce that all was for the best, that, indeed, 'the landlord is better, the farmer is better, the cottager is better' (Vincent 1977: 204–7). In fact all three were beginning to feel the draughts of depression and farmers in particular had already for some years been actively organizing clubs of a political sort the better to bemoan the failures of land reform and to support the electoral endeavours of Home Rule (Clark 1979: 214–20).

III

The depression of the late 1870s became politically formidable not only because a sudden drop in incomes created discontent but because an effective political leadership was in place to take advantage of a situation which might otherwise have run into the sands of atomistic confusion. By the time the Land War broke out in 1879 Parnell had already achieved a powerful position in Home Rule affairs. By collaborating with American Fenians and more immediately with Michael Davitt (who, after early Fenian imprisonment, had emerged as the most effective exponent of the aspirations and discontents of small farmers) Parnell was able, partly by luck and partly by utilizing some awesomely-tuned political skills, to assume the leadership of a combined agrarian and nationalist movement in which the former was for a time to prove very much the dominant element.

The conjunction of bad harvests and falling prices made it difficult for tenants to pay their rents. Evictions rose to levels not seen since the Famine. Rural violence, as measured by the official index of 'agrarian outrages', began to increase in 1879 and reached a peak in 1881 (Moody 1981: 562–6). Notable was the way in which the initial unrest was centred upon the poorer counties of the West for previously Connacht had proved itself the least disturbed and politically active part of the country (Hoppen 1984: 372–4). It was not long before the agitation spread to almost the whole of southern and also to parts of northern Ireland so that the Land League established by Davitt and Parnell in 1879 was able to draw both external strength and internal contradictions from the very fact that its activities reflected unrest throughout all parts of the agricultural community. Soon, however, it became apparent that the differences within agrarian society could not be permanently overwhelmed by common experience alone; and even in disturbed

Mayo it was only for a few heady months that 'the Nationalist and anti-landlord coalition of Fenians, farmers and townsmen' was able to obscure the splinterings hacked into the social fabric by that 'conversion to agrarian capitalism' which had been under way for a century or more (Jordan 1987: 347).

What is, however, in the end most remarkable about the whole episode is not the revelation of all kinds of tensions between farmers of various kinds (Bew 1978), but that, if only for a brief moment, it proved possible to sustain a united front (Clark 1971 and 1979). The Land War only seems a kind of failure to those who persist in believing that a different and more permanently unifying species of politics was somehow 'in the air' ready to be used had only contemporaries possessed sufficient wit and insight. Apart from being quite unrealistic such views also involve an enormous condescension by the present upon the past. That during the early 1880s the small farmers of the West were at all prepared to follow the lead of the hated graziers (Jordan 1987), that the local branches of the League attracted not only a representative membership from the whole economic spectrum of the tenantry but also from labourers so long hostile to farmers of most kinds (Hoppen 1984: 475–9) is evidence that something unusual and important had taken place, even if its import could as yet be perceived only as through a glass darkly.

Gladstone's eventual Land Act of 1881 granted the 3 Fs and ushered in that spatchcock period during which the land of Ireland was, in reality and to some extent in law, held in co-partnership between tenants and 'proprietors'. Parnell, now Butt's successor as Home Rule chief and leader of a parliamentary following rendered more effective by increased discipline and by the results of the general election of 1880, was determined to support the measure through the Commons even though some of his lieutenants feared it might castrate the fierceness of popular protest. By adopting the ingenious device of urging farmers to 'test' the act and by enjoying the good fortune of imprisonment Parnell was able to avoid having to make a more considered or detailed response. As he himself is supposed to have predicted, 'Captain Moonlight' (i.e. uncontrolled violence) took over the leadership; but although he and his imprisoned associates felt it necessary to give the extremists at least one bite of the cherry by issuing a fruitless 'No Rent' manifesto, the agitation soon began to fall apart. And in May 1882 Parnell was released after having come to an unofficial agreement with the government: he to counsel good behaviour, it further to extend the scope of land reform.

With agitation now virtually at an end – though it was to experience revival later in the decade and in succeeding decades also – it is time to assess the nature of what had happened. Two conclusions emerge with particular force. Despite the western origins of the Land War it is clear that the main rural beneficiaries of the affair were soon 'revealed to be the already substantial strong farmers of Ireland' (Bew 1982: 88). In the second place, Parnell was now in a position to devote himself more exclusively to the great aim of his life, namely, Home Rule, and in doing so to reassert the primacy of political over economic considerations. The Land League had been proclaimed unlawful in October 1881 and the Irish National League which was set up to replace it in the following year, though locally drawing upon an almost identical personnel, was entirely under central control and was 'dominated by parliamentarians, preoccupied with parliamentary objectives, and committed to constitutional rather than agrarian agitation' (Lyons 1977: 237).

A series of by-elections in the early 1880s showed that Parnell's Home Rule politics could attract an electorate virtually unchanged since 1850 as regards the franchise upon which it was selected and that the overwhelming triumph at the general election of 1885 – when the party won every Irish seat outside north-east Ulster and Trinity College Dublin – was only in modest part the result of the third Reform Act of 1884/5 having given the vote to small farmers and landless labourers in Ireland. The successful candidates were selected by conventions at which the central leadership played a decisive role (O'Brien 1964: 126–33). They included seventeen journalists, seventeen lawyers, nine merchants, seven licensed traders, six farmers, five landlords, four physicians, as well as single representatives of occupations not hitherto thought acceptable in such a context: tailor, grocer, draper, cattle dealer, teacher, money-lender, and manager of an aquarium at New Brighton (Hoppen 1984: 339). Those who needed it were given financial assistance: a new development in British as well as Irish parliamentary life. Yet, however much they differed from the landed MPs of former years, the irony remained that they were still not merely unrepresentative of the 'people' at large but even unrepresentative of their own most active grass roots supporters, for, even if one includes the lone cattle man, no more than eight per cent were in a position to claim farming as their principal avocation. Tenants (with the substantial men as usual to the fore) were, however, to achieve a more significant presence with regard to the election of poor law boards – bodies of growing administrative importance – where they captured an increasing number of seats between 1879 and 1886 and thus foreshadowed those later gains which were to flow from the Local Government Act of 1898 (Feingold 1975 and 1984).

Although it has been suggested – not altogether convincingly – that public opinion at this time was less universally in favour of Home Rule than is commonly supposed (Loughlin 1986), there can be little doubt that the mid-1880s marked the high point of Parnell's influence. Already in 1884 the Catholic bishops had at last bestowed their imprimatur and entrusted the parliamentary party with responsibility for pressing Catholic educational claims (Larkin 1975a: 235–66). June 1885 brought about a constellation of good luck as William Walsh succeeded the cautious Cardinal McCabe as archbishop of Dublin and at Westminster Gladstone's Liberal administration, worn down by foreign disasters and domestic disputes, was defeated by a combination of Parnellites and Conservatives (Cooke and Vincent 1974: 173–254). Though much more had been at stake than Irish matters alone this latter development briefly allowed Parnell to assume a pivotal role in British party politics by the very fact of his possessing not only the willingness but also the lack of attachment required for independent action. Already a few maverick Conservatives in England had been dropping hints of a vaguely sympathetic nature and, indeed, Salisbury's caretaker government lost no time in passing what in retrospect can be seen as perhaps the most important legislative intervention of the half century, Ashbourne's Land Purchase Act, by which the complete cost of buying farms was lent to tenants on attractive terms – effectively the first of many such schemes which were together to shift the pattern of landownership in Ireland in an entirely new direction.

Those who believed that Ashbourne's Act marked some fundamental change in Conservative opinion were, however, rapidly disappointed. Parnell's manifesto calling on the Irish in Britain to vote against Liberal candidates at the general election of 1885 was at bottom little more than a tactical manoeuvre in a complicated and developing situation. Although its effect is not easy to determine the election produced a result (Liberals 335, Conservatives 249, Nationalists 86) which allowed Parnell to hold the balance, 'either doubling the Liberal majority or destroying it utterly as circumstances might dictate' (Lyons 1977: 302–6). But when Gladstone's son announced on 17 December that his father had been 'converted' to Home Rule all previous calculations ran into the sands. Gladstone's motives – complex, obscure, and involving far wider dimensions than those of Ireland alone – need not concern us here. Their results, however, undoubtedly succeeded in attaching Parnell's forces to the Liberal Party with rods of steel, so much so, that constitutional nationalism's freedom of action as regards British party politics was to remain closely circumscribed for thirty years and more. Although some have seen this as simply making formal what had earlier been just as much the case informally (O'Day 1986), this is to exaggerate the inevitability of the pre-1885 Liberal alliance well beyond its reasonable deserts.

With Irish support Gladstone became prime minister for the third time in February 1886. Although he made no great efforts to select a cabinet sympathetic to Home Rule and must have known that parliament would never pass any significant repeal of the union, he introduced a Home Rule Bill in April which at once revealed the enormous technical, administrative, and financial problems involved. There was to be an Irish legislature with an executive responsible to it, but with a long catalogue of 'imperial' matters excluded from its jurisdiction: peace and war, defence, foreign and colonial affairs, customs and excise, trade and navigation, the post office, coinage, the list went on and on. As a result even Gladstone was obliged to think again about his initial insistence that Irish representation at Westminster be brought to an end, but did so too late to affect the issue. The Conservatives remained antagonistic and enough Liberals voted against the bill to ensure its defeat in June by thirty votes. Many of the so-called Liberal Unionists knew little of Ireland and cared less. But they scuppered Home Rule all the same and ensured that the resulting general election of July 1886 ushered in two almost-solid decades of Conservative hegemony at Westminster and in Whitehall.

For the rest of the 1880s Parnell played a meandering game. With 'independent opposition' no longer a runner a certain opaque inertia was perhaps the most sensible response to what had happened, and opaque inertia had few greater exponents than Parnell. In 1886 he and his mistress, Mrs O'Shea, decided to live together permanently, with the result that he was often virtually incommunicado at Eltham in south-east London rather than available for leadership and advice in Ireland or the House of Commons. What, however, this did enable Parnell to achieve was a degree of beneficial aloofness from the second phase of the Land War, the so-called 'Plan of Campaign' orchestrated after October 1886 by his lieutenants John Dillon and William O'Brien (Lyons 1968: 82–112) in the face of a renewed downturn in the economy. Essentially the Plan was an attempt at collective bargaining on individual properties: the farmers offered a reduced rent, which, if the landlord refused to accept it, was paid into an 'estate fund' and, together with nationally-raised monies, used to support the tenant cause. Although some successes were obtained, the campaign proved expensive and was eventually ground down by the skill of Arthur Balfour (chief secretary 1887–91) in putting a last backbone into landed resistance and combining this with effective coercion, on the one hand, and practical concessions, on the other – the latter soon christened the policy of 'killing Home Rule by kindness' (Curtis 1963; Geary 1986). Yet, even if a minority of landlords were able to mount something of a counter-attack (Donnelly 1975: 308–76), this was to prove a swansong rather than the herald of things to come. Overall the coincidence of rural agitation and economic depression undoubtedly hit landlords with stomach-churning intensity, and the continuation of the latter well beyond the more dramatic efflorescence of the former ensured that landlordism was not accorded that breathing space which alone might have enabled it to recapture – even if only temporarily – the ground it was so obviously losing and would continue to lose.

Parnell gave the Plan just enough support to maintain an image of sympathy but not so much as to be too closely identified with its comparative failure. His general reputation, if not his actual power to influence events, was never higher than in 1889 after the humiliating collapse of *The Times*'s vindictive attempt to prove him a political liar on the basis of forged letters had briefly made him the incongruous darling of English Liberalism (Bew 1980: 100–108). But just as a wave reaches its crest at the moment of imminent collapse so for Parnell the peak of popularity was soon engulfed in a personal and political crisis of epic intensity. In December 1889 Mrs O'Shea's husband, who had long known of his wife's liaison, filed suit for divorce and named Parnell as co-respondent. In November 1890, when the case came for trial, Gladstone, under pressure from those Nonconformist saints who supplied the Liberal Party with its most effective support, told Parnell's associates that the 'Chief' would have to go. Already too a number of Catholic bishops in Ireland had begun to make threatening noises and were only being held in check by

Archbishop Walsh's sensible advice that they had better wait and see what the parliamentary party would do (Larkin 1979: 191–232). There all was confusion. At first Parnell was re-affirmed as leader by acclamation. But when some of those who had acclaimed most loudly found that, contrary to expectations, he not only refused to retire but actually issued a stridently anti-Liberal manifesto, they insisted that a more formal judgement be undertaken. After a week of bitter debate in Committee Room Fifteen at Westminster the MPs split 45 to 27 against Parnell – if those absent could have voted the result would have been 54 to 32 (Lyons 1960: 118–49 and 1971: 192).

Parnell, now in a minority and deprived of the help of his ablest subordinates, at once carried the war to Ireland. As the political temperature reached boiling point rational calculations became subsumed in a general atmosphere of moralistic vituperation. Parnell – his avenues of escape now blocked as much by his own actions as by those of his opponents – embarked on a series of increasingly extreme declarations culminating in a famous appeal issued in his name, but apparently without his permission, to 'the hillside men'. 'Will you', it asked, 'give him up to the Saxon wolves who howl for his destruction? Or will you rally round him as your fathers rallied round the men of '98?' (Lyons 1977: 539). Though by no means all of the priests adopted an anti-Parnellite stance the hierarchy was virtually united; and in by-elections at Kilkenny, Sligo, and Carlow Parnellite candidates went down to decisive, if not overwhelming, defeat.

For some years Parnell had been in indifferent health. Now the strain proved too much. His physical degeneration became obvious; his speeches coarse and repetitive; his appearance unkempt; his behaviour wild. He was only forty-five years old when he died on 6 October 1891. And the manner and the youth of his departing immediately gave him honorary status among those who had suffered death for Ireland's sake.

Though the precise contours of Parnell's ideology are almost impossible to delineate (for simple consistency had never been among his faults), there is ample evidence to suggest that cautious political and social conservatism represented a more authentic mode than did those occasional bouts of radical rhetoric characteristic especially of his last years. And while a cold eye might observe that he had in large measure been the architect of his own misfortune, yet myths far removed from the mundane world of actuality soon encrusted his memory and 'it was as the proud man overthrown by base men that Parnell's name was to echo through Irish literature and politics with a passion that has not even yet entirely died away' (Lyons 1971: 195).

IV

The efflorescence of nationalist and agrarian moblization in the South of Ireland during the 1880s inevitably produced a matching reaction on the part of Protestant Conservatism. At first there was a good deal of confusion. Protestant farmers too wanted redress and it is significant that most of the eighteen Ulster Conservative MPs returned in 1880 adopted comparatively radical positions on the matter in parliament (Thompson 1985). But the legislation of 1881 satisfied many in Ulster, so that, with Home Rule soon adopting a more prominent profile, it became less difficult to induce a real sense of Protestant solidarity (Kirkpatrick 1980). Just as popular politics in Catholic Ireland consisted of a multitude of often contradictory elements, so Irish Conservatism had long been a loose alliance of landed gentlemen, urban populists, farmers, industrialists, evangelical enthusiasts, Orangemen, southerners and northerners, Episcopalians and Presbyterians. As the threat of Home Rule seemed to become more formidable so cohesion became more important among its opponents. By 1885 the Liberal revival which had been evident in some Ulster constituencies had come to an abrupt end. Though internal tensions remained and though the larger Ulster farmers (who had constituted the chief supporters of rural Liberalism) were never able to achieve that dominance characteristic of their Catholic counterparts elsewhere (Gibbon 1975: 119–20), solidarity was more and more becoming the order of the day. Similarly in the northern towns class considerations, while always potentially and sometimes actually important, were subordinated to sectarianism in an increasingly fierce and effective manner (Patterson 1980: 1–41). Earlier traditions of urban violence reached new heights during the great Belfast religious commotions of 1864, 1872, and 1886, so much so, that the physiognomic claims of a local police committee chairman – 'I could tell a man's religion by his face' – had begun to seem neither incongruous nor bizarre (Hoppen 1984: 388).

What, however, rendered all of this especially formidable and

125

also helped, for example, to contain the discontents of Presbyterians at what many of them still saw as continued exclusion from the corridors of power (McMinn 1981) was the emergence of a new leadership prepared to adopt a demotic pose and prepared also to render Irish Conservatism less subservient to British party control. Ironically, therefore, the appearance of formal rather than informal unionism was made manifest not so much by a close identification with British models but with the reverse.

The last gasp of aristocratic Conservatism's attempt to repel the nationalist hordes of the South expired at the general election of 1885 when the Irish Loyal and Patriotic Union put up large numbers of no-hope candidates against Parnell (Savage 1961). Henceforth southern Unionists would have to depend upon the charity of the good and the great in England and though this seemed reliable enough at the time it necessarily implied a clear distinction between patrons and supplicants. But because the life of the gentry continued much as before – indeed, as political power faded social exclusiveness became more intense than ever (d'Alton 1973 and 1975) – so sufficient deluding arrogance remained to allow one scholar to describe the period 1885–1914 as one of 'confident opposition' (Buckland 1972: 1–28). In reality, however, the slow journey towards internal exile was already well under way.

For Ulster the Patriotic Union's electoral defeats constituted a powerful confirmation of the old truth that in Conservative politics, as in Irish affairs generally, there existed a clear boundary between the imperatives of South and North. More directly worrying was the fact that even in Ulster the opponents of Home Rule had been divided in 1885 and had allowed Parnell's men to pick up no less than seventeen of the thirty-three Ulster seats. This and the shock of Gladstone's conversion to Home Rule led to the foundation in January 1886 of the Ulster Loyalist Anti-Repeal Union which was soon able to enter into fruitful collaboration with the Orange Order and the Protestant churches of the province (Buckland 1973: 1–21). In February Lord Randolph Churchill, who had hitherto shown a notable lack of enthusiasm for Ulster intransigence but was now anxious to lay his hands on any weapon which might propel him towards the leadership of his party (Foster 1980), told an enthusiastic Belfast audience that in this their darkest hour 'there will not be wanting to you those of position and influence in England who are willing to cast in their lot with you – whatever it may be, and who will share your future and your fate' (Buckland 1973: 10). And though Churchill was in no position to deliver so flamboyant a promise, his rhetoric undoubtedly helped to raise the political temperature. Already the Ulster Unionist MPs had effectively formed themselves into a distinct parliamentary group. In April the majority of northern Liberals turned against Home Rule and joined the laager. When the next general election took place in the sacred Orange month of July (1886) the Unionists were able to present a coherent front. At the same time newspapers were full of reports that Orangemen were planning to purchase arms and certainly the leader of the new Ulster Unionist Party, the witty, intransigent, evangelical yachtsman and horse fanatic Edward Saunderson, was busily urging his followers to drill, arm, and put their uniforms on (Savage 1961: 203; Buckland 1973: 2–3).

It was impossible to sustain so high a pitch of united intensity for more than a few years. The defeat of Gladstone's second Home Rule Bill in 1893 and splits within nationalist ranks helped to encourage the re-appearance of unionist mavericks and frondeurs. Protestant farmers and landlords did not always agree and labour relations in Belfast often led to bitter internal disputes. During the twenty years after 1890 Ulster politics – like those of the South – exhibited sporadic reversions to the free-wheeling localism of former days. In 1903 an Independent Orange Order broke away from the main body (Boyle 1962). Its leader, Tom Sloan, a shipyard worker, combined extreme sectarianism (he made much of Saunderson's failure to support the state inspection of convent laundries) and popular radicalism in a manner hardly designed to smooth over those economic antagonisms Unionism had so successfully begun to realign. But in the end such hybrid phenomena were, like the mule, unable to father effective progeny (Patterson 1980: 19–61). And even though Unionism's party machinery wound down during the quiet years around the turn of the century it needed only renewed threats to call it back into life.

Not the least remarkable aspect of the whole business was the continued blindness of nationalist leaders. Though unlike O'Connell, Parnell was occasionally capable of reaching real insights into the nature of unionist politics, his lieutenants remained sunk in an ignorance at once invincible and dangerous (Bew 1980: 127–43). Not for the first and not for the last time did nationalist opinion sustain – against all the evidence – the comfortable belief that Orange intransigence was the exclusive preserve of vulgar mobsters and colourful cranks (Foster 1980: 271; Kee 1972: 401–2). And in this matter history was to repeat itself with cyclical regularity: first as tragedy and then as tragedy again.

V

To British politicians and their fellow countrymen generally Ireland in the nineteenth century presented the curious aspect of a country at once near in distance but remote in understanding, at once part of the United Kingdom but demonstrably foreign. A growing distaste at what was regarded as Irish fecklessness and love of disorder coloured the minds of leaders and masses alike. As time went on caricatures did increasing service for reality – on both sides of the Irish Sea. Stereotypes became woven into a framework of mutual incomprehension: dirty, benighted, simian Paddy, on the one side, dull, stupid, mercenary John Bull, on the other (Curtis 1968 and 1971). As Queen Victoria put it in 1867: 'These Irish are really shocking, abominable people – not like any other civilized nation' (O'Farrell 1975: 49). While Disraeli confined himself to jokes and accounted Irishmen 'imaginative' beings driven to discontent by living 'on an island in a damp climate, and contiguous to the melancholy ocean' (Monypenny and Buckle 1910–20: v, 91), Peel thought them simply corrupt and during the Famine capable of 'gross exaggerations of suffering' (Hoppen 1984: 302 and 334), Russell was appalled by their Popish superstitions, Melbourne preferred to think about them as little as possible, and Gladstone believed the Scots and Welsh far more deserving of national recognition (Vincent 1977: 231–2). All of this helped to ensure that, whenever Ireland should have been seen as another country where things followed a different path it was viewed as no more than a querulous appendage of England, and whenever it should, indeed, have been seen as an appendaged reflection it was regarded as wild, *sui generis,* and remote (O'Halpin 1987).

In this context it was perhaps above all in the matter of violence that myth and reality became most damagingly intertwined. In English eyes Irishmen were 'naturally' violent and that was an end to it. As such they deserved and were accorded special consideration in the shape of a centralized and armed constabulary larger by far than the locally-controlled and unarmed police forces of the rest of the Kingdom and of a significantly more substantial complement of military might as well (Hoppen 1984: 414). Yet all this investment merely brought about a state of things in which the government almost invariably got the worst of both worlds by appearing 'to rest on force while seldom exerting enough force to secure real control' (Townshend 1983: 410).

VI

After Parnell's death nationalist politics unravelled into mutual hostility as normalcy reasserted itself in the shape of dances around local gods: 'issues tended to be downgraded, and great emphasis was put on the personalities, charisma or popularity of the factional leaders' (Garvin 1980: 263). The general election of 1892 exhibited virtually all the characteristics (save landlord influence) which had marked the decades between O'Connell and Parnell (*South Meath Petition* 1892; Woods 1980). Though the anti-Parnellites emerged triumphant with seventy-one seats as opposed to the Parnellites' nine, they were far from a united force and were themselves informally divided between the very different styles of leadership espoused by John Dillon and Timothy Healy. While Dillon fought for central control, Healy, with all the vituperative skill at his disposal, stood for the diffusion of authority and the sovereign rights of the constituencies, in other words, for localism raised to a principle (Lyons 1951: 41–3). Throughout the 1890s localist sentiment also coincided with clerical opinion and the decline of power at the centre and its growth elsewhere tended to increase the influence of the priesthood. In this sense there was, indeed, 'no real dichotomy between clericalism and localism in Irish politics' (Bull 1972: 41). Although Healy was expelled from the party in 1900 the fierceness of the struggle between such very different views was evidence that immediate and pragmatic imperatives had not been driven out of political life by Parnell's transitory success in constructing a centralized hegemony (Jordan 1986; Murray 1986a).

The party's position was made no easier by the efforts, however cynical and confused, of the Unionist (Conservative) governments of 1886–92 and 1895–1905 to 'kill Home Rule by kindness' (Gailey 1987) while the defeat of Gladstone's second bill in 1893 did nothing to paper over nationalist disunity – quite the reverse. Various Land Acts provided more and more cash with which tenants could purchase their holdings. In 1891 the Congested Districts Board was set up to tackle the economic problems of the West. Legislation in 1898 at last provided Ireland with a fully elected system of local administration. In the following year a Department of Agriculture was set up to encourage improvements in efficiency and farming techniques. Even if such developments were politically speaking little more than chimeras Dillon became anxious lest his followers be diverted from the paths of devolutionist rectitude (Lyons 1968: 175–8, 187–8). His fears were the more acute because the leader of a new land agitation, his friend and associate, William O'Brien, seemed to be prepared to cooperate pragmatically with unionists if tangible benefits might thereby be obtained. In January 1898 O'Brien founded the United Irish League at Westport, the very place where Parnell had first given his blessing to the infant Land League in 1879. However, even more than the earlier movement, the new body shed much of its radicalism once it began to move beyond the impoverished fastnesses of the West, where, in any case, the main objects of attack had been and often continued to be rich graziers rather than landlords as such (Garvin 1981: 93; Bew 1987: 75–80). Although the authorities became nervous and although the League was claiming 60,000 to 80,000 members by the Spring of 1900 it was far less successful than its predecessor had been in creating anything approaching a general mobilization of the countryside (O'Brien 1976: 107–14). Indeed, its comparatively restricted geographical and economic base was a reflection of how deep the divisions between those with something and those with little to lose had become (Jones 1983) as also of the undoubted fact that the 'declining relevance of antilandlordism in the aftermath of tenurial reforms' had 'removed an important unifying' factor from the political algebra of rural Ireland as a whole (Kennedy 1983b: 367).

What the activism of the League did, however, help to bring about was the reunification of the Parliamentary Party in 1900 under John Redmond previously the leader of the small Parnellite group. Although this juncture marked the temporary marginalization of Healy's factionalism it did not produce any notable increment in political effectiveness. If anything the Land Act of 1903 once again brought nationalist divisions to the surface (O'Brien 1976: 142–60; Boyce 1982: 269–70). In November 1903 O'Brien actually resigned from the party and, after a brief interlude, re-entered politics as a kind of agrarian Healy to fight elections with a following of his own.

Even the long-awaited return to power at Westminster of the Liberals in December 1905 did little to alter the situation, for the results of the 1906 election allowed first Campbell-Bannerman and then Asquith to govern without Irish support. Home Rule, it soon became clear, was far from ministerial thoughts (Lyons 1968: 292–5). In short, the Parliamentary Party seems to have reached a position in which it enjoyed the worst of all worlds: tied irrevocably to the Liberal alliance it gave an impression of spinelessness, of being a Lazarus forced to make do with no more than crumbs from the

Liberal table. Clinging to nurse for fear of something worse and hoping to weaken the power of the House of Lords, Dillon and Redmond felt obliged to support Lloyd George's budget of 1909 even though that measure's increase in liquor taxes was deeply offensive to many of their red-blooded and retailing supporters at home. At the general election of January 1910 O'Brien resumed his free-booting activities and succeeded in having seven of his followers returned as independent nationalists. Yet overall the election at last gave the party the balance of power in parliament and this was reaffirmed at another election held in December largely over the issue of the Lords' veto of the government's financial legislation.

VII

By then, however, other tendencies and movements had begun to challenge the party's hegemony. The most important of these involved that fusion of culture and politics which the Young Irelanders had proposed as essential to a sense of national identity. Although they themselves had failed to achieve this in their own day their literary remains continued to exercise a strong fascination especially when read in conjunction with the stories and songs produced by the early Fenians of which Charles Kickham's inchoate but powerful novel of rural life, *Knocknagow* (1873), was the most important (Comerford 1979: 197–203). But if the new nationalism of the late-nineteenth century was heavily dependent upon the concurrent triumph of the English language (by 1901, though one person in seven still knew Irish, only one in two hundred was not bilingual) it also drew strength from the activities of those who, distressed by what they saw as the anglicization of Irish culture, set about attempting a Gaelic revival (Hutchinson 1987). Only in a superficial sense was this a paradox, for the Gaelic revival in all its linguistic, social, and sporting forms was above all a profoundly *modern* phenomenon. It looked quite as much to the future as to the past, and, though undoubtedly involving much romantic emphasis on real or imagined traditions, radiated a dynamic modernity far removed from mere nostalgia and antiquarianism.

The Gaelic Athletic Association was one of the earliest manifestations of this new approach. Founded just after the Land War it organized young men into football and hurling clubs, was rapidly infiltrated by the Irish Republican Brotherhood (Mandle 1977), and, by combining the provision of recreational facilities with a framework in which traditional local leaders could operate, was able to attract widespread support. Although not immune either to the recrudescence of localism in the 1890s or to a certain amount of clerical suspicion it survived sufficiently successfully to be able to greet the twentieth century with some confidence (Garvin 1981: 87–94; Greene 1960). More generally the GAA formed part of that congeries of movements and attitudes which revolved around the ideas expressed so elegantly by its chief ecclesiastical patron, Archbishop Croke of Cashel, in his anathema of 1884 against England's 'fantastic field sports . . . [and] accents, her vicious literature, her music, her dances, and her manifold mannerisms' none of them 'racy of the soil, but rather alien, on the contrary to it, as are, for the most part, the men and women who first imported and still continued to patronise them' (Boyce 1982: 236).

A somewhat more cerebral line was adopted by the Gaelic League founded in 1893 by Douglas Hyde (son of a Church of Ireland parson), Father O'Growney of Maynooth, and Eoin MacNeill, a Catholic intellectual from County Antrim. At first this differed little from earlier scholarly societies, but before long its essentially political case – the preservation and growth of a national identity based entirely upon Gaelic culture – was to become clear. At a time when Ireland was 'riddled by secret societies and fraternities of all sorts, ranging from local agrarian groups to well-developed lawful' bodies such as the Freemasons, the Orange Order, and the Ancient Order of Hibernians (a kind of green Orange Institution), the Gaelic League proved not merely the most popular but also the only 'one of these organizations to gain' full 'clerical approval and participation' (Garvin 1986a: 73).

Hyde's contacts also, however, embraced a very different group then actively engaged in emphasizing a peculiarly idiosyncratic version of Irish identity. But although *its* chief proponent, William Butler Yeats, stood head and shoulders above his contemporaries as a writer of power and brilliance, the so-called Anglo-Irish literary renaissance was, in political terms, a comparatively marginal phenomenon. While for Yeats literature could be both national and international, both a vehicle for change and true to its own inner promptings, those identified with the Gaelic League acknowledged a more utilitarian creed. 'Thomas Davis', a critic of Yeats declared in 1892, 'was as fond of literature, qua literature, as any other man, but when he wrote for Ireland it was not the book he was thinking of but what the book might do.' More direct still was the question posed in 1899: 'What is the meaning of this rubbish? How is it to help the national cause? How is it to help any cause at all?' (Boyce 1982: 246; Lyons 1979: 51). Fiercest of all was the brilliantly vituperative journalist, D. P. Moran, who, in his periodical *The Leader* hoisted the flag of 'Irish Ireland', denounced the 'sham' patriotism of the Parliamentary Party and the 'West Britishism' of the literary renaissance, fought for industrial and language revivalism, for Catholicism, and in favour of withdrawal into a redoubt of parochial self-sufficiency in everything from brain work to boot straps (Lyons 1979: 58–62; Hutchinson 1987: 173–8). Amidst such attacks the brief moment of Anglo-Irish cultural activism soon flickered into darkness, snuffed out as effectively as were the concurrent efforts of 'constructive' unionists like Horace Plunkett to create a new rural climate in which efficiency might draw strength from a common appreciation of the importance of agrarian improvement and change (West 1986).

More directly political were the efforts of Arthur Griffith to develop a movement able to capitalize on the Parliamentary Party's seeming impotence. An aloof but able journalist, Griffith, though a separatist in the fullest sense, was adept at putting up a plenitude of proposals designed to catch some or all of the various nationalist winds then blowing through political life (Davis 1974). In 1905 he announced a detailed policy soon accorded the name Sinn Fein meaning simply 'Ourselves' though often mistranslated as 'Ourselves Alone'. But while Griffith had discovered a kind of middle path between constitutionalism and physical force the new life injected into the Liberal alliance by the elections of 1910 short-circuited his efforts and the political and electoral appeal of Sinn Fein proved, in the short run, 'virtually non-existent' (Boyce 1982: 298–9). On the one side, the Parliamentary Party recaptured a more effective centrality; on the other, the regrouping of the IRB in 1907 under the old Fenian, Tom Clarke, though a very modest affair, further divided up those sympathetic to a more advanced position (Younger 1981: 41–2; Ó Broin 1976: 133–50).

The same kind of marginal fermentation was also experienced by the small labour movement in Ireland. Here too there were numerous divisions: between Protestant and Catholic workers in both Belfast (Patterson 1980) and Dublin, between those who belonged to British trade unions and those who joined the dynamic James Larkin's Irish Transport and General Workers Union of 1908 (Larkin 1965), between those who favoured some kind of rapprochement with the Parliamentary Party and those who rigorously refused to have anything to do with it, between those who preferred Larkin's syndicalist 'one big union' approach and those who found the nationalist Marxism of James Connolly, Irish socialism's leading theoretician (not a position for which there were many contenders), more to their taste (Mitchell 1974: 11–30). Although Larkin's paper, the *Irish Worker,* had a circulation ten times greater than that of Griffith's *Sinn Fein* (Kee 1972: 494), the first really serious confrontation between capital and labour – the Dublin general strike/lock-out of 1913 – ended in total defeat for Larkin and his union. At no time did the Parliamentary Party seriously attempt to bring about a compromise settlement and it was a matter of considerable significance that the employers' intransigent but effective leader, William Martin Murphy, was a prominent supporter of the party both directly and as owner of the *Independent* newspaper which appealed especially to the more prosperous sections of the Catholic middle class. Larkin, never the most equable of men, lurched into increasing cantankerousness and – rather like one fleeing the cinema just as the big picture gets under way – left for America in October 1914 for an absence of more than eight years. Connolly became more convinced than ever that only a republic brought to birth by violence could provide sufficient scope for his ideals, and, though well aware of the dangers of giving separatism temporal priority over socialism, moved closer to those advanced nationalists who, unlike Dillon, Moran, or even Griffith, had shown sympathy for the workers' cause and were later to provide the organizing leadership for the Easter Rising of 1916 (Mitchell 1974: 48–9).

VIII

Important as all this was to prove in the longer run the centre of the stage was still occupied by the Parliamentary Party. However, amidst all the wrangling between constitutionalists and republicans a resurgent unionism – galvanized into new energy by the real possibility of Home Rule legislation – began to throw an increasingly powerful spanner into the political works. In 1910 the Dublin lawyer, Edward Carson, though himself a man of liberal views on some issues, emerged as the brilliantly relentless leader of what had now, even more than before, become an overwhelmingly northern movement. But Asquith as prime minister knew little of Ulster and entirely failed to seize the opportunity of even attempting to deal with its problems on what might still – just possibly – have been fruitful terms when in 1912 he brought forward a Home Rule Bill to pay off his obligations to the Parliamentary Party (Jalland 1980: 261). Matters swiftly moved well beyond the contents of the bill itself. That these were again modest – many things remaining under 'imperial' control – meant less than the universal conviction that they represented the thinnest possible end of the nationalist wedge.

The government's blindness over Ulster contrasted strongly with the febrile excitement displayed by its Conservative opponents. Conscious that the Lords could now only delay the measure for three years at most, Bonar Law, the Conservative leader, announced in July 1912 that he could 'imagine no length of resistance to which Ulster can go in which I should not be prepared to support them' (Buckland 1973: 85). A few months later, amid scenes of emotion and excitement, thousands of Ulstermen signed a Solemn League and Covenant against Home Rule, and thus, as nationalists too so often had done, combined present politics and historical allusion into a potent gesture of defiance and solidarity. In January 1913 the Ulster Unionist Council established a Volunteer Force with the aim of keeping the Home Rule wolf from Ulster's door, if need be by force of arms (Stewart 1967). By the time the cabinet began to take all this seriously it was too late; and soon Asquith's Ulster 'policy' was completely overwhelmed by the Curragh 'Mutiny' of March 1914 when a number of military officers declared their unwillingness to take action against northern Unionists even if ordered to do so by their legitimate superiors (Fergusson 1964; Ryan 1956).

By then the nationalist Irish Volunteers were also in place. Rapidly penetrated by the IRB they too, like their Ulster counterparts, were soon importing arms from abroad. The outbreak of war in August 1914 made things more complicated still. When, therefore, in September the bill itself was passed but postponed until peace should come, the government – under the impress of necessity – simply allowed a whole jumble of loose ends to dangle dangerously in the winds of battle.

Redmond, who believed the war would soon be over, called on Irishmen to fight for the rights of small nations 'wherever the firing-line extends'. The Volunteers at once split. About 170,000 stayed with Redmond (the National Volunteers). The remainder

135

– 11,000-strong – kept the original title and soon came under the control of Eoin MacNeill as chief of staff and of a number of members of the IRB of whom Patrick Pearse, Thomas MacDonagh, and Joseph Plunkett were the most prominent. These three and especially Pearse held almost mystical views of republicanism's potential as a redeeming and cleansing force amidst the corrupt compromises of constitutional politics. While, therefore, the bulk of the new Irish Volunteers saw violence only as a last resort, Pearse and his associates – almost from the first – were set on revolution at all costs (Edwards 1977: 222–3). For tactical reasons, however, Connolly, now in command of a tiny Citizen Army of 200 men, had to be restrained from premature explosion while negotiations with Germany over the supply of arms dragged on.

Before long Pearse emerged more and more forcefully as the epicentre of future rebellion. A *mélange* of Gaelic Catholicism, mythical history, oratorical drive, and a deep belief in the solvent qualities of violence led him to see the 'blood sacrifice' of even a hopeless rising as the culmination of earlier revivalist work in education and literature. Of the Great War and its heroisms he wrote in December 1915 'It is good for the world that such things should be done. The old heart of the earth needed to be warmed with the red wine of the battlefields. Such august homage was never before offered to God as this, the homage of millions of lives given gladly for love of country' (Edwards 1977: 245). Here and in the writings of Plunkett and MacDonagh are revealed the imperatives of passionate men virtually talking themselves into some final dramatic and self-destructive act. MacNeill, on the other hand, looked primarily, not to some hopeless demonstration during the war, but towards the possibility of action thereafter. However, by early 1916 the inner circle of IRB men in the Volunteers had definitely decided on a rising for the following Easter and on collaboration with Connolly who then himself joined both the Brotherhood and the Military Council set up the previous year.

The immediate background to the rising was one of confusion abounding (Martin 1967a and 1968; Wall 1969). MacNeill was cruelly deceived. In Dublin Castle few took seriously such information as was available to the authorities (Ó Broin 1970). The rifles and ammunition despatched by the Germans never reached the conspirators. On Easter Monday, after desperate efforts by MacNeill to countermand the whole affair, Pearse read to a sceptical audience outside the General Post Office in Dublin a declaration of independence signed by himself and six others. It promised religious and civil liberties, that 'all the children of the nation' would be cherished equally, and referred, not only to the 'six times during the past three hundred years' when the 'Irish people' had asserted its national freedom in arms, but also to the support provided by exiles in America and 'by gallant allies in Europe'. With a few minuscule exceptions little took place outside Dublin. Probably no more than 1600 individuals were actively involved. There was no popular enthusiasm save on the part of enterprising looters. But, against all the odds, the rebels held out for a week during which about 450 people (soldiers, police, civilians, and revolutionaries) were killed and 2600 were wounded (Lyons 1971: 374; Martin 1967b; Nowlan 1969; Ryan 1949).

Had things ended then and had the government behaved as after the rising of 1848 little might have come of it all. But the actual response, with its unpredictable swerves from severity to leniency, its lack of clarity, its failures to see the consequences of certain actions, created that bizarre congeries of accidents which almost alone gave the rising an effective after-life. It is of course easy to forget the popular outrage in Britain against what many saw as a stab in the back. Yet official reactions managed with monotonous regularity to get the worst of all possible worlds, involving as they did far more even than the strung-out execution of fifteen rebels – a procedure calculated 'to rouse maximum resentment and minimum fear' (Lee 1973b: 156) – and the internment of several thousand others.

By some curious and illogical process the rising was immediately attributed to Sinn Fein though Griffith had not been directly involved at all. But the new Sinn Fein was a very different body from its pre-war original (Laffan 1971). Taken over by republicans it soon emerged as a vigorous political force – a process accelerated by threats to extend conscription to Ireland during the last months of the war. At the general election of December 1918 (when women over thirty were able to vote for the first time) it won seventy-three seats to the Unionists' twenty-six and the Parliamentary Party's six. Although this exaggerated its actual share of the vote there could be no doubting that constitutionalism had suffered a major defeat. Sinn Fein had been able to appeal to a wide spectrum of opinion in part by the simple but effective expedient of presenting no policy worth the name beyond abstention from Westminster and plans for attending the Versailles peace conference to demand Ireland's rights to independence. Even Eamon de Valera, the senior surviving leader of the rising and now Sinn Fein's president, confined himself to platitudes and to promises that no further military action would prove necessary. If, therefore, the people had voted for something more than Home Rule they had by no stretch of the imagination voted uncompromisingly for 'The Republic' of Pearse's dreams.

But it was precisely the more extreme representatives who dominated the constituent assembly (Dail Eireann) called together in January 1919 and boycotted by both Unionists and Home Rulers (Farrell 1971). Less than thirty Sinn Fein MPs were able to attend under the presidency of Cathal Brugha, a militant if ever there was one. Those present briskly ratified the 'establishment of the Irish Republic' and, by abandoning the fruitful ambiguities of the previous year, left little room for compromise. They also produced a 'Democratic Programme' full of those ringing declarations against poverty which were soon to become a substitute for real social reforms. When in April de Valera, now at large, was chosen as president (prime minister) and provided with a cabinet the first shots had already been fired in what later became known – depending on one's point of view – either as the 'War of Independence' or the 'Anglo-Irish War'. During 1919 the Volunteers in effect became the 'army' of the new 'republic' – the IRA – and as such turned their initial attention to attacks upon the Royal Irish Constabulary. De Valera's cabinet met secretly and found it difficult to function with any degree of administrative efficiency though sums of money were collected and eventually an alternative system of 'Dail courts' was set up with some success. Although nominally subordinate to Brugha (the Defence Minister) it was Michael Collins who enjoyed the dominant influence over the IRA, something which did nothing to improve relations between the two men (Forester 1971). As incident followed incident so the government's initial desire to dismiss the whole thing as no more than a set of isolated 'outrages' became less and less convincing (Holt 1960: 169–95). The terror of republican assassination was met with counter-terror mounted by special forces recruited to assist the military and police – the Auxiliaries and the 'Black and Tans' (so named after a famous hunt on account of their spatchcock uniforms). By the middle of 1920 there could be little doubt that a guerrilla war had come into being in which the republicans exhibited a relentlessness and an efficiency which the authorities found it difficult to match (Townshend 1975: 202).

December 1920 saw both de Valera's return from a long tour of the United States and the passing of the Government of Ireland Act setting up separate parliaments for the six north-eastern counties of Ulster and the twenty-six counties of the South. Though in the latter the act remained a dead letter, the Unionists – soon to be led by the dour and wily Sir James Craig (unlike Carson, himself an Ulsterman) – had now in effect been given what, rather reluctantly, they had come to see as the best deal circumstances would allow. And with sympathetic support from the dominant Conservative element in Lloyd George's coalition government they were able to ensure that the fiefdom assigned them would be as large as the maintenance of Protestant hegemony would permit (Laffan 1983). Eventually in July 1921, with the IRA short of arms and the government made more anxious than ever to heave itself out of Irish quagmires by growing criticism at home, a truce was arranged (Boyce 1972: 118–41; Lawlor 1983: 68–98).

The six months that followed were marked by tortuous contacts between the British and the Irish camps, neither of them entirely of one mind and both containing some fully paid-up members of the Awkward Brigade. Within Sinn Fein guerrilla war had clearly strengthened the power of the more extreme. Yet the truce had also injected a certain slackening of fervour by encouraging large numbers of naked opportunists to demand membership – the so-called 'sunshine soldiers', Hibernian precursors of those *Märzveilchen* (or March violets) who flocked to the Nazi Party in the Spring of 1933. Although de Valera had proved unsuccessful in earlier efforts to search for an accommodation with the Ulster Unionists – his one meeting with Craig in May 1921 proved a fog-bound episode (Bowman 1982: 47–8) – he did, nonetheless, make some attempt to retain flexibility within the strait-jacket which the Dail tied around his shoulders in August when it demanded that all its members take an oath to 'the Irish Republic and the government of the Irish Republic which is Dail Eireann' (Murphy 1975: 27–8). But his linguistically complex and perhaps deliberately vague proposals for an independent Ireland in *external* association with the Commonwealth failed to elicit much in the way of a positive response from London. Eventually in September Lloyd George struck upon a formula which the Irish were prepared to accept as a basis for negotiation, upon which delegates were sent to England 'with a view to ascertaining how the association of Ireland with the community known as the British Empire may be reconciled with Irish national aspirations' (Macardle 1968: 478).

The most surprising feature of what followed was de Valera's refusal to be one of the delegates. Certainly he was well aware that any agreement would involve compromise and his aim seems to have been to 'render any outcome *compatible with minimum republican claims*' so that future generations might at least find themselves in a position 'to complete the work' (Bowman 1982: 60). Those who did go were Griffith, a reluctant Collins (seen by de Valera as crucial in being able to influence the 'hard men' of the IRA), and three others of lesser stature, with the hard-line Erskine Childers as secretary (Lawlor 1983: 110–12). The negotiations were long and emotional. Bonar Law, the Conservative leader, scotched any lingering ideas Lloyd George might have entertained of preserving some form of thirty-two county unity. The only alternative was to persuade Sinn Fein to accept Dominion status without Ulster, a pill Lloyd George sweetened by the promise of a Boundary Commission which would later redraw the border with, it was assumed by and suggested to the Irish delegates, the effect of rendering the northern 'state' too small for long-term viability (Pakenham 1972; Curran 1980). The British prime minister, with brilliant legerdemain, waved now carrots now sticks in front of Griffith and Collins whose position was deeply weakened by the failure of de Valera's government to make that really decisive thrust through the veil of wishful thinking – about external association and Ulster in particular – which alone could have led to clarity of mind. And the refusal of the most rigid republicans like Brugha and Stack to go to London meant that, while 'moderation' was perhaps over-represented during the negotiations, it was certainly under-represented among those who stayed behind.

While the problem of British defence requirements was settled with remarkable ease, those of national unity and constitutional status caused enormous difficulties. Many and ingenious were the ideas canvassed in an effort to produce some Houdini-like escape from the seemingly irreconcilable imperatives of the two sides in which, as so often, symbols counted for as much, if not more, than realities. Eventually, with the help of a good deal of theatricality, Lloyd George bludgeoned the delegates into signing on 6 December 1921 the 'Articles of agreement for a treaty between Great Britain and Ireland'. This gave the latter Dominion status under the title of the Irish Free State and required that its parliamentarians swear an oath to the crown. Northern Ireland was, however, to be allowed to 'opt out' whereupon a Boundary Commission would be appointed. In peacetime the Admiralty was to control certain southern Irish ports, while in time of war it could claim 'such harbour and other facilities as the British Government may require' (Canning 1985: 7–8).

De Valera reacted with something close to panic. He called a cabinet meeting for 8 December to be followed by a discussion in the Dail and thus 'slipped into the course from which he subsequently failed to extricate himself: he did not take a decision himself, but probably hoped that the cabinet and the Dail would share his feelings: the cabinet rejecting the document, and the Dail following suit' (Lawlor 1983: 147). In fact the reverse occurred and in cabinet de Valera found himself in a minority with only Brugha and Stack on his side. When the Dail met he at last produced his alternative which soon became known as 'Document Number 2'. But this, despite, or perhaps even because of, its confusions and ambiguities, pleased almost no one. With all the initial signs indicating that popular reaction to the treaty was favourable, the Dail eventually agreed to accept it by 64 votes to 57. The debate itself was prolonged and increasingly rancorous towards the end. Most of the discussion revolved around constitutional matters; remarkably little around partition. Childers delivered the best speech against. Collins, with that realism which was his hallmark, insisted that Ireland had indeed been given freedom, 'not the ultimate freedom that all nations aspire and develop to, but the freedom to achieve it' (Lyons 1971: 442). Brugha, however, would have none of this and mounted an abusive personal counter-attack by way of reply (Curran 1980: 154).

If such bitterness was hardly surprising, there can be no doubt that the treaty itself represented a spectacular advance on anything that had been offered before as also the maximum any British government could possibly have conceded at the time. Not only that, but partition was the only option left if Britain was to be able to withdraw without coercing the North-East. To blame the border for all subsequent trouble is to forget that by 1921 it had already (in *de facto* terms) existed for a century or longer – a state of things brought about far more by the behaviour of all kinds of Irishmen than by the unhelpful and often ignorant interventions of Westminster and Whitehall.

What can, however, be too easily overlooked amidst the excitements of these last days of full colonial rule is the manner in which political life at the local level remained far less dramatically altered than national events alone would seem to indicate. Of course things had changed and sometimes substantially so. But much also remained the same and continuity provides as important a prism for illuminating the period as does alteration. 'Because the Home Rule organisations had worked, because their collapse was evidently caused not by internal rottenness but by a bizarre series of accidents,

141

the architects of the new mass movement [simply] rebuilt those organisations under different names' (Fitzpatrick 1977: 283). Just as the Liberals of old had sometimes transformed themselves into Home Rulers without by any means always taking on much new ideological baggage, so too many old Home Rulers were happy to find refuge in the potentially capacious portmanteau of Sinn Fein.

While the bewildering tergiversations of the years 1918–21 allowed politics for a time to become 'the preserve of small, often clandestine bodies of a sort which had never [before] won such influence', the assumptions which lay behind the continuing aspirations of farmers, labourers, small-town shopkeepers and the like had suffered no sea change. Over the whole period from the outbreak of the Great War a strong element of continuity survived in local political leadership with all the continuities in the primacy of the immediate and the tangible which that implied (Fitzpatrick 1977: 284, 138). And the cautiousness of the new Free State in social and economic matters, its failure to consider seriously (let alone deliver) a social revolution to match the constitutional revolution which had taken place reflected the survival in Irish society and political culture of those superiorities and inferiorities which had long marked the actual experiences of rural and urban life. When, in his famous Commons speech of 16 February 1922, Churchill remarked how the 'integrity' of Irish quarrels had so fully survived the alarms of global war that, as the deluge subsided and the waters fell short, one could see 'the dreary steeples of Fermanagh and Tyrone emerging once again' (*Hansard* 3rd Series: cl, 1270), percipient observers might well also have espied the simultaneous return to obsessive prominence in both parts of Ireland of that less elevated but no less cherished structure – the parish pump.

CHAPTER 6
Religion

Triumphs and Stockades

The seven decades that followed the Famine saw the Catholic Church successfully resolving many, but not all, of the contradictions and ambiguities which had marked its experience of the previous half century. In the sphere of spirituality and morals its clergy moved relentlessly towards further reform and control and in the process accentuated that sense of professionalism and exclusiveness which had constituted the main thrust of earlier attempts at religious modernization. By contrast, the world of politics – the last important area where the secular and the religious activities of the priesthood remained not merely connected but mutually indistinct – presented a markedly different picture. There, after something of a false lurch into ineffective hegemony during the 1850s and 1860s, the clergy eventually settled, with some reluctance and occasional dissent, into an essentially ancillary role.

I

It was above all the activities of Paul Cullen as Archbishop of Armagh (1849–52) and of Dublin (1852–78) which provided the crucial point of contact between individual endeavour and the imperatives of the wider world at large. Cullen, one of the towering figures of modern Irish history, had spent virtually all his earlier career in Rome, where he had been inoculated against liberalism in its continental form. He returned home with exaggerated notions of Ireland's ecclesiastical and spiritual backwardness, with legatine authority to refashion the local church along ultramontane lines, and with the confidence that he enjoyed real influence amidst the Vatican's meandering corridors of power and delay (Bowen 1983a). Himself of prosperous Leinster farming stock Cullen was the personal embodiment of the kind of Catholicism which many middling and larger farmers were already beginning to espouse and make dominant: modern, formal, shorn of 'magic' and older folk customs (Hynes 1978; Larkin 1975b). Like so many energetic reformers he tended to divide the world into sheep and goats. Those who were not for him he perceived as irretrievably hostile and among the Cullenite circles of the damned were virtually all Protestants, all Englishmen (especially English Catholics), Gallican ecclesiastics, political revolutionaries, and anyone associated with Archbishop MacHale of Tuam, who, after first welcoming Cullen as an ally against politically moderate members of the episcopate, soon became a dogged, though in the end, defeated adversary capable of driving Cullen (who combined authoritarianism with hypochondria) into acute bouts of depressive rage.

By the narrowest of margins Cullen was able to obtain support at the Synod of Thurles of 1850 – the first national synod of bishops held in modern times – both for his trenchant hostility to the Queen's Colleges set up by Peel in 1845 and for a reaffirmation of earlier, but still only partly successful, attempts to cleanse the church of folk religion and the organizational abuses of former times. Patterns now stood condemned as potentially immoral. Wakes were to be sanitized and all the other rites of passage – funerals, baptisms, weddings – brought under clerical auspices alone (Corish 1985: 195–7; Larkin 1980: 27–57). Like some ecclesiastical actuary Cullen lost no time in telling Rome of the advanced age, ill health, and imminent demise of bishops opposed to his cause, so that, already by the end of the 1850s, his enormous influence over appointments had consolidated a generally sympathetic majority on the episcopal bench (Larkin 1980 and 1987).

Yet, however important Cullen's influence undoubtedly was in shaping the nature of modern Irish Catholicism, it should be remembered that he was building upon foundations already laid by others – notably Archbishop Murray whose achievements he invariably denigrated and ignored – and that even his own new broom was never able to sweep entirely clean. On his arrival the heroic period of church building was almost over and in the eastern dioceses ultramontane practices and devotions were already firmly established (Keenan 1983). In addition, his task was made the easier, firstly, by the gathering importance of those elements in society most sympathetic to religious reform (Miller 1975; Hynes 1978) and, secondly, by the enormous population collapse of the late 1840s which greatly improved the ratio of parochial priests to Catholic people from 1 to 2773 in 1845 to 1 to 1783 in 1861 and eventually 1 to 1126 in 1901, even though the relevant clerical numbers only rose from 2393 just before the Famine to 2938 at the century's end. Thus did the grim reaper and the emigrant ship combine to make the clergy more ubiquitous and, in logical if not necessary consequence, more powerful than before.

On the whole priests also became increasingly well-off and in so doing first anticipated and then matched the late-nineteenth-century prosperity experienced by their kinsfolk in the ranks of the substantial farmer class (Hoppen 1984: 227–32). Some, indeed, did well enough to drive an astonished foreign visitor in the 1880s to record their interest in fine wines: 'they each have their favourite claret: one likes Léoville, another Château Margaux'[1] (Connell 1968: 154). In new parochial houses and dressed now invariably in a recognizable clerical uniform they could exercise their functions not only within a world rendered less spiritually ambiguous than before but from citadels which physically and metaphorically proclaimed their growing distinctiveness and power. And in their mission of moral purification and influence they were also, as time went on, increasingly assisted by rising cohorts of regulars (members of religious orders) and above all of nuns – from about 120 in 1800 and 1500 in 1850 the number of nuns in Ireland rose to no less than 8000 as the century came to a close (Corish 1985: 203). Whereas before the Famine financial exigencies had limited the recruitment of priests, thereafter Ireland was to export large numbers of 'surplus' clergy to minister to emigrant communities in Britain and North America and later to those yet lesser breeds without the law in tropical and eastern lands. Here, indeed, was a Hibernian spiritual empire to surpass Britain's money-grubbing imperialism. And Cullen, exulting in the enterprise, remained ever ready to view all things through remorselessly denominational lenses, so much so, that for him even the Crimean War became, above all else, a great and essentially *Catholic* crusade (MacSuibhne 1961–77: ii, 215).

One of the new ultramontanism's greatest domestic triumphs was its success in obtaining almost total control over the running of the church's major seminaries. Cullen had long been suspicious of Maynooth with its government grant and alleged (though in practice insubstantial) tendency towards Gallican particularism.

Before the 1850s were out he had imposed draconian loyalty oaths upon the staff and ensured that both Maynooth and the new seminary founded for his own diocese at Clonliffe in 1859 were henceforth to produce only priests totally committed, at least in theological and social terms, to his own vision of the clerical role (Corish 1979; Hoppen 1984: 188). While this did nothing to encourage intellectual endeavour within the church, it proved highly efficacious in producing a steady stream of those dogged pastoral moralists who, armed with a rule book at once precise and immutable, could alone have furnished the kind of religious justification and guidance which important sections of the laity increasingly demanded and required.

What was at issue here was the gathering post-Famine shift to the impartible inheritance of land, for, although few farmers actually *owned* their holdings until the turn of the century, most tenants were allowed by landlords to choose their successors. Already before 1850 many eastern farmers had begun to select a single (usually male) heir who was then found a suitable dowried wife by means of a formal 'match' so that marriage became above all a 'symbol of the pooling of property' (Fitzpatrick 1985b: 120–1). With the demographic collapse of the labourer class this practice became more and more widespread although it was not until the last third of the century that impartible inheritance and the resulting 'stem family' succession system were generally to be found in the West of the country. Because this meant that only one heir could succeed and he could wed only one bride non-inheritors found themselves excluded from the marriage market. And although it was above all emigration which allowed this increasingly mercenary marriage system to flourish so successfully, there can be little doubt that the church's ability to furnish a coherent moral and psychological framework to support those who remained behind also provided crucial lubrication for the machine. While, then, the initial point of departure consisted of a growing awareness of the link between marriage and personal living standards – something by no means confined to Ireland – the Irish combination of a continuingly agrarian society, large-scale emigration, and the church's ability to supply both individual solace and general prescriptive support yielded a particularly striking outcome in both social and cultural terms (Kennedy 1973).

The characteristic puritanism of late-nineteenth and early-twentieth-century Irish Catholicism developed, therefore, not simply out of some purely theological set of compulsions, but directly in response to a situation in which widespread celibacy was more and more becoming the rule. While in industrial England it was the discipline of regular working patterns which helped to shape the Victorian experience, in Ireland the discipline 'necessary to mobilize the labour of family members while subordinating their aspirations to the long-term ability of the family land to support those dependent on it at an acceptable standard' proved far more important (Hynes 1978: 150). All the consequent clerical denunciations of immodest dances, company keeping, and fleshly sins in general (Connell 1968: 113–61), however restrictive for particular individuals, involved, in the end, a kind of invited repression. Before the Famine the clergy's attempt to demolish the 'extravagances' of folk religion had been only very partially successful because then the church had, in effect, been kicking against the pricks. Thereafter the priesthood was moving *with* the grain of social and economic development and laying siege to fortresses of behaviour already under energetic demolition from within.

Unsurprisingly there developed a reciprocity of both power and tension between priests and people. As the clergy became more effectively the moral guardians of certain governing desires so their immediate social authority became increasingly visible. If in certain cases economic imperatives produced an at best muffled response to the church's injunctions – notably those in favour of early marriage and on the moral dangers of emigration – it is, nonetheless, significant that most of the men and women who did marry continued to have large numbers of children. Indeed, the marital fertility rate actually rose between the 1870s and the Great War at a time when the level of postponed marriage was also going up. In part this may have been because the most 'deferential' Catholics were to be found among those who married late, remained celibate, or emigrated overseas (Kennedy 1973: 194–9). But perhaps more significant was the church's success in forging a powerful ideological link with that increasingly influential figure – the Irish mother. While the decline of the domestic textile industry and the shift from tillage to pasture undoubtedly reduced the economic independence of many Irishwomen, the simultaneous transformation of what had formerly been crude mud cabins into modern and 'civilized' homes, although it certainly inaugurated a new drudgery of domestic manners and expectations, also gave mothers an altogether more prominent role as homemakers and as the purveyors of values and attitudes to younger generations (Lee

1978; Inglis 1987: 187–214). The national school system placed enormous emphasis on training girls to be good housewives and the definition of what that meant was increasingly based upon an agenda drawn up by priests and by nuns who thereby helped to make mothers one of the main organizational links between an institutionalized church and the individual farming families of the time (Inglis 1987: 194).

Intermingled with such developments was the clergy's deep-seated fear of the modern and of urbanism, a curious matter in the light of the church's espousal of much that can be regarded as 'modern' in post-Famine society – the decline of folk religion, the growth of nationalism, politer manners, impartible inheritance, even (though here lurked obvious dangers) increasing literacy. Having sucked dry, as it were, the useful juices of modernization, the clergy proceeded to emphasize the importance of a whole series of largely invented 'traditions'. Thus could representative priests like Father Peter O'Leary (1839–1920) – in his famous autobiography published in Irish in 1915 as *Mo Scéal Féin (My Own Story)* offer a 'simple-minded, evil-city–*versus*–virtuous-village polarity, tied up . . . with an identification of England and English modes with the former and Ireland and Irish-language traditions with the latter' (Garvin 1987: 59). 'If people', declared O'Leary, 'would only throw away the tea and the white loaf and start taking potatoes and milk as their food and drink again . . . they'd have teeth and stomachs and health every bit as good as their fathers had' (Goldring 1982: 33–4). Others, like the prolific novelist Canon Sheehan (1852–1913), wanted above all to 'preserve' rural Ireland as a fortress of anti-materialism and identified women and priests as the chief regimental forces in the fight against urban Anglo-Saxon paganism. Both Sheehan and O'Leary contributed to D. P. Moran's *Leader* in the years before the Great War and in its pages joined others in denouncing the mixing of the sexes in schools, *Tit-Bits*, Darwin, and the English language itself as poisonous to faith and fatherland alike (Garvin 1986a: 69–71; MacDonagh 1970).

Although, therefore, a good deal of anxiousness underlay the triumphalism of contemporary Irish Catholicism it is, nonetheless, remarkable that many of the moral propositions of the new Irish-Catholic ideology, rooted as they were in rural social organization, became almost as widely adopted by townspeople as by farmers and their kin (Fitzpatrick 1987: 195). That in the matter of marriage and related phenomena like divorce Catholic priests were indeed responding to the deep social and economic requirements of post-Famine life is further made clear by the fact that within the Protestant communities too were to be found very similar patterns of celibacy, large families, and sexual puritanism (Kennedy 1973: 191; Hepburn 1978: 92–5). In truth, despite certain obvious differences, the cultural thrust of late-nineteenth and early-twentieth-century religious experience in Ireland was shared by important elements within all the major denominations, as can be seen, for example, in a universal lack of complaint over the failure to extend England's more liberal divorce legislation of 1857 across the Irish Sea (Fitzpatrick 1987: 185–7).

The Catholic hierarchy's official denunciation in 1875 of 'dangerous amusements in theatres . . . improper dances [the waltz and the polka] . . . imported into our country from abroad' was echoed by the Orange demagogue, Rev. Thomas Drew, rector of Christ Church Belfast, who campaigned in the 1850s and 1860s against the stage and drama as pollutants of true faith, and echoed also by repeated and urgent reminders in Edwardian Ulster that 'plays inflame the passions, excite the imagination and depict vice' (Hoppen 1984: 223; Budge and O'Leary 1973: 79; Baker 1973: 806). The well-known public outrage which greeted the first production of J. M. Synge's *The Playboy of the Western World* at Dublin's Abbey Theatre in 1907 was, in such a context, not simply a matter of parochial Catholic rage against what the *Freeman's Journal* called a 'protracted libel upon Irish peasant men and, worse still, upon Irish peasant girlhood' (Lyons 1979: 69), but grew out of a general distrust of all but the safest and most deferential literary representations of social behaviour and morality. Indeed, in some respects, priests had a firmer grasp of the boundaries of their influence than did many Protestant ministers and especially so in that other important contemporary question of social discipline, drink and its abuse. Here the Catholic authorities adopted a cautious approach and were happy enough to commend such bodies as the Pioneer Total Abstinence Association of the 1890s more warmly than they had ever supported Father Mathew's pre-Famine campaigns in part because the later movement saw the complete renunciation of alcohol as an act of 'devotion by a heroic few, rather than the desired behaviour' of the nation as a whole – a nation in which, of course, publicans constituted one of nationalism's and Catholicism's most important organizational and financial props (Connolly 1985b: 55; Malcolm 1982 and 1986).

The Catholic clergy's nimbleness of foot depended greatly upon this kind of ability to paper over the cracks between a repeated elevation of something that might best be called rural anti-materialism and a ruggedly realistic appreciation of social and economic realities. By translating the latter into the language of the former the church achieved a high measure of acceptance for its status as the repository of Ireland's dominant values and aspirations. Theory, therefore, was constantly tempered by pragmatism. Support for the true underdogs of rural life, the agricultural labourers, never developed much beyond pious ejaculations in favour of universal goodwill (Kennedy 1978a: 70–1; O'Shea 1983: 119–35). Father Walter McDonald, from 1881 a professor at Maynooth, recognized with unusual clarity, that priests did 'not spring from the labouring class' and, just as before 1850, failed to 'sympathize with labourers as much as with farmers' (McDonald 1925: 334, 23, 169). By 1871 Bishop Nulty of Meath was, indeed, entirely typical in having decided exactly upon whose shoulders Holy Ireland must rest (Hoppen 1984: 181).

> The purest, the holiest, and the most innocent of society in this country, at least, certainly belong to the class of small farmers. They are high enough, in the social scale, to be above the temptation of extreme want and poverty; and they are below the reach of the seductive and demoralising influences of great wealth and affluence.

As so often, of course, it all depended upon what was meant by 'small' farmers, for, despite a joint episcopal pastoral of 1900 full of ringing sympathy, the clergy in general adopted an extremely cautious policy towards later proposals for the break-up of cattle ranches in favour of the poorer tenants of the West. And the same was true of attitudes towards the agricultural co-operative movement whose theories might be thought to have contained much to attract a church ostensibly wedded to concepts of the common good. However, neither large graziers nor rural shopkeepers and traders looked kindly upon land redistribution or the spread of co-operation into the retailing sector. And with the church depending heavily upon financial support from such quarters and many priests locked into kin relationships with such people the clergy often proved unsurprisingly eager to acknowledge the virtues of moderation and compromise – something rendered less difficult than it might otherwise have been by the way in which nationalist leaders like Dillon and Davitt denounced co-operatives as a Tory plot and expressed fears that land redistribution might deflect popular enthusiasm from the great and central issue of Home Rule (Kennedy 1978a). It was, therefore, not so much, as one historian has suggested (Kennedy 1978b: 55), that the religious and economic spheres were simply autonomous, but rather that the church's ability to balance the priorities involved allowed it to strengthen and render legitimate that integration of piety and ruthless self-interest which developments in the secular world were also making attractive to all concerned. Like Janus the church may have had two faces. But both of these were, as with the ancient god, firmly attached to the same skull.

II

If the flavour of Irish Catholicism undoubtedly changed it would be as wrong to exaggerate the completeness of these later transformations as to deny their prefiguration in the years before the Famine. In matters like church building and liturgical reform earlier trends were strengthened and driven to completion, although progress was often slow in the western dioceses. Clerical discipline, while improving, continued to present problems even to bishops prepared to use their powers to the full. The bishops themselves remained stubbornly individual and neither Cullen nor his successors found it easy to enforce a centralized authority (Corish 1985: 227). In particular Archbishop MacHale of Tuam (who did not die until 1881) fought a bitter rearguard action against many aspects of ecclesiastical modernization. Others too simply ignored Cullen's endless demands that the practice of stations be brought to an end, while as late as 1884 Archbishop Croke of Cashel still found it necessary to confirm 300 *adults* who had presumably failed to receive the sacrament in childhood as the church had long demanded should be the case (Hoppen 1984: 190–1, 208–9; Larkin 1975a: 228).

Some contemporaries admittedly talked apocalyptically of sudden and imposed reform. The 'coloured races' of America, wrote one student of popular culture in 1873, 'have not receded before the advances of the white men of Europe with greater celerity than the national observances of Ireland [wakes, patterns etc.] have been obliterated by the unsparing hand of social progress, and the stern utilitarianism of modern times' (Hogan 1873: 261). In fact, however, folk religion lingered on, particularly among those farm servants and labourers so ostentatiously by-passed in the march of ecclesiastical modernity (Carbery 1973: 158). Priests were still not infrequently credited with 'magical' powers and were still on occasion happy enough to trade on the fact (Kennedy 1979a). In 1868 a woman was charged in court for having 'held constant communication with the fairies' (Hoppen 1984: 220). As late as 1 May 1890 virtually all the houses in Sligo Town were decorated with blooming gorse to please 'the good people', while the county infirmary regularly admitted patients wearing 'straining strings' designed to cure dislocated limbs (Wood-Martin 1902: i, 299–302 and ii, 29, 72–3, 262). In a notorious instance in 1895 a woman was killed near Clonmel by relatives in the belief that she was a fairy, the parish priest revealingly defending his lack of intervention by saying 'the priest is very often the last to hear of things like that' (Jenkins 1977: 47–8; McGrath 1982).

Undoubtedly, however, such practices were seeping towards the margins – both socially and mentally – of Irish life as the clergy proved generally if not completely successful in overcoming them by a mixed process of abolition and assimilation. Many traditional places of popular pilgrimage were simply abandoned. Others were sanitized and made safe for ultramontane orthodoxy such as those at Lough Derg in Donegal and Croagh Patrick in Mayo (O'Connor 1910; MacNeill 1962). Both the Catholic and Protestant Churches augmented such assimilations by means of popular rituals of an imported kind. The former established entirely novel centres of piety, notably at Knock – only some thirty miles from Croagh Patrick – where in 1879 the Virgin Mary (having hitherto made herself manifest chiefly in France: at Paris in 1830 and 1836, La Salette in 1846, Pontmain in 1871, and Lourdes in 1858) appeared arrayed in ultramontane splendour. 'I distinctly beheld her', recalled one thirteen-year-old, 'life size . . . clothed in white robes, which were fastened at the neck . . . She wore a brilliant crown on her head, and, over the forehead, where the crown fitted the brow, a beautiful rose' (MacPhilpin 1880: 32). Such novelties were reinforced by the new practice of parish missions during which members of religious orders descended upon individual neighbourhoods and for perhaps a month repeatedly called the people to penance and mortification. So successful were these that in some cases local 'bad characters' were run out of town by pious mobs and in one famous instance Rev. Vladimir Percherin, Russian revolutionary turned Redemptorist, held a great burning of immoral books at Kingstown in 1855 only to be (unsuccessfully) tried for blasphemy when it was discovered that maddened evangelicals had persuaded a young boy to smuggle some Protestant bibles among the volumes to be destroyed (Corish 1985: 210–11).

Important elements within Irish Protestantism responded to post-Famine change in much the same way. Their counterpart of parochial missions was the street preaching of a long line of evangelical firebrands. These condemned popery and nationalism in equal proportions while presenting a religious rhetoric powerfully reminiscent of those rhythms of eternal damnation which the Redemptorists in particular knew so well how to beat out (Baker 1973: 803). And just as ultramontanism was imported from abroad, so evangelicals four times between 1867 and 1892 welcomed the American revivalists Moody and Sankey to Ulster (Connolly 1983b: 46), an Ulster which a few years earlier had already witnessed one of the most extraordinary phenomena of modern Irish religious history – the revival of 1859. This too was sparked off by news of enormous enthusiasm in the United States and spread rapidly throughout eastern Ulster. Its chief adherents were the rural proletariat and factory workers (especially female mill hands) who responded to dynamic preaching with prostrations, cries, groans, weeping, and speaking in tongues. Although the large farmers remained generally aloof the now dominant evangelical ministers within northern Presbyterianism were quick to express their approval and had little difficulty in crushing 'moderate' criticism of these physical and (sometimes literally) naked expressions of divine immanence (Gibbon 1975: 45–65; Carson 1958). But if in one sense such developments exhibited certain obvious parallels with what was happening within contemporary Catholicism – for Catholic missionaries too harped constantly on the crucial question 'Am I saved?' – the differences were as striking as the similarities. In particular, while the preachers of 1859 were often uneducated laymen who still talked in strongly millenarian terms, such things had by the late 1850s become anathema to the tightly-organized clerically-dominated ultramontanism of the Cullenite church.

We are, therefore, left with a set of what at first seem somewhat curious developments in the course of which Catholicism, far more than Protestantism, succeeded in ridding itself of certain popular practices repugnant to the apostles of polite belief and reformed manners. Indeed, the revival of 1859 not only looked back to the harsher joys of pre-Famine millenarianism but also forward to the late-Victorian proliferation of independent gospel halls in Ulster and the establishment of the only significant international religious denomination ever actually founded in Ireland – the pentecostal Elim Foursquare Gospel Church which came into being in that unlikeliest of Meccas, Monaghan Town, during the

153

early years of the Great War (Wilson 1961: 30–5). While, then, post-Famine Catholicism constituted an increasingly homogeneous phenomenon, Irish Protestantism remained, in the religious sense, an unusual coalition of disparate elements: gentry and professional Church of Irelandism, respectable evangelicalism, fierce popular revivalism, and much else besides.

As Catholicism became more confident and Protestantism more defensive so inevitably the stockades which marked the boundaries between the two grew increasingly prominent. The former, adopting the appurtenances of something not far short of an unofficial establishment, demanded ever completer and more formal allegiance; the latter, fearful of being overwhelmed, reacted with a mixture of continuing exclusiveness and protective anxiety. Cullen was determined to make 'mixed' marriages as difficult as possible and when in 1870/1 changes in civil law rendered such marriages lawful before a Catholic priest the bishops imposed the humiliating condition that they henceforth take place in the sacristy (rather than in the body of the church), without mass or the nuptial blessing then becoming common at Catholic marriages. When, therefore, in 1908 the screw was tightened even further and the papal decree *Ne temere* (which insisted that the offspring of mixed marriages be brought up as Catholics) was extended to Ireland Protestants of all kinds reacted with unsurprising anger and dismay (Corish 1985: 220–2).

However, long before this the disestablishment of the Church of Ireland in 1869 had confirmed the suspicions of many of its bishops that, in truth, they were conducting little more than a long retreat from the uplands of former times (Bell 1969). In the South Anglicanism was entering a quiescent, in the North a combative, cultural ghetto, something which many seem to have found a thoroughly congenial development (Bowen 1978: 272–82). Mrs Alexander, the famous hymnodist and wife of the Bishop of Derry, caught the mood of despair and disdain with uncanny authenticity in lines sung in her husband's cathedral the day disestablishment came into force (Bell 1969: 158).

> Look down, Lord of heaven, on our desolation!
> Fallen, fallen, fallen is now our Country's crown,
> Dimly dawns the New Year on a churchless nation,
> Ammon and Amalek tread our borders down.

After the Land War the stream of Protestant energy in the South was to flow almost entirely into the maintenance of a separate social identity and a strategic defence of economic interests. The 'more the gentry's economic power shrank, the more important the comforting sense of status became', so that, within the world of hunt balls, tea parties, and bazaars, an increasingly particular and minute appreciation of hierarchy was demanded and obtained (Fitzpatrick 1977: 52; d'Alton 1973 and 1975). In the bigger towns, where Protestants still loomed large in commerce and the professions (the 1901 census shows that more than half Dublin's doctors and more than a third of its bankers and merchants were Protestants), a pattern of life was sustained which rarely necessitated any real breach in the sectarian divide. 'We were told', recalled the Church of Ireland Bishop of Ossory in 1899, 'that the Act of 1869 would kill jealousy, and draw all Christian folk together. The very opposite has been the case. The prophecy of Archbishop Whately has been realised to the very letter, all Ireland has been divided into hostile camps, with clerical sentries pacing between' (Bowen 1978: 257).

Although tensions still remained, an accelerating sense of pan-Protestant identity gathered further pace and especially rapidly so during the Home Rule crisis of the mid-1880s. In northern towns political resentment and religious suspicion heightened the walls of segregation between Catholics and Protestants. Educated in their own schools and colleges, patronizing their own shops, playing separate games, reading different newspapers 'a great part of Belfast's white-collar workers and middle class, and most of their wives and children, knew "the other sort" only as stereotypes' (Baker 1973: 803–4) and much the same was true elsewhere as well. The poet Louis MacNeice, in describing his Edwardian Ulster rectory childhood, encapsulated a wider experience when he remembered how 'The cook Annie, who was a buxom rosy girl from a farm in County Tyrone, was the only Catholic I knew and therefore my only proof that Catholics were human' (MacNeice 1965: 41).

III

The most important stockade of all was that produced by the increasing sectarianism of education. Here all the denominations had vested interests which each pursued with relentless energy if in rather different ways. Especially for the Catholic bishops a growing literacy – those able to read rose as a percentage of persons aged five and over from 47 in 1841 to 75 forty years later (Hoppen 1984: 457)

– induced fears that unless their flocks were firmly enclosed within the walls of truth the errors of the written word might well tempt younger generations into disobedience, indifference, or (worse still) Protestantism. Almost from the very beginnings of the national school system introduced in 1831 both Catholic and Presbyterian authorities proved themselves brilliantly successful in turning what was in theory a non-sectarian state-supported enterprise into one which eventually provided denominational schools at the taxpayers' expense. In this they were greatly assisted by the myopic fears of the Church of Ireland which for three decades poured effort and treasure into its own independent Church Education Society (Kelly 1970). The Presbyterians, on the other hand, had been the first to realize that an initial general acceptance followed by a series of truculent demands was the best way of achieving what they wanted, with the result that, already by the 1840s, almost all their requirements had been fulfilled (Akenson 1970: 187; Ó Raifeartaigh 1955).

The Catholics, with their fiercer antagonism to denominationally mixed education, were slower off the mark. While Archbishop Murray of Dublin agreed to serve as a national commissioner and adopted a generally eirenic approach, those who looked to his chief episcopal opponent, Archbishop MacHale, denounced the schools as violently as they did the 'godless' university colleges set up by Peel in 1845. But, while in the latter case successive governments long proved reluctant to meet Catholic demands, already by the middle of the century the national schools had become denominational in all but name (Akenson 1970: 257). By the early 1860s half the Education Board's members were Catholics. By 1870 half of all Catholic children were attending schools devoid of even a *single* Protestant and another 45 per cent schools with an average Protestant enrolment of one in fifteen (Corish 1985: 205; Murphy and Ó Súilleabháin 1971). Not only that, but reformatories and so-called 'industrial' schools were in the 1850s and 1860s put under clerical auspices and in the 1880s denominational teacher training colleges were also established. Because each school came under a 'manager' with considerable powers and as, in the Catholic case, such managers were invariably priests, clerical control, let alone denominationalism, soon became the order of the day. And the power of the bishops was further increased in the 1870s when a notorious legal wrangle concerning an independently-minded parish priest named O'Keeffe, who insisted that his suspension by the Bishop of Ossory in no sense involved his ceasing to be manager of the local national school, was effectively decided in their favour. In consequence it became tacitly accepted that a priest's role in a school 'depended primarily on his nomination to his parish by the bishop, not on his nomination' as manager by the National Board (Corish 1985: 206; Bowen 1983a: 235–44). Small wonder, then, that by 1900 even the bishops (though on autocarp to the end) had to admit that the 'system of National education, instead of spreading secularism or indifference, has itself undergone a radical change, and in a great deal of Ireland is now in fact, whatever it is in name, as denominational almost as we could desire' (Murphy and Ó Súilleabháin 1971: 46).

The secondary sector (usually referred to in Ireland as 'intermediate') involved altogether fewer children and remained substantially a matter for private – usually religious – enterprise. In 1878 the state began to give grants and, though these in no sense offended sectarian sensibilities, they long remained very modest indeed (Murphy and Ó Súilleabháin 1971). It was, in any case, the lack of university provision acceptable to the hierarchy which attracted the bulk of attention. Cullen's establishment of an independent Catholic University in Dublin in the 1850s under the rectorship of the eminent English convert, J. H. Newman, collapsed amidst opposition from MacHale and chronic financial difficulties. And although Peel's colleges at Cork and Galway attracted – despite Cullen's best efforts – enough Catholic students to continue in being, they were never able to achieve the success of their northern sister in Belfast let alone match that of the Elizabethan foundation of Trinity College in Dublin (Flanagan 1978). After endless plans and proposals had been canvassed and rejected a National University of Ireland was eventually established in 1908 to encompass the existing institutions in Cork and Galway as well as a new University College in Dublin (but while Peel had provided enough money to build mini-Oxbridge colleges in 1845, the Dublin college in appearance long resembled a Potemkin village – all façade and little else). Trinity was left untouched while the Belfast foundation was transformed into the Queen's University. Although it and the National University remained theoretically non-denominational, in practice the demands of both Ulster Protestants and the Catholic hierarchy had now been met and, as with the primary schools, met at the public expense (McGrath 1971; Miller 1973: 195–204).

Overall it was a remarkable triumph and one the bishops utilized to the full. What above all they had succeeded in making distinctive about the Irish case was not simply that denominational schools

157

received substantial support from state funds (in Scotland even more money was provided), but that such schools were completely under clerical control (Corish 1985: 229). As, in addition, education was the issue on which the bishops in the 1880s came to enter into formal alliance with the Parliamentary Party the hierarchy was thereafter always able to secure the support of constitutional nationalism for its aspirations and demands. Parents, however, were given no more than walk-on parts because, as every right-thinking person realized, schooling was 'somewhat outside their competence' (1904), while lay teachers, especially in secondary schools, were ill-used, badly paid, and denied either security or influence (Titley 1983: 20–51). Plans drawn up in the very last years of British rule to provide additional resources from local taxation drove the hierarchy into paroxysms of fear lest ratepayers demand some say in how such monies were spent, the mere thought of which made Cardinal Logue predict in 1919 the imminent arrival of all 'the impiety, corruption, and materialism of the age' (Titley 1983: 56). By jumping as it did into the back carriages of the republican train just before these receded along the tracks of independence the church managed both to overcome such proposals and to enter the Free State 'with school systems at both primary and secondary levels largely under its control and with a certain confidence that changes would only take place with its consent' (Titley 1983: 70).

IV

If education constituted the most important link between the Catholic Church's immediate priorities and the world of politics in general, the priesthood's political activities were of course never confined to it alone. Increasingly successful in adopting the character of religious specialists and unscrambling that mixture of sacred and profane which had marked the mores of pre-Famine times, priests proved unable or unwilling to assume a similarly unambiguous role when it came to politics where for them the secular and the eternal remained locked in close, almost inseparable, embrace. After the death of O'Connell in 1847 clerical politics entered a rudderless phase and the great truth soon became apparent that priests were always politically most effective in a national sense when they acted as auxiliaries rather than on their own account. Cullen's attempts to continue O'Connellism without O'Connell ran, therefore, rapidly into the sands. Never, as was once commonly supposed, particularly determined to keep priests 'out of politics', Cullen was, if anything, all too keen on clerical participation so long as this followed lines congenial to himself (Whyte 1958 and 1967a).

Whatever Cullen and his episcopal supporters may in fact have desired the reality of the clergy's political behaviour during the quarter-century after the Famine reflected the fissiparous localism of the time. At elections, for example, priests had never been more active (Hoppen 1979; O'Shea 1983: 43–51; Whyte 1960); but, deprived of any overarching secular movement to which they could relate, they now operated as little more than one interest group among many others – the gentry, shopkeepers, artisans, farmers, merchants, and so forth. Repeated attempts by the hierarchy in the 1850s to strengthen earlier injunctions against political excess were widely and openly ignored, not least by the hierarchy itself (Larkin 1980: 170–349; Whyte 1967a: 25–6). Individual priests built up impressive connections in particular districts which depended for their effectiveness more upon the patterning of local conditions – employment, better drains, kin relationships, mercantile rivalries – than upon any governing ideas of a more general kind (Hoppen 1979 and 1984: 232–56; O'Shea 1983: 48). Although most bishops and priests shared the opinions and prejudices of the rising class of farmers on matters ranging from land reform to anti-British and indeed anti-Semitic attitudes (Steele 1975: 241–2; O'Shea 1983: 46–7), an inability to present a united front dissipated their efforts into little more than a kaleidoscope of recrimination and particularism. Especially remarkable is how little was made of the land question. Although a few clergymen were certainly to be found agitating this crucial matter and although the bishops from time to time acknowledged its importance 'their response to agrarian movements between 1850 and 1876 was limited to a few meagre petitions, and certainly was not in proportion to their interest in education' (O'Shea 1983: 65).

When, therefore, the arrival of Fenianism as a potentially significant force in the 1860s persuaded Cullen to take centre stage and establish, for the first and only time in modern Irish history, a formal all-Ireland political movement under almost total clerical control – the National Association of 1864 – this was more an admission of powerlessness than the reverse (Norman 1965: 135–89; Corish 1962). The Association's main aims were the disestablishment of the Church of Ireland and increased denominationalism in education, with some very modest proposals for land reform tagged on as a kind of unavoidable afterthought. Somehow this failed to set the country ablaze and within a few months the clergy of Meath (who had long put greater emphasis on the land issue) withdrew entirely from a movement notable from the start for its lack of energy, cash, and organizational drive (Corish 1967: 23–6; Norman 1969: 9–13). Even on the Fenian issue the bishops failed to pull together, though the actual rising of 1867 was widely condemned. Some like Moriarty of Kerry proclaimed that hell was not hot enough nor eternity long enough for members of the Republican Brotherhood. Others, Cullen among them, though they tried – at first with little success – to galvanize Rome into public condemnation, adopted a less extreme position. A few like MacHale gave comfort to maverick priests such as Father Lavelle who led a Fenian front organization, delivered sermons at Fenian funerals, and gave public lectures on 'The Catholic Doctrine of the Right of Revolution' (Ó Fiaich 1968; Gilley 1984).

Although on the surface Gladstone's Irish legislation of 1869–70 could be interpreted as a response to the demands of the National Association, in reality it had more to do with fears of Fenianism and with the Liberal leader's perception that it represented the most efficient way of knitting together his new parliamentary following at Westminster. In a foreshadowing of what was to happen after 1916, the failed Fenian Rising of 1867 quickly achieved a significant afterlife, with the result that the widespread Amnesty movement for the release of those Fenians still in prison represented the first extensive popular political agitation in Ireland since the days of O'Connell (Hoppen 1984: 465–8). Just as in the early-twentieth century so now also a revolutionary organization long feared by dominant elements within the ecclesiastical leadership was, at least for some, brought within the canon of popular Catholicism by British executions (in this case of the so-called Manchester Martyrs in November 1867) and by stories of how piously the revolutionaries had met their end. 'I never', reported the priest who visited the 'martyrs' in jail, 'had more devotional penitents in my life . . . My poor boys, how they did pray!' (O Fiaich 1968: 92).

V

The 1870s represent, indeed, a decade of transition as regards the clergy's involvement in politics. Cullen's new departure of the

1850s, that is, his efforts to make the church act 'not as auxiliary to nationalists, nor as guide to the people, but as driver and commander' (Boyce 1982: 181), had clearly broken down. With his death in 1878 and that of Pius IX in the same year an initially confused and then more clearly defined return to what had been the norm in the quarter-century before the Famine took place. The appointment of the Hamlet-like figure of Edward McCabe to the archbishopric of Dublin after Cullen's death signified the Vatican's strong preference for caution, 'moderation', and a distinctly hands-off relationship with the rising force of Home Rule. For the next six years until his death in 1885 McCabe sought, with diminishing success, to follow the path Pope Leo XIII so clearly desired, only to find himself increasingly out of tune, not only with Parnell's new nationalism and its agrarian base, but also with other bishops (notably Thomas William Croke appointed to Cashel in 1875) who felt that Rome was seriously misreading the portents of the time (Larkin 1975a; Tierney 1976).

The Land War of 1879–82 elicited an at first cautious and then more dynamic clerical response. In Tipperary, for example, almost three-quarters of the priests attended Land League meetings in 1880 and 1881, though few actually joined the organization (O'Shea 1983: 74–5). All in all the clergy played a skilful role, giving support and sympathy, leaving the crucial administrative work to the laity, placing one foot on the accelerator and the other more firmly still on the brake. McCabe's battle to maintain a critical stance became more and more a lonely one as bishops and priests (whose incomes, like those of the farmers, fell as a result of agricultural depression) briskly decided that their own best interests lay in movement rather than repose. While undoubtedly the church as a whole felt more comfortable with the National League set up under Parnell's control in October 1882 than it had with the more independently-minded Land League outlawed by the government the previous year, Rome's clumsy attempts to earn brownie points from the British government by condemning the testimonial collection for Parnell in May 1883 and by appointing some bishops hostile to agrarian agitation increased rather than diminished clerical enthusiasm for land reform and Home Rule.

Parnell, with considerable dexterity, not only exhibited a sudden interest in denominational education but struck a variety of attitudes congenial to episcopal tastes on such matters as the atheist Bradlaugh's attempts to take his seat at Westminster and Davitt's plans for land nationalization. He was rewarded when in

October 1884 the bishops decided to place the education question in the hands of the 'Irish Parliamentary Party' and doubly fortunate when in 1885 Rome (temporarily dismayed by Britain's failure to acknowledge its efforts in Ireland) appointed the able, dynamic, and firmly nationalist William Walsh to succeed McCabe (Larkin 1975a: 241–300). With impressive legerdemain Parnell made priests *ex officio* members of the county conventions called to select candidates for the general election of 1885 while seeing to it that the convention system was soon effectively abandoned and real power given into the hands of the central lay-dominated party machine (O'Shea 1983: 205). And this new departure in party–church relations, as important as the new departures properly so-called which had realigned constitutionalism, agrarianism, and Fenianism in the 1870s, was formally confirmed when in February 1886 the episcopate publicly and finally announced its 'firm conviction' that only Home Rule could satisfy 'the wants and wishes of the Irish people' (Larkin 1975a: 363).

Walsh and Croke fully lived up to their promises when in 1888 the Vatican, once more lured by siren songs from London and worried about the 'dangerous' turn the land agitation was taking, issued its famous decree against the refusals to pay rent associated with the Plan of Campaign. From the start both men had been happy to deploy some exceedingly nimble theological footwork in justification of the Campaign and they did not falter now. With the skill of a trapeze artiste Walsh kept the choleric Croke in check, tried to explain Irish realities to Rome, drew all kinds of distinctions between pronouncements on *moral* and on *political* matters in an effort to render the decree harmless (Larkin 1978), and in effect succeeded in providing yet further evidence that the church in Ireland had now moved quite decisively into a new political relationship. And while this undoubtedly meant a considerable reduction in the clergy's freedom of manoeuvre it also yielded a considerable increase in clarity of purpose and comparative unity all round, the church acknowledging the party's political primacy as a prop and defence of its own primacy in the broader field of morals and religious culture generally.

As, however, the achievement of complete harmony is rarely given to any collection of individuals there still remained a few irreconcilables determined to insist that any number of plump and desirable babies were being thrown out with the bathwater. On the one side sea-green Fenian incorruptibles denounced new departures of all kinds. On the other the episcopate still contained its unavoidable complement of rugged political individualists, though these had now been effectively reduced to two: Healy, the coadjutor Bishop of Clonfert (and later Archbishop of Tuam), still kept the Moriarty–McCabe candle alight, while, far more dramatically, Thomas Edward O'Dwyer, Bishop of Limerick since 1886, was already beginning to plough those idiosyncratic furrows which, during the next three decades, he was to make so compellingly his own. Angry that the bishops had conceded any power at all and mindful that Parnell himself was no son of the church, O'Dwyer, like some spectre at the feast, lost no time in denouncing the Plan of Campaign as dangerous to faith and morality. 'I don't care what advantage it brings to the farmers or others – if it puts a gold mine in the heart of every farm and abolished all rent for ever, if it is condemned by the Church I will not have it . . . Roma locuta est, causa finita est' (Larkin 1978: 255–6). But if now magnificently out of step (and that not for the last time) O'Dwyer was also laying the foundations for that heroic sense of confident self-assuredness which, towards the end of his life, was to prove instrumental in helping the hierarchy as a whole to execute, with some semblance of public conviction, one of the most daring and important political somersaults of modern times.

In one respect O'Dwyer was able to have a preliminary laugh a good deal earlier than that. While most of his colleagues had by the late 1880s reconciled themselves to the view that when faced with widespread popular agitation it was best to bend with the wind and thus, in Bishop McEvilly's words, 'keep the people attached to them' (Larkin 1975b: 1265; O'Farrell 1971: 189, 192), O'Dwyer consistently maintained a higher view of episcopal rights and responsibilities. Throughout the Summer of 1890, therefore, he and leading parliamentary nationalists like Dillon and O'Brien conducted a public dispute of notable abusiveness. At a huge meeting in Limerick itself Dillon declared that all right-thinking men knew well 'how to draw the line between politics and religion', a remark which merely elicited further O'Dwyerite attacks on the Plan of Campaign (Larkin 1979: 165–77). Soon even Walsh and Croke came to realize that unless attention was once again concentrated on constitutional rather than agrarian issues the delicate equilibrium between the church and the party might well tip altogether too far in the latter's favour. In order to secure their position they conciliated the Vatican, while at home emphasizing their support for Parnell rather than the more truculent Dillon and O'Brien. When, therefore, the bombshell of Parnell's involvement in the

O'Shea divorce case hit Ireland, O'Dwyer – never one to miss an opportunity for saying 'I told you so' – happily left his colleagues in the lurch by refusing to sign their various anti-Parnellite manifestos on the grounds that he had 'never been either a follower or ally of Mr Parnell, whom the true instincts of our Holy Father condemned years ago' (Larkin 1979: 302–3).

It is difficult, amidst the maelstrom of mutual abuse, to reach any satisfactory assessment of the clergy's influence in the whole affair. If in the crucial by-elections which followed the 'split' many priests proved themselves untiring interpreters of what the correct nexus should be between political worthiness and marital fidelity and if men like Bishop Nulty lost no opportunity to denounce Parnellism as a barrier to 'the diffusion of the divine knowledge', there is little evidence to suggest that voters were in any great need of clerical pressure to propel them into the anti-Parnellite camp (Woods 1980).

With the firm smack of Parnell's leadership gone the church entered an environment which, though it bore certain similarities to that of the 1850s and 1860s, was in many respects unprecedented. The see-saw plank connecting priesthood and politics had, indeed, moved again but in a somewhat different manner than before, so that now the church was obliged to face, not so much a political vacuum, as a situation in which a variety of hostile – often very hostile – factions and interests were engaged in bitter wrangles for supremacy and dominance.

Things were rendered more complicated still when in 1893 Walsh's commanding position was undermined by Rome's awarding a cardinal's hat, not to him, but to Archbishop Logue of Armagh. Logue, an altogether less able man, represented that element within the church most anxious to return to the (rather futile) clerical 'dominance' of the immediate post-Famine years. As such he gave his support to the Healyite faction within the Anti-Parnellite Party which emphasized the independence of constituencies at the expense of strong central leadership – in effect a return to the free-wheeling particularism of earlier times (Miller 1968: 76). But though localism always remained an important strand in Irish political life, Healy proved unable to deliver and after 1900, when the party was reunited under Redmond's leadership, he collapsed into the role of irritating gadfly without any considerable influence or following. Logue, however, continued to yearn for Healyite impossibilities; Walsh became entirely consumed by the question of higher education; while a small minority of bishops went so far as to declare their disenchantment with the Home Rule cause as a whole. That, indeed, a working relationship with the Parliamentary Party was kept in some kind of repair flowed more from the failure of the Unionist governments of the time to solve the education question than from anything connected with Home Rule itself (O'Farrell 1971: 219; Miller 1968: 78–9).

All the tensions and problems which underlay the activities of the reunited party had their counterparts among the clergy. Thus the agitations connected with the United Irish League at the turn of the century and with the Ranch War thereafter required a public balancing act between the 'legitimate' aspirations of small western farmers for land redistribution and the 'rights' of the large graziers whose financial and cultural importance to the church demanded proper respect. It was, in any case, not until 1905 that the bishops as a body could bring themselves to repeat the declaration of 1886 and urge the country to 'rally round our Parliamentary representatives and give them the whole strength of the nation's support in their endeavour to secure ordinary civil rights for Irish Catholics' (Miller 1973: 124–5). Bishops like Logue, O'Dwyer, and Healy of Tuam remained deeply suspicious of any alliance with the English Liberal Party and even many of their colleagues supported Redmond in no very enthusiastic way, with the result that the Parliamentary Party and the church came to resemble nothing so much as partners at a ball, who, while sharing the congenialities of long acquaintance, still keep looking over their shoulders in the hope that some more exciting and energetic dancer might yet invite them to take a turn upon the floor.

VI

What rendered such glances on the church's part more than merely theoretical was the fact that, in certain important respects, the cultural nationalism identified most closely with the Gaelic Athletic Association and the Gaelic League touched the temperamental heartstrings of contemporary clericalism more directly than the down-to-earth charms of Dillon and Redmond let alone those of their Liberal allies in England. Both the new cultural nationalists and the priesthood, however practical their *behaviour* often was, shared a certain ethereal sense of what Ireland should be and must become. In 1895, for example, the important clerical periodical, the *Messenger of the Sacred Heart,* in proposing a new prayer for 'toilers in the fields, that remaining in their country homes, by their labours, simplicity and holiness they may counter-balance the corruption and irreligion of towns and cities' resonated some of the deepest chords of cultural nationalism's glorification of the simple life. And matching afflations were becoming increasingly frequent and increasingly capable of providing sweet music for ecclesiastical ears, as when the republican language enthusiast, Eoin MacNeill, declared that 'When we learn to speak Irish, we soon find that it is what we may call essential Irish to acknowledge God, His presence, and His help, even in our most trivial conversations' (O'Farrell 1971: 224–33; Coldrey 1988).

While, therefore, the clergy still voted for the Parliamentary Party the form of nationalism which was beginning to capture priestly affections had more to do with D. P. Moran's Irish-Irelandism than with the wheeler-dealing factionalism which continued to mark the constitutional movement's attempt to gain Home Rule. By 1906 Walsh had become so disillusioned that he ceased to contribute to party funds and it is significant that when in 1908 the MP for Leitrim North resigned his seat in order to stand again as a Sinn Feiner there was no ecclesiastical suggestion that Sinn Fein was not a proper 'potential claimant to national leadership' (Miller 1968: 83; Miller 1973: 221). Admittedly the rise of Ulster Protestant intransigence and the outbreak of war in 1914 brought about some clinging together on the part of the bishops and the party, but such rain-induced sheltering under a single umbrella proved no more than a passing phenomenon (Whyte 1967b).

The Easter Rising of 1916, whatever the initial shock given to sacerdotal sensibilities, soon confirmed the belief of many clergymen that the torch of political Catholicity might now be transferred to other hands. While rebellion in 1798 and 1848 had been flawed by Anglo-Irish and Protestant participation and in 1867 by that of a secret society under grave ecclesiastical suspicion, in 1916 the continued involvement of the IRB was rapidly overlooked amidst the pious intensity of those who had laid down their lives for their beliefs. Pearse's messianic Catholicism struck a responsive chord as did the later pronouncements of Terence MacSwiney – shortly before he embarked upon his hunger strike to death – that the liberty for which he strove was 'a sacred thing, inseparably entwined with the spiritual liberty for which the Saviour of man died'. Within weeks of the rising's end hagiographical accounts of its executed leaders (not excluding even the socialist Connolly) appeared in the Catholic press. And no occasion was lost to stress how constantly the rosary had been recited in the General Post Office by revolutionaries fortified by the sacrament of holy communion and fully convinced, as one of them put it, that they 'were renouncing the world and all the world held for them and making themselves worthy to appear before the Judgement Seat of God' (Newsinger 1978; O'Farrell 1971: 285).

If at first the hierarchy found it difficult to present a united front and seemed paralysed into inactivity, the junior clergy and certain individual bishops had little hesitation in declaring where their sympathies lay. In September 1916 the inimitable O'Dwyer, now convinced that his own triumphalist vision of an all-embracing and exclusivist Catholicism had at last found a worthy political receptacle, declared himself a Sinn Feiner, while the ageing Walsh, together with 200 priests, followed the funeral cortège of a hunger striker (Thomas Ashe) who, at his death, had actually been the president of the Supreme Council of the IRB (Miller 1968: 87; Newsinger 1978: 619). Though some bishops took a more cautious line, the bulk of the clergy moved away from constitutional and towards 'revolutionary' politics, their journey made easier by de Valera's brilliant ability to genuflect to the church while still reassuring his more militant colleagues that renewed violence could not be long delayed. At the 1918 elections the Parliamentary Party left many seats, especially in the South-West, uncontested because it could see that in such areas the priests were no longer to be relied upon (Miller 1973: 393–4, 424). More generally the undoubted social conservatism of Sinn Fein defused fears that revolution might spill over into matters the church was determined to keep uncontaminated by radical change.

By 1919 the episcopal chorus in favour of the new order was swelling to a greater sonority as Bishop Fogarty of Killaloe praised the 'young men of my diocese who belong to Sinn Fein' for being 'most exemplary in attending to their religious duties and living good, Christian lives' (Larkin 1975b: 1272). As guerrilla war became widespread the bishops' language in condemning atrocities was usually fierce in relation to government and bland in relation to republican incidents. In October 1920 the hierarchy issued a statement likening the behaviour of the crown forces to 'the horrors of Turkish atrocities' and the 'outrages attributed to the Red Army in Bolshevist Russia'. Even Bishop Cohalan of Cork's famous excommunication of December 1920 applied to both sides and grew out of real personal despair at the anarchy of his diocese rather than from any animus against Sinn Fein as such (Keogh 1986: 49–51, 60–1). If cautious to the end, the hierarchy still refused de Valera's pleas fully to endorse the 'republic', few that had ears to hear and eyes to see could any longer doubt where its sympathies and those of the clergy generally had come to rest.

Of course there was a good deal of calculation in all this as the church exhibited its customary skill in providing retrospective benediction for revolutionary violence and did so on this occasion with considerably greater expedition than before. It would, however, be wrong to see the clergy's move to Sinn Fein as based solely on a 'canny adulation of success'. Many priests shared a genuine disgust concerning the Parliamentary Party, a fear of socialism if Sinn Fein were not allowed its head, a fellow feeling with rebel dreams, and a gratitude to the revolutionaries for 'adopting the terminology if not the principles of the Gospels' (Fitzpatrick 1977: 140; Larkin 1964). But whatever the motivation, the church, by its success in making last-minute political adjustments, ensured that its prominent role in the Irish moral and cultural firmament would be securely protected for the future.

Social changes, such as the post-Famine apotheosis of the farmer, cultural changes, such as a decline in the 'magical' beliefs of the countryside, economic changes, such as those which made possible a growth in clerical incomes, had all combined to provide a framework within which the fruits of ecclesiastical reform could the more easily be harvested. But if in cultural terms much had changed, in the sphere of politics the clergy's experience was marked by a recurrent oscillation between the extremes of rudderless independence and effective attachment to and constriction by the powerful lay forces led by O'Connell, Parnell, and Sinn Fein (Gilley 1988). What had undoubtedly become more and more evident was the increasingly confessional nature of Irish life as a whole. And this was something to which the Protestant communities contributed with similar, if not always identical, zeal. Indeed, Protestant clergymen often proved no less prominent in shaping the rhetoric of cultural and political distinctiveness than their Catholic counterparts. Small wonder, therefore, that, when the advent of partition after the Anglo-Irish Treaty of 1921 forced both Catholics and Protestants to share in defeat as well as in victory, in minority as well as in majority status, it finally became apparent that even the most ruthless harvesting and the most relentless use of sectarian chemicals had entirely failed to prevent a universal accumulation of nettles amidst the corn.

NOTE

1. In the original five-tier 1855 classification of the most expensive red Bordeaux wines Margaux was one of the four first growths while the three Léovilles (Lascases, Poyferré, and Barton) were assigned to the fourteen-strong group of second growths.

PART THREE

Promised Lands: Ireland since 1921

CHAPTER 7
Politics

An Island Now Formally Divided

If partition represented the least bad and perhaps the only practical policy in the circumstances of the early 1920s it also ensured that many wounds would continue to be available for vituperative display by those in Ireland dedicated to rejecting the proposition that half a loaf is better than no bread. At first, however, it quite failed to occupy the centre of the political stage. There were several reasons for this. In the first place, the border which now separated the six counties of the North-East from the rest of Ireland represented no more than a precise geographical delineation of that deep fault line which had long divided North from South, Protestant from Catholic, unionist from nationalist, and had done so in cultural and social as much as in political terms (Heslinga 1962). In the second place, the chief thrust of the bitter arguments that split the nationalist camp in 1922–3 related to disagreements over sovereignty rather than to the less ethereal matter of partition on which myopia and naive faith in the Boundary Commission provided for in the Treaty persuaded many that in due course a truncated northern statelet would collapse into economic ruin and Ruritanian farce. In the third place, there was the undoubted but unacknowledged fact that partition allowed almost all concerned – pro- and anti-Treaty elements in the South as well as northern unionists, though *not* northern nationalists – to create closed and relatively satisfying environments in which they could feel confident that their prejudices would always fall within the limits of a shared understanding.

As a lowest common denominator, partition suited a far wider range of opinion than would have admitted the fact. Without it northern unionists could not have used their initially unwanted

173

devolution to create a 'Protestant parliament for a Protestant people' (as the first prime minister, Sir James Craig, put it), the earliest Free State administrations could not have operated without effective parliamentary opposition, republicans would have found their stand on the sovereignty issue even more exposed, while the South generally could never have clung with such limpet fidelity to that species of cultural Catholicism which rendered its anti-partitionist aspirations simultaneously extreme and unrealizable. Partition, in other words, allowed many groups to have their cake and to eat it as well: to posture about the wickedness of divisions 'imposed' by Britain while enjoying the psychological, economic, and political comforts which the border provided (O'Halloran 1987). If, in the role of Lazarus at the rich man's gate, northern Catholics and (in a different manner) southern Protestants were, however, denied the self-indulgent mental luxuriance which partition reinforced, like the other Lazarus, Ulster nationalism was to prove itself capable of later resurrections and of returns from the grave which would come to haunt both the enemies and the 'friends' who had once so easily consigned it to the catacombs of political invisibility.

I

The Irish Free State which came into existence soon after the Treaty had been narrowly accepted by the Dail in January 1922 was faced almost immediately with civil war against those who objected to the constitutional compromises reached the previous December, so that little time was available for the formulation of a considered policy towards the North. Its effective head, Michael Collins, at first supplied the IRA in the six counties with weapons in the belief that an ability to resist unionist attack (and in certain areas murderous incidents had been common for some time) outweighed the danger of giving arms to groups containing elements antagonistic to his own Treatyite position. But, as civil war spread in the South, so the affairs of Ulster became increasingly regarded as no more than an irritating side-show to the main business in hand (Fanning 1983: 34–6). After some preliminary limbering up during which both Collins and de Valera made ineffective attempts to keep things from falling entirely apart (Williams 1966) a curious pause ensued in the shape of the 'pact' election of June 1922 when both sides agreed to allow incumbents a clear run. The result reflected widespread popular support for the Treaty: the republicans (who refused to sit in the new lower house) were reduced to 36 out of 128, the formal pro-Treaty group numbered 58, while the remainder (who had not participated in the pact) took their seats as Labour, Farmer, or Independent deputies (Gallagher 1979).

Strengthened by the additional public legitimacy the election had conferred and prodded repeatedly by the British (Towey 1980) the Free State authorities eventually decided to crush the anti-Treaty elements of the IRA which had since April occupied the Four Courts in the centre of Dublin. With borrowed British artillery this was rapidly achieved amidst the simultaneous destruction of Ireland's rich official archives housed in the adjacent Public Records Office – a loss that did not, however, prevent the new state from clinging tightly to the bureaucratic procedures developed in colonial times.

In military terms the civil war hovered uneasily between personal tragedy and strategic farce. In August 1922 Collins, the towering genius on the government side, was killed in an ambush only ten days after his colleague, Griffith, had died of a stroke. Their deaths not only removed two of the chief negotiators of the Treaty settlement but also severed the close links which Collins's multi-faceted abilities had maintained between the conduct of political and military affairs. William Cosgrave – 'I've been pushed into this. I'm not a leader of men' (Ervine 1949: 480) – succeeded as head of the provisional government and in December 1922 became president of the Executive Council (i.e. prime minister) but left everyday military affairs to others. On the republican side, however, it was precisely de Valera's lack of a military role which rendered his position peculiarly difficult because, by the time he came round to reconstituting a 'government' in October, there was not much left for him to govern and the IRA (its pro-Treaty members having departed for the new Free State army) showed little deference to anything but its own commanders. Though the republican forces did not abandon the field until May 1923 their defeat had been inevitable from the start. Poorly equipped and on the whole poorly led, they entirely failed to evoke that measure of support which had kept the struggle against the British alive between 1919 and 1921. The church and the press were overwhelmingly hostile and so – as far as one can judge – were most of their fellow citizens. Although probably no more than 600 of 700 deaths resulted from the civil war (Murphy 1975: 58) the harvest that followed was bitter indeed and helped to divide nationalist politics and society in deep and obstinate ways.

The years immediately after the civil war were marked on the victorious side by doggedly successful efforts to ensure that the governmental procedures of the new state should be distinguished by continuity rather than experimentation. Admittedly a written constitution was adopted and the nomenclature of offices and office holders underwent certain striking alterations. However, little of this affected more than the brass plates on the doors and the heart of the machine continued to beat to the rhythms of Whitehall (Barrington 1967; Fanning 1986b). In particular, the Department of Finance's success in achieving Treasury-like dominance meant that the mighty banner of cheese-paring probity soon came to constitute the Free State's most authentic and revealing heraldic device (Fanning 1978). It was, indeed, attempts to curtail expenditure and demobilize the inflated forces of the civil war that led in 1924 to the so-called 'army mutiny' during which a number of officers dressed up their worries about pay, promotion, and jobs in principled persiflage concerning the abandonment of Collins's ideals (Valiulis 1983). Their comparatively easy defeat not only allowed the Minister for Home Affairs, Kevin O'Higgins, to emerge as the government's man of iron but strengthened the ascendancy of a new civilian leadership over the old fighters who had been out with Collins between 1919 and 1921. Apart, however, from the young O'Higgins, whose caustic tongue and grim aptitude for taking the hardest of lines during the civil war (when firing squads executed seventy-seven IRA men and many others were jailed without trial) shed a certain magnetic fascination over his activities, the Free State ministers were so immersed in the agonizing task of holding the new polity together that their natural lack of charisma was allowed to flourish unchecked. Nor did either O'Higgins's laconic insistence that 'the ceasing of the bailiff to function is the first sign of a crumbling civilization' (Lyons 1971: 482) endear the cabinet to those many Irishmen who had got into the habit of presuming that it would prove possible to combine peaceful stability with the laxer financial disciplines of rebellion and unrest.

Despite manifold difficulties Cosgrave's administration did more than simply survive, though it never lost the ability to ensure that its failures and parsimonies were remembered long after its achievements had been forgotten. When in 1925 newspaper leaks indicated that the Boundary Commission was not going to hand over large parts of Northern Ireland Cosgrave moved rapidly to defuse the situation by patching up an agreement with London and at least obtaining some cash for acquiescing in the inevitable.

As if to compensate for such humiliations the government tried hard to disguise its essentially grey political image by adopting a messianic cultural policy, especially as regards the revival of the Irish language. Irish became compulsory in schools, required for the civil service, some of the professions and certain university appointments, and all at the hands of an administration led by a man who delivered his official St Patrick's Day greetings with the help of phonetic cards without which he could not even have pronounced the language he did not know (O'Callaghan 1984; Ó Cuív 1966).

The problems facing de Valera were in many respects greater still in that his opponents could at least propose and dispose over a real ministry. Already in August 1923 he was beginning to embark upon that pilgrimage of power which was to mark the next stage of his career when he expressed his distaste for those who saw 'principles where they do not really exist' (O'Neill 1976: 157). At another general election in 1923 the republicans (who had appropriated the title Sinn Fein) were again defeated, though the very fact of their putting up candidates at all seemed to betoken a reluctance to remain entirely aloof. However, they still refused to take their seats in the Dail which continued to be composed of Cosgrave's party (now formally launched as Cumann na nGaedheal – Band of the Gaels) and a 'loyal' opposition of Labour, Farmers, and Independents.

What kept the republicans out was the requirement that all deputies (Teachta Dala or TDs) take an oath declaring faithfulness to George V 'in virtue of the common citizenship of Ireland with Great Britain and her adherence to and membership of the group of nations forming the British Commonwealth of Nations'. But, though the oath seemed an insurmountable barrier, few republicans could have been entirely unaware that de Valera's own record as guardian of the sacred flame had never lacked either cloudiness or ambiguity. In particular, his position during the Treaty debates, when he had produced alternative proposals known as Document No 2, had been far from intransigent and in many ways closer to the framework accepted by Collins than to the ideal of an independent republic (McMahon 1984: 13). Again, de Valera – however aloof his behaviour sometimes appeared – never shared in that contempt for the 'undeserving' mass of the people which has from time to time constituted so marked a feature of irreconcilable republicanism (Garvin 1986b: 493–4; Bishop and Mallie 1987: 32). His imprisonment without trial under emergency legislation from

August 1923 to July 1924 allowed extreme elements to assert themselves and in November 1925 – under the shock of the Boundary Commission fiasco – the IRA formally declared itself free from political (i.e. de Valera's) control. The next year de Valera called an extraordinary meeting of Sinn Fein to discuss a motion that, if the oath were removed 'it becomes a question not of principle but of policy whether or not Republican representatives' should enter the Dail (O'Neill 1976: 168). When this failed to secure unambiguous acceptance he immediately resigned as president and, at the urging of one of his closest lieutenants, Sean Lemass, established a new party named Fianna Fail (Warriors of Destiny or Soldiers of Ireland) to provide a more pragmatic focus for those who opposed the government but were still reluctant to participate in parliamentary affairs.

The general election of June 1927 was a crucial test of strength, not so much between Cosgrave and his republican opponents as between Fianna Fail and Sinn Fein. The result could not have been more decisive. Among the outgoing deputies twenty-three had stayed with Sinn Fein and twenty-two had joined the new party. Now the latter doubled its size to forty-four while the former collapsed to a humiliating rump of five. Although Cumann na nGaedheal also did badly (dropping from sixty-three seats to forty-seven) the question as to whether it could continue in power against the existing 'constitutional' opposition was overtaken by the dramatic murder of O'Higgins on 10 July 1927 (probably by an IRA splinter group) and the reintroduction of fierce emergency legislation outlawing the IRA, setting up military courts, and requiring candidates to declare before being nominated their willingness, if elected, to take the oath. This last provision – Cosgrave's greatest gift to the preservation of democracy in Ireland – changed everything and accelerated Fianna Fail's entry into the Dail.

In August de Valera marched towards the parliament building and led his deputies past the squat statue of Queen Victoria which dominated the forecourt until the late 1940s. On being shown the book which contained the oath and required signature de Valera – having first removed the Bible to the far end of the room – solemnly tried to wash away the dirt by telling the clerk (in Irish) that

> I wish to inform you that I am not going to take an oath or to give any promise of allegiance to the King of England or to any other power apart from the Irish people. I am putting my name here to obtain permission to enter among the deputies elected by the Irish

people. Understand that there is no other meaning in what I am doing (Grogan 1967: 165).

However humiliating, such incantations were unavoidable given the strait-jacket into which de Valera had tied himself and necessary too as a mantra with which to ward off the evil eye of republican extremism. And while Sinn Fein rapidly faded away from any proximity to power de Valera was slow to kick down the ladder by which he himself had climbed to prominence. Fianna Fail continued for a time to march in the same parades as the IRA and in 1929 de Valera (using words that were to haunt him for many years) declared that those republicans who still remained in the 'Organization' could 'claim exactly the same continuity that we claimed up to 1925' (Nowlan 1967: 15). Sean Lemass too still found it politic to answer the pertinent question whether Fianna Fail was or was not a 'constitutional' party with the unforgettable apophthegm that it was in fact 'a slightly constitutional' one (Lyons 1971: 495). But as the new departure started to bring home the political bacon so the warriors of the slightly constitutional began to place less stress on the qualifying adverb and more upon the adjective unadorned.

Fianna Fail's entry into the Dail and the uncertain results of June 1927 made another election in September unavoidable. From this both of the main parties benefited at the expense of the smaller groupings, though Cosgrave was, in the event, only able to continue in power with the increasingly precarious support of a shrinking Farmers Party and a fissiparous collection of Independents. Amidst the death-wish that seems to have over-come the Cumann na nGaedheal administration in its final years many undoubted achievements are easily overlooked. Greatest by far was making constitutionalism work at all and taking the risk of subjecting the military to civilian control and introducing an unarmed police force (in sharp contrast to what was happening in the North). In Commonwealth affairs Cosgrave's governments also proved a creative influence by helping to reshape the formal and informal relationships between Britain and the 'empire' so as to render London more a Constantinople than a Rome (Harkness 1969: 256). Land purchase legislation too was extended while important innovations were made in setting up what became known as 'semi-state bodies' to provide electricity (a large hydro-electric plant was built on the Shannon in the 1920s) and supply reliable credit to the farming community.

Much of this was, however, overwhelmed by the memorable acts

179

of meanness for which Cumann na nGaedheal became notorious. Cutting teachers' salaries by ten per cent in 1923 and reducing the old-age pension from ten to nine shillings a week in 1924 (the Minister of Finance would have preferred eight) were among the most striking examples. Memorable too was the announcement by another minister in the latter year that, with only limited funds available, 'people may have to die in the country and die through starvation' (Fanning 1983: 100). Reshaping the Commonwealth buttered few parsnips among the poorer farmers of the West who beheld a government closely allied to grazier interests and believed that free trade benefited only the biggest agricultural battalions. Fianna Fail – in a curious reversal considering the prominence of Griffith (the great apostle of autarky) on the Free State side – adopted the cause of protective tariffs and increased its popularity as the great depression of the late 1920s gathered pace. In addition, de Valera's party had, from the beginning, devoted itself to building up an effective organization, in sharp contrast to Cumann na nGaedheal whose leaders remained indifferent to the very notion that they should soil their hands in cultivating anything as soil-encrusted as grass roots.

II

Depression brought with it renewed activity outside parliament. The IRA became for a time radicalized and a new socialist republican movement, Saor Eire, demanded 'an independent revolutionary leadership for the working class and working farmers towards the overthrow in Ireland of British imperialism and its ally, Irish capitalism' (Nowlan 1967: 16–17). This was a programme notably fiercer than the usually mild lucubrations of the trade union orientated Labour Party (and Irish trade unionism was, in any case, riven by disputes between pragmatists and derring-doers) which until 1927 had constituted the chief and generally genteel opposition in the Dail. In 1931 the government declared a host of organizations (including Saor Eire and the IRA) unlawful and tried its best to remain in power by increasingly intense efforts to mount a 'red scare'. But the depression and de Valera's judicious interweaving of nationalism with promises of a more equitable social order allowed him to form a Fianna Fail administration with unofficial Labour support after the general election of February 1932.

The comfortable classes expected the skies to fall in as red republicans led by the archfiend himself turned the world upside down. But as usual the comfortable classes had got it wrong. After a few brisk genuflections to the gods who had blessed the last months of his progress to power – a pensions bill, reductions in ministerial salaries, the release of some prisoners convicted under Cosgrave's recent legislation – de Valera concentrated upon the quest which had always constituted and was always to constitute the core of his politics, namely, the quest for sovereignty. Most other things could happily be allowed to remain the same. There was no slaughter of the Innocents within the civil service, the army, or (with one important exception) the police. The judges were not sent to the salt mines. Just as the Free Staters had in 1922 continued to walk the administrative road laid down by the British, so de Valera continued to walk it too.

In order to counter what they considered Fianna Fail's dalliance with the left and to resist the undoubted violence being used against their meetings significant elements within Cumann na nGaedheal began to exhibit enthusiasm for an Army Comrades Association set up in 1931, which, partly in response to de Valera's remarkable victory at a snap election in January 1933, was more and more obviously decking itself out in some of the trappings of European fascism. In February de Valera dismissed the police chief, Eoin O'Duffy. Within months the latter had become leader of what was now called the National Guard or, in popular parlance, the Blueshirts – black and brown having already been appropriated elsewhere. At its peak some 100,000 were supposed to have joined its ranks: the disgruntled lower middle class, the fearful upper middle class, anxious graziers, plus a handful of genuine eccentrics from the groves of academe and the pastures of literature (Manning 1970). The tone-deaf W. B. Yeats composed unsingable marching songs and instructed a bewildered O'Duffy in the mysteries of Spengler and Hegel. Professor Michael Tierney of University College Dublin informed the public that it was 'a complete mistake to suppose that Italian Fascism is merely a crude individual or party dictatorship', while a more humble supporter urged his fellows to greet their leader with shouts of 'Heil', 'pronounced sharply', or, better still, with shouts of 'Hoch' (Thornley 1967). Much of this was mere confusion and reflected an interest in the curiosities of contemporary papal corporatism as much as in the wilder shores of fascism *pur sang*. Nonetheless, Cumann na nGaedheal's real sense of desperation was revealed when, in September 1933, it actually

181

merged with the National Guard to form the United Ireland Party (soon to be better known as Fine Gael) with the increasingly dotty O'Duffy at the helm. After a brief interlude the putative man of iron was, however, obliged to resign and in 1935 normal service was resumed under Cosgrave's leadership, O'Duffy helpfully departing for Spain at the head of a pro-Franco Irish Brigade.

Although in retrospect the episode was not lacking in comedy it was serious enough at the time. Above all it demonstrated the bankruptcy of Cumann na nGaedheal while not in any serious way impeding de Valera's solemn progress towards the dismantlement of the Treaty settlement. And with protectionism bringing about a so-called 'economic war' with Britain Fianna Fail was able to play the patriotic card more effectively than ever before. Over the next few years the oath disappeared, the governor general was reduced to a cipher, appeals to the judicial committee of the privy council in London were brought to an end, the crown was effectively taken out of the constitution, and the second chamber – the Senate, which, though weak, had long proved a thorn in de Valera's side – was abolished.

The firmer he was settled in the saddle the more confident did de Valera become in dealing with the IRA and he skilfully used the Blueshirt menace to revive emergency laws which it would otherwise have been difficult to justify. Moreover, by the end of the decade he had, in a series of Anglo-Irish agreements in 1938, settled the economic war and persuaded a previously hostile Neville Chamberlain – 'Mr de Valera's mentality was in some ways like Herr Hitler's. It was no use employing with them the arguments which appealed to the ordinary, reasonable man' (Harkness 1983: 57) – that the Treaty ports should be handed over to the Dublin government. Chamberlain was not, however, as Churchill declared, recklessly abandoning vital defence facilities because, as the British cabinet well realized, the dangers of trying to render the ports operative 'if war broke out would be exactly the same as if they had been returned to the Irish government without securing an assurance about access' (McMahon 1984: 29).

By then too de Valera had already summarized and codified the changes undertaken since first coming to power by means of a new constitution adopted in 1937. This turned the Free State into a republic in all but name and rendered the British and Commonwealth connection little more than an insignificant convenience, though the sacred word itself was omitted because partition still survived and because of worries about what might happen to the large Irish community in Britain. London regarded Eire – now the official Irish language name for the South – as still in the Commonwealth. De Valera believed rather that his old project of 'external association' had at last been realized. It suited both to leave it at that.

Ireland now had a president – the old Protestant Gaelic Leaguer, Douglas Hyde. The head of government was gaelicized into the Taoiseach and the senate was restored, though in an even more powerless condition than before. Two aspects of the constitution deserve particular attention. The first is its now-you-see-it-now-you-don't juxtaposition of articles 2 and 3. The former announced that the 'national territory consists of the whole island of Ireland, its islands and the territorial seas', the latter, more pragmatically, that 'pending the reintegration of the national territory' the con-stitution applied only to the twenty-six counties – a classic case of causing maximum annoyance to northern unionists for minimum returns from southern irreconcilables (Bowman 1982: 148–50). Such irritations were not reduced by the strongly Catholic ethos of the document as a whole and in particular article 44 which declared that 'the state recognizes the special position of the Holy Catholic Apostolic and Roman Church as the guardian of the faith professed by the great majority of the citizens' while also 'recognizing' the major Protestant churches and 'other religious denominations existing in Ireland at the date of the coming into operation of this constitution'.

Few at the time realized how much of a compromise the document was. The word republic was omitted. Senior Catholic churchmen would have liked something a good deal stronger than article 44 (Keogh 1986: 208–20). The senate had not been permanently abolished. The corporatist notions then so busily being canvassed in ecclesiastical and intellectual circles obtained no more than a few verbal salutes (Lee 1979a). The fact that the whole business aroused comparatively little controversy at the time reflected perhaps, not simply the myopic sense of Catholic triumphalism which infected all major political groups in the South, but also a shrewd realization that the constitution did no more than encapsulate something which all already knew to be the case. But even if this was true and even though de Valera undoubtedly *believed* his policies towards northern Protestants to be conciliatory and generous, they in turn saw him in a very different light. And, in any case, gracious admissions that unionists too were 'fundamentally Irish' were constantly being annulled by a dogged insistence that their continued Irishness depended upon renouncing unionism and opting for 'Irish' citizenship instead (Bowman 1982: 317–18).

If partition had always been one of de Valera's pivotal preoccupations, the settlement of his other constitutional priorities in the 1930s meant that it was made to stand forth even more single-mindedly upon his mental horizons. Both then and during the war he seldom refrained from pointing out to British representatives that so long as the border remained Anglo-Irish relations could never be regarded as normal (McMahon 1984: 288, 293; Carroll 1975: 53). Paradoxically, however, it was the very existence of that border which, together with the return of the Treaty ports, allowed de Valera to enter upon his finest hour: the declaration and maintenance of neutrality during the Second World War – or the 'Emergency' as it was officially known in the South (Nowlan and Williams 1969).

Had the Allies not been able to use naval and other bases in Northern Ireland or, indeed, had they been able to use the Treaty ports, neutrality could hardly have survived. What, therefore, the hated border gave de Valera the opportunity of doing was to unite the southern population behind him (for almost all supported neutrality) and thus turn himself from merely a brilliant politician into a national leader. It was not so much that all was forgiven. Many still distrusted him with undiminished rancour. But for the public at large the emergency placed de Valera securely in a special category of his own. Already legends had grown up about his ascetic abstemiousness ('for his evening meal, for example, he took nothing except a cup of black tea') and El Greco features ('Tall as a spear, commanding, enigmatic, his eyes so dark and deep that it is difficult to see their expressions') heightened by a liking for long black cloaks and remarkable wide-brimmed black hats (McMahon 1984: 16, 42). Already too de Valera's sympathy for the anti-materialist strand in Irish nationalism had been displayed with metronomic regularity. Now, in time of war, the failure of his administrations to achieve more than modest improvements in prosperity and social welfare (Murphy 1975: 87), the losses some had suffered during the 'economic war', the dissatisfaction of small farmers at the pace of land redistribution (Ó Tuathaigh 1982), though not dissipated, were rendered less prominent by a more immediate and universal predicament.

It seems almost as if de Valera rejoiced that an enforced austerity had arrived. In a famous wireless address for St Patrick's

Day 1943 he described the 'Ireland which we dreamed of' as one that

> would be the home of a people who valued material wealth as the basis of right living, of a people who are satisfied with frugal comfort and devoted their leisure to the things of the spirit – a land whose countryside would be bright with cosy homesteads, whose fields and villages would be joyous with the sound of industry, with the romping of sturdy children, the contests of athletic youths and the laughter of comely maidens, whose firesides would be the forums of wisdom and serene old age. It would, in a word, be the home of a people living the life that God desires that man should live (Gallagher 1985a: 38).

Although it has proved easy to ridicule such sentiments and to contrast them with many of the actions of him who spoke them, they were, in truth, neither ignoble nor mean of spirit. Certainly no other European statesman of his generation – save perhaps the equally enigmatic de Gaulle who also believed that he had only to look into his heart to see what his people desired – could have presented them as a serious contribution to public political discourse in the modern age (Prager 1986: 63).

Draconian wartime emergency powers enabled de Valera to crush those elements in the IRA which wanted, with more fervour than efficiency, to replay the old tune that 'England's difficulty was Ireland's opportunity' (Longford and O'Neill 1970: 347–68). Censorship, more rigid even than in Britain, allowed the government to maintain a stance of scrupulous equal-handedness between the belligerents while privately leaning overwhelmingly towards the allied side and more and more overwhelmingly as German victories receded into oblivion. Allied planes were allowed to fly over Irish air space, German submarine activity reports handed over, weather forecasts supplied, wireless direction-finding aids made available to allied aircraft, joint staff talks held on the question of co-operation against possible German invasion, allied personnel washed ashore or parachuted on to neutral soil quietly sent up to Belfast, and much more besides (Fanning 1983: 124–5; Fisk 1983: 282–3).

To many in Britain and to the unionists of the North de Valera's lop-sided neutrality remained hidden or despised or both. With liberty's back against the wall in 1939–41 it seemed to them that Catholic Ireland had merely weaseled its way into a dishonest and parasitical invulnerability. Remembered were the IRA's dalliance with the Nazis and above all de Valera's famous call on the German minister in Dublin to express his condolences at the death of Hitler in May 1945. Churchill, who might have known better, could not stop himself, even in his victory speech, from congratulating 'His Majesty's Government' on having refrained from invading 'Eire' and having left 'the Dublin Government to frolic with the Germans and later with the Japanese representatives to their heart's content'. It was de Valera's broadcast reply to this outburst which finally confirmed his standing as a national figure without equal in Ireland. Calm and restrained he praised Britain's 'stand alone, after France had fallen and before America entered the war' and went on to ask Churchill

> Could he not find in his heart the generosity to acknowledge that there is a small nation that stood alone, not for one year or two, but for several hundred years against aggression; that endured spoiliations, famines, massacres in endless succession; that was clubbed many times into insensitivity, but that each time on returning [to] consciousness, took up the fight anew; a small nation that could never be got to accept defeat and has never surrendered her soul? (Carroll 1975: 163–5)

Of course these words represented a particular interpretation of Irish history. But the spontaneous gathering of crowds around the radio station even before de Valera had finished speaking to cheer him as he left and the many congratulations given throughout the next days show that it was an interpretation with a very general resonance throughout nationalist Ireland. In its romantic language and emphasis upon the ultimate power of David over Goliath it is an interpretation which cannot, it seems, be denied a grip upon the imagination. That it helped to create a widespread response to de Valera's words in 1945 is undoubted. That it still operates so powerfully upon the public mind is at once the strength and the tragedy of nationalist Ireland's imprisonment within a special version of the past.

III

Just as the 'Emergency' finally confirmed the South's sovereignty and independence so the war rendered Northern Ireland's place within the United Kingdom secure. It had not been so to begin with. An irredentist neighbour to the south, the general hostility of that Catholic third of the population largely opposed to partition, and a good deal of disapproval from not unimportant elements in British political life gave six-county governments a sense of beleaguerment and obduracy. Sir James Craig (Viscount Craigavon from 1927) remained prime minister until his death in November 1940. Although himself neither excessively narrow of mind nor lacking in ability, the hot-house atmosphere within which his administrations operated made it tempting to ride the sectarian tiger for all it was worth (Buckland 1980). The crucial difference between South and North was of course that, whereas the Protestant minority in the former was too small to matter, the Catholic minority in the six counties was substantial, resentful, and potentially disruptive. From the narrow perspective of unionist triumphalism Craig's relentless success in winning handsome majorities at all five general elections between 1921 and 1938 and seeing to it that his own 'people' consistently enjoyed a psychological and often also an economic place in the sun were no more than reflections of the natural order of things. In a wider view they were deeply divisive and potentially dangerous.

The Free State may not have been the home of abundant administrative talent, yet its leading politicians and bureaucrats between the wars were giants when compared with all but a handful of their counterparts in the North. Again and again the necessity of pandering to the wishes of the extreme unionists meant that other noses were quite unnecessarily rubbed in the dirt. The system of proportional representation which the British had insisted upon as a means of protecting minority interests was abolished in local (1922) and parliamentary (1929) elections – to no great purpose save the gaining of a handful of additional local authorities (Buckland 1981: 52; Lyons 1971: 684, 707; Whyte 1983a). Sir Basil Brooke (later Viscount Brookeborough), who became prime minister in 1943, expressed what many believed, when, in the 1930s, he sadly admitted that 'There are a great number of Protestants and Orangemen who employ Roman Catholics. I feel I can speak freely on this subject as I have not an RC about my own place . . . I would appeal to loyalists, therefore, whenever possible, to employ good Protestant lads and lasses' (Darby 1976: 147). And on both sides of the border classified newspaper advertisements revealed the great mystery that some lawns demanded cutting only by Protestant gardeners and that many objects of common use – carpets, sofas, linen, and so forth – clamoured for similarly sectarian attention. It was of course the imperatives of demography which rendered the northern examples dangerous instead of merely shameful and helped to turn the six counties into what one contemporary has called a 'factory of grievances' (Buckland 1979: 1).

One thing can, however, be said in favour of unionist polemics, namely, that, while much energy was put into rebutting charges of discrimination, little was wasted upon positive claims of angelic fair-mindedness. By contrast, nationalists in the South have always been driven by some inner compulsion to descant without end upon how two of their presidents have been Protestants, how Dublin once had a Jew as lord mayor, how thirteen fire engines were sent to Belfast during the Blitz, how, indeed, in some hidden and subcutaneous way, all Irishmen are the same – as the Belfast riots of 1932, when all denominations took to the streets in protest against benefit cuts (Campbell 1967), are again and again held to have shown. But such molehill peaks of togetherness stand out merely because of the flatness of the surrounding countryside. Douglas Hyde may have become president in 1938 but the service held in St Patrick's Church of Ireland Cathedral to mark his inauguration took place without the attendance of the Catholic taoiseach, Eamon de Valera, who, some years before, had told the Dail that 'if I had a vote on a local body, and there were two qualified people who had to deal with a Catholic community [as, for example, librarians], and if one was a Catholic and the other a Protestant, I would unhesitatingly vote for the Catholic' (Whyte 1975: 101, 109).

Though none can reasonably claim that the minorities North and South were treated with similar harshness, both Catholics and Protestants found it an easy matter to retain unflattering perceptions of how the other actually behaved. The whole ethos of the two states constantly drove home the immutability of local superiorities and inferiorities. In the South, censorship, laws against divorce and contraception, the introduction of compulsory Irish, in the North, the official role of the Orange Order in Unionist Party circles and discrimination in public employment, electoral practices, and policing, all in their different ways announced who was in charge. And just as southern Protestants felt abandoned by Britain and Ulster, so did the much larger Catholic community in the North rightly perceive that, after an initial flurry, Dublin wanted to have as little to do with it as possible (O'Halloran 1987: 57–92).

In general and unsurprisingly things were rawer in the North where men and women continued to be killed in sectarian riots and where state power was used far more openly in favour of those who controlled the bureaucracy, the government, and the police. But the circumambient cultures often functioned in almost indistinguishable ways. The same kind of parsimonious conservatism characterized all of Ireland until well after the Second World War, while the Catholic puritanism of the South bore certain remarkable similarities to the Protestant puritanism of the North. Unionists might often denounce the clericalism of southern society (while happily allowing two Presbyterian clergymen to join Brooke's cabinet of 1943), yet, save in rhetorical usage, all but a handful shared that same clericalism's reactions to dirty books and films and (especially in earlier years) to contraception and divorce as well. If anything, Protestants stressed 'respectability' with greater fervour and, notwithstanding all the denunciations of Dublin's laws on moral questions, were deeply suspicious of the secularism and laxness evident elsewhere in the United Kingdom.

Almost as pressing for the early political leaders in Belfast as simple survival and the maintenance of unionist superiority were the problems created by the six counties' feeble economy. In theory the North was supposed to pay for the many services still supplied on a United Kingdom basis by means of an annual 'imperial contribution'. By 1934–5 hard times had reduced this to a derisory £24,000 and Northern Ireland seemed to be approaching the condition of a rentier state (Johnson 1985a: 8). Not only, however, did such things create violent disagreements within the upper echelons of government in Belfast, but they also revealed how dependence on Britain could be used by pragmatic politicians to suspend the laws of classical economics. Thus, while finance ministers in Belfast argued firmly for retrenchment and tried 'to press the state along a *via Britannica* of a pre-Keynesian kind', an ultimately victorious group around Craig adopted an unashamedly populist line according to which substantial expenditure of public funds was essential if the pan-Protestant appeal of unionism was to be maintained (Bew, Gibbon and Patterson 1979: 76–82). In this matter, as in not a few others, it was Dublin that proved the more faithful disciple of Whitehall.

Such disputes were, however, generally hidden from public view, while the attacks of maverick unionists at elections and other times, though irritating and not without result, were regularly defused by either the old policy of assimilation or the new one of financial largesse. Ulster's constitutional nationalists provided vapid opposition and acted in the Stormont parliament (so called after the completion of its architecturally domineering buildings in 1932) more as individuals than members of an organized group when, that is, they were not looking anxiously over their shoulders to see what the more extreme republicans were up to. Labour proved even more divided than in the South and socialist candidates fought elections under an almost Heinzian variety of banners designed to appeal to different sectarian groups in different constituencies. Unionism, in short, had little difficulty in maintaining the pan-class alliance which had been both its chief strength and the major constraint upon its manoeuvrability since the middle of the nineteenth century.

When the war broke out in 1939 Craig was an old and tired man. Not long after declaring staunch support for an embattled Britain – 'We are King's men, and we shall be with you to the end' – he was dead. J. M. Andrews, the long-standing heir apparent, proved neither popular nor effective and was replaced in 1943 by Sir Basil Brooke who then remained in office for twenty unbroken years. While the war proved predictably dismal and air raids on Belfast exposed both the city's puny defences and the low morale of its inhabitants, victory, when it came, yielded rich fruit in the shape of yet further financial subsidies to bring Northern Ireland into line with post-war British social reforms and implicit – and later explicit – recognition from London that the six counties had now fully worked their passage as an integral part of the United Kingdom.

IV

The North's constitutional position was, in the event, rendered even more secure by developments in the 'other' Ireland now greeting the post-war world with pent-up economic expectations, strikes, rising prices, and bad harvests. Although wartime metamorphosis may have transformed de Valera into a special kind of political being, yet, as in the case of Churchill, not all his fellow citizens believed that the man for the emergency was necessarily also the man for the peace. There were even signs that Fine Gael, for years the somnambulist of Irish politics, was beginning to stir itself (Gallagher 1978: 6), while the foundation in 1946 of a new party called Clann na Poblachta (Family of the Republic) under the leadership of a former IRA chief of staff, Sean MacBride, meant that at last Fianna Fail was faced with a 'constitutional' group able and willing to play the green card with more energy than itself.

To say that Fianna Fail was disturbed is an understatement. As de Valera called a snap election in 1948 in an effort to prevent the Clann from consolidating itself his lieutenants desperately denounced MacBride's 'pseudo-Communist and Fascist philosophy' (Gallagher 1985a: 110–14). They almost succeeded: Fine Gael actually fell back and with 19.8 per cent of the vote notched up its worst result ever, while MacBride, with ten seats, did less well than his more sanguine supporters had anticipated. Yet, in triumphant vindication of the mighty axiom that many of the most important political turning-points are sharpened in smoke-filled rooms, the jumbled collection of parties which shared only a sincere desire to dethrone Fianna Fail managed to coalesce and form the first so-called inter-party government. This curious construct consisted of the traditionally conservative Fine Gael, the new green radical Clann na Poblachta, a recently formed party representing small farmers called Clann na Talmhan, two separate Labour parties, plus a majority of the dozen independents returned by an electorate determined to spread its favours in all directions. John A. Costello of Fine Gael emerged as taoiseach because that party's leader, Richard Mulcahy, proved unacceptable to MacBride's republican sensitivities. In the event, the government functioned as well as it did more because of inter-locking family, educational, and temperamental affinities among its more important members than because of anything so mundane as agreement over aims and policies (Fanning 1983: 165).

The two things for which Costello's government is best remembered are, first, its declaration of a republic in 1948 and, second (for which see Chapter 9), its climb-down when faced with ecclesiastical opposition over a scheme for providing medical treatment to mothers and children introduced by its Minister of Health. The former was perhaps the more bizarre, though not the more interesting, of the two. MacBride had long wanted to repeal the External Relations Act of 1936 by which de Valera had neatly placed the Free State into a limbo-like relationship with Britain, but Fine Gael of course represented a tradition quite opposed to forward movement on such matters. The precise background is still unclear but so much confusion surrounded the decision that the intended declaration was first made public by Costello on a visit to Canada. While some reacted as if Savonarola had proclaimed his support for free love, in practical terms it did not amount to very much. Indeed, as de Valera rather unkindly pointed out, Costello was merely acknowledging that the state existing 'under the 1937 constitution' had really been a republic all along (Fanning 1983: 175).

Belfast, however, quickly demanded that London produce new and stronger constitutional guarantees. Attlee's Labour government – by no means the least pro-unionist of British administrations – responded with the famous provision in its Ireland Act of 1949 that 'in no event will Northern Ireland or any part thereof cease to be part of His Majesty's dominions and of the United Kingdom without the consent of the parliament of Northern Ireland' (Fanning 1982a). Although the status of the republic's citizens in Britain remained virtually unchanged – they could work and vote as a matter of course – the Dublin government's expressions of surprise at the vigour of the British response were fully in tune with the dim-sighted insularity that had governed southern attitudes to the North since 1921. There was, for example, little grasp that Costello's declaration was itself almost designed to alienate unionist opinion beyond even its normal condition of simmering paranoia. And just in case anyone might still not have heard the good news both the inter-party government and de Valera's opposition assessed it expedient to mount an international campaign against the evils of partition and the 'Quisling Irish' who supported it (Bowman 1982: 273–6). Indeed, this issue so dominated the foreign policy of the 'new' republic that its continued reiteration upon any and every international platform served both to embarrass Irish diplomats and render Ireland ludicrous abroad, though the refusal to join NATO on the grounds that this would involve alliance with a state 'which supported undemocratic institutions in the north-eastern corner of Ireland' was a more substantial matter (Fanning 1982b). When in 1956 Ireland at last took its seat at the United Nations there followed a more sophisticated period of diplomatic endeavour, even if, in retrospect, an oft-repeated sympathy for ex-colonial third-world countries and involvement in UN peace-keeping operations seem rather less significant than many then supposed (Lyons 1971: 582–7; Keatinge 1973). More recently horizons have narrowed once again and entry into the European Economic Community in 1973 has tended to concentrate minds (and sometimes very effectively so) upon the crucial task of putting as little in and getting as much out as possible.

Elections in 1951 led to the return of de Valera, in 1954 to another inter-party government, and in 1957 again to de Valera, who eventually 'retired' two years later to the presidency leaving Fianna Fail to enjoy another long period in office (until 1973) to match that of 1932–48. The most important developments of these years were in the economic sphere as the classical frugalities of Cosgrave's Cumann na nGaedheal administrations and de Valera's cosy homesteads were abandoned amidst much worship at the Keynesian shrine of demand-led growth. Living standards rose dramatically and certainly Ireland in the 1960s exhibited a confidence and a sense of purposive excitement it had never known before.

Although the new prosperity undoubtedly led to increased slickness on the political front, with mohair suits replacing the 'legendary seatless trousers' as a badge of party authenticity (Murphy 1979b: 9–10), what is most striking about the whole period since the war is not how much but how little has changed as regards the nature of Irish political life. Even those who bewail the advent of a more grasping crudity miss the point that 'materialism' had always been rampant; it now simply became more blatant than before. Admittedly, a hint of the 'rat race syndrome' began to emerge, but that was not 'because there were more rats about. "Traditional" Ireland was crawling with rats. They just couldn't race' (Lee 1979b: 177). More specifically, politics remained to a considerable degree caught within the net of localism, kin relationships, and the reciprocity of favours which had been so marked a feature of the century before independence (Hoppen 1984; Fitzpatrick 1977). Indeed, that parting gift from the British – proportional representation by means of the single transferable vote – ensured that the net would remain in good repair. Under this system all constituencies return at least three (and often more) members and voters are allowed to rank candidates in order of preference and thus in effect to prefer, for example, one Fianna Fail man over another or (more rarely) to mix up party choices amidst a jumble of individual likes and dislikes (Chubb 1982: 350–3; O'Leary 1979). The result has not been to make Ireland a country of weak party ties, quite the reverse, but rather to ensure that very few TDs can ever relax in the knowledge that theirs is a safe seat. By combining a primary along American lines and an election proper in one process the single transferable vote (STV) procedure has kept TDs in a state of constant anxiety lest a rival *within* their own party might emerge to replace them next time round.

For a brief period in the early days of independence the effect of this was disguised by the national prominence which so many fighters for freedom had achieved in the years before 1922. Such men were, therefore, able to represent constituencies with which they had no connection and to eschew that endless round of social work activity which had been required of their Victorian

193

predecessors and was to be even more urgently demanded of those who rose to prominence once the revolutionary generation had died away (Garvin 1972: 360–3; Marsh 1981: 267). As time went on party candidates found it increasingly necessary to carve out particular geographical 'bailiwicks' within which they could then proceed to act as 'grievance men and as intermediaries between local society and central government' (Garvin 1981: 197). In a few places successful TDs actually turned themselves into local bosses of a kind common in the clientelist political systems of underdeveloped countries by, in effect, obtaining direct leverage over the way in which local administration conducts its employment, planning, and contracting functions (Bax 1976). More commonly, however, such men adopted the role of broker rather than patron and acted as 'friends at court', both locally and nationally, for their constituents (Sacks 1976). Certainly almost all backbenchers have spent and still spend the bulk of their time in what has been described as 'going about persecuting civil servants' (Chubb 1963). Ireland's central administration may indeed be apolitical and upright beyond reproach, but the voters as a whole have a consistently low view of public officials and *believe* that only personal contacts and 'pull' will yield swift and favourable results (Collins 1985; Komito 1984; Carty 1983: 23). Partly by choice and partly out of necessity TDs have, therefore, tended to ignore their legislative functions and concentrate on a parochial level of representation (Farrell 1985).

The whole business exhibits, however, not so much the political 'power' of professional politicians, as their increasingly enfeebled dependence upon an electorate which has largely succeeded in making its representatives the victims of a kind of perceptual fraud. Especially in the larger towns even the most active TDs cannot assume that any particular service will automatically be repaid in terms of a vote given at election time. Yet, the performance of such services still remains vital as a means of maintaining a general reputation in the community. If, therefore, power is 'measured by the ability to determine the rules of exchange, then we must question the assumption that politicians have much power', for it would seem that in general it is not they but the voters who 'collectively determine the rules' (Komito 1984: 184).

Within the culture which encourages so particulate and localist an approach to the conduct of everyday politics it has, nonetheless, been possible for strong and cohesive parties to emerge. This, together with the fact that brokerage rather than outright patronage represents the characteristic mode of behaviour for both TDs and party leaders, is what in the end differentiates the Irish case from that of the much stronger clientelism to be found, not only in the 'third world', but also in European countries such as Greece where political parties 'regardless of labels, programs, or other paraphernalia of modernity, merely consist of unstable coalitions of patrons for the conquest of office' (Mavrogordatos 1983: 12). In Ireland, by contrast, the single transferable vote has allowed the electorate to fashion – even more than in earlier times – both parish pump *and* party into the joint totems of political life (Carty 1983).

If the main Irish parties have proved stable they have not, however, been separated from one another by deep differences in ideology or in the social bases of their support (Gallagher 1985a). Indeed, if such things are supposed to rank among the appurtenances of modernity, then Ireland – North as well as South – has not only rejected, but actually moved steadily further and further away from, many of the most important characteristics of political modernism. In no significant sense do either Fianna Fail or Fine Gael represent clearly different elements or 'classes' within society at large (Whyte 1974). Initially they were built upon strongly opposed attitudes to the Treaty of 1921 and, to a considerable extent, this particular disagreement has subsequently achieved almost a life of its own. This does not, however, mean that existing divisions were 'invented' in the 1920s but simply that they were then given the essential form they still retain today. Of course diligent investigators have, at various times, been able to detect other distinctions as well, but these have usually proved transitory or marginal or both. Certainly the better-off sections of society in 1921–2 tended to support the Treaty more than did the less well-to-do. Certainly too Cumann na nGaedheal tended to perform best among large farmers, graziers, and professional people, while de Valera's early appeal was to the poorer men of the West (Whyte 1983b; Rumpf and Hepburn 1977). But over time Fianna Fail turned itself into a brilliantly successful catch-all party appealing, not only to poor farmers, Irish language enthusiasts, and the like, but to almost all sections of the population. Although its chief rival still perhaps retains a more sectional support, occasional 'progressive' lurches by elements within Fine Gael have torpedoed any possibility that party politics might be rearranged on the basis of left versus right (O'Leary 1979: 93–6; Lee 1979b: 176). By splitting over a nationalist rather than a class issue the elite of early-twentieth-century Ireland not only aligned political life firmly to that localism which had long been important but also helped to prefigure those patterns which have subsequently become so characteristic of post-colonial successor states generally (Garvin 1980: 269).

The two leading parties are not of course identical. But the differences between them have rarely been so sharp as to prevent either from making attempts to appeal to a very wide spectrum of opinion and affluence. Nor does the history of Labour, the only other constitutional party to achieve permanence, alter the picture to any significant extent. Although at times – notably in the late 1930s and the late 1960s – it has made noises of a socialist kind, in general its tone has been moderate, reformist, and, in cultural terms, conservative (Gallagher 1985a: 68–92). Indeed, in 1953 a future leader, Brendan Corish, made a statement in the Dail which even some bishops might secretly have found extreme. 'I am', he declared, 'an Irishman second; I am a Catholic first . . . If the Hierarchy gives me any direction with regard to Catholic social teaching or Catholic moral teaching, I accept without qualification in all respects the teaching of the Hierarchy and the Church to which I belong' (*Dail Eireann Parliamentary Debates*, cxxxviii, 840: 29 Apr. 1953).

Although at first little more than the political arm of a splintered trade union movement the Labour Party maintained an electoral presence largely through the good offices of a handful of local political chieftains capable of attracting the votes of agricultural labourers, who, then as before, had gathered no more than crumbs from the nationalist table (Rumpf and Hepburn 1977; Mitchell 1974). And even when, after years of trying, Labour at last managed to gain a foothold in Dublin City, it still remained too small to be able to form a government single-handed and was obliged to enter into coalitions with the larger Fine Gael in 1948, 1954, 1973, 1981, and 1982. Nationally Labour has always occupied third place. Since 1923 its vote has oscillated between 17.0 per cent (1969) and 5.7 per cent (1933). Little wonder that political theorists have sometimes referred to the republic as having a two and a half party system (O'Leary 1979). In fact, up to the mid-1950s (though less so thereafter), the system is more accurately seen as a multi-party one in which Labour had constantly to compete with other groups to retain its number three position. Although such minor parties have covered a wide range of enthusiasms, they have tended to fall into a number of recognizable categories: sectional, like Clann na Talmhan, reincarnations of the old Parliamentary Party, like the National League of the late 1920s, republican, like Clann na

Poblachta, or simply bizarre, like Ailtirí na hAiséirghe (Architects of the Resurrection) which in the early 1940s unsuccessfully put forward a combination of Salazarism, gaelicism, and messianism under the slogan that, 'in co-operation with Divine Providence', it would 'settle the affairs of the universe for another 2000 years' (Gallagher 1985a: 107–9).

In an important sense both the alignments of post-independence Ireland and the manner in which these have been articulated reflect the fact that the two major parties in the South are not only the children of a once united Sinn Fein but the grandchildren of the often disunited Parliamentary Party that preceded it. More generally still, the environment which has helped to make such apostolic successions possible continues to revolve around those local issues which nineteenth-century voters regularly placed at the forefront of political discrimination. Thus, both the candidate who in 1859 announced that his 'politics and principles' were 'all embraced in the advancement of Galway – the erection of a breakwater in its harbour' and his Sligo contemporary who ensured success by obtaining 'appointments for, or otherwise substantially benefiting, a greater number of individuals than compose the present constituency' (Hoppen 1984: 83, 446) would have felt quite comfortable in the shoes of the politician who, a century later, evoked the following newspaper puff.

> He has consistently fought in the Waterford County Council (of which body he has been a member for many years) for amenities for the town, and it was due to his representations that the long-suffering residents of the old road had a foot-path provided in front of their homes to prevent flooding. Also the provision of an extra light at the entrance to Chapel Street and at Tuckey's Corner, and the provision of a public convenience which, through no fault of his, has not yet been erected (Chubb 1963: 277).

V

One of the more notable features of the violence which has so savagely re-entered Irish life since the late 1960s in the shape of the 'troubles' of Northern Ireland is that it has in no sense diminished this kind of concentration upon limited horizons. Not that there is anything inherently despicable (or indeed unique) in the localism which has so long marked the politics of North as much as of South (Buckland 1981: 25–6; Bew, Gibbon and Patterson 1979: 165).

What has, however, been so damaging recently is the manner in which it has coexisted with inspirational and unreal rhetoric from nationalists and unionists alike. Successive Dublin governments, by strengthening those aspects of law, education, and culture which unify the Catholic 'nation', have, in effect, adopted a kind of regional localism, which, despite repeated claims to the contrary, has simply excluded the North from serious consideration. In this they have of course accurately enough reflected that consensus of opinion in the republic which has always wanted to have its cake and eat it too: to indulge traditional nationalist emotions while, in the 'real' world, simultaneously consigning Northern Ireland to the margins of vision and keeping the main chance firmly in view.

Unsurprisingly there have been some who really do place traditional republican concepts at the forefront of their priorities. Yet, until the late 1960s, the majority in both North and South could easily enough believe that the irreconcilables of the IRA had been relegated to the lumber room of history from whence they might occasionally sally forth to irritate – as during the Second World War or when they mounted a military 'campaign' against the North in the 1950s (Coogan 1970; Bowyer Bell 1970) – but could never return to the centre of the stage. Increasing prosperity and the unprecedented meetings in 1965 between de Valera's successor, Sean Lemass, and Brookeborough's successor, Terence O'Neill, seemed to herald the dawn of a new age. Yet, what is most remarkable about these meetings is not the small practical results which flowed from them but the fact that even so modest and late a coming-together should have created so wide and intense an excitement. Also symptomatic of the strait-jacket into which minds on both sides of the border had come to be encased was the way in which O'Neill, though already viewed with distrust by fellow Unionists as a dangerous liberal, was himself quite unable to abandon those deep suspicions of Catholics which had long represented a central part of the Protestant inheritance (Darby 1976: 147). Thus, when, four years after the Lemass meetings, he talked on the wireless about his recent enforced resignation from the premiership, his choice of words revealed the old Adam still lurking beneath the skin. 'It is frightfully hard', he told his listeners,

> to explain to a Protestant that if you give Roman Catholics a good job and a good house they will live like Protestants, because they will see neighbours with cars and TV sets. They will refuse to have eighteen children, but if the Roman Catholic is jobless and lives in a most ghastly

hovel he will rear eighteen children on national assistance (Hepburn 1980: 182).

The immediate background to the removal of the cork from the Ulster bottle in the late 1960s had as much to do with the international growth of the civil rights movement as with anything particularly Irish. Marches by the Civil Rights Association and the more militantly socialist and nationalist People's Democracy in 1968 and 1969 were handled by a government and a police force to whom the arts of presenting a sophisticated response were as foreign as ballet steps to a lumber-jack. In a rapidly changing situation O'Neill and his immediate successor, Chichester-Clark, tried desperately to conciliate Catholics without alienating Protestants, but were ground down in the attempt (Lyons 1971: 748–55). Organized Unionism itself began to crack under the strain as reincarnations of figures familiar to any student of Ulster history trundled out the traditional call of 'No Surrender', most notable among them Ian Paisley, whose opinions, stentorian voice, physical bulk, and political dexterity are eerily reminiscent of nineteenth-century unionist men of God like 'Roaring' Hugh Hanna and Thomas Drew. At the same time all those major as well as petty discriminations from which Catholics had long suffered (Whyte 1983a) were being articulated so loudly that even the self-serving deafness of Westminster was eventually overcome. As sectarian tensions rose so the first of many deaths occurred in July 1969. When in August severe disturbances began in Belfast (which contains the largest concentration of Catholics outside the border areas themselves) the British army intervened to separate the two sides and especially to protect Catholics from sustained Protestant attack. The taoiseach, Jack Lynch, appeared on television to say that the republic could 'no longer stand by'. In the event, that is more or less precisely what it has continued to do.

If the authorities in Belfast, Dublin, and London were totally unprepared for what was taking place, so too was the IRA. Indeed, the feebleness of its initial response to Protestant attack led the inhabitants of the Catholic areas of Belfast to augment the iconography upon their house walls with the derisive motto 'IRA – I Ran Away'. This 'failure' was in large part the outcome of earlier decisions by the IRA's Dublin-based leadership to adopt a broadly socialist and political (rather than military) stance. Soon, however, the movement split and the 'Provisionals' emerged to 'inherit the traditional IRA mantle, leaving the "Official" IRA to concentrate on its goal of a socialist Ireland' (Harkness 1983: 160–1). And by early 1971 the Provisionals had armed and organized themselves sufficiently to be able to 'go on the offensive' (Bishop and Mallie 1987).

The years that followed were marked – though over a comparatively small area – by fluctuating outbreaks of violence, murders of a most savage sort, intimidation, extortion, and blackmail. In 1972 direct rule from London was imposed when Brian Faulkner (a more cunning, but no more successful, prime minister than O'Neill) refused to accept the transfer of security to Whitehall. Since then abortive attempts have been made by various British administrations to find a way out of the dead end which their predecessors had so largely helped to create. The most notable was the formation of the so-called 'power-sharing' executive of December 1973 to May 1974 in which Faulknerite Unionists and members of the Social Democratic and Labour Party (founded in 1970 and since then the main vehicle for non-violent nationalism) and of the non-sectarian Alliance Party participated. But this soon collapsed, as have all subsequent efforts along similar lines, in the face of fierce opposition from loyalists and republicans alike (Rose 1976: 96–100).

The South has reacted with a mixture of fear, triumphalism, and concern, together with not a little *Schadenfreude* in some quarters (Coogan 1987). And with all six general elections between 1973 and 1987 producing defeats for the outgoing government an atmosphere of unease seems to have taken hold of the political elite. Charles Haughey, who succeeded Lynch as leader of Fianna Fail, has usually been prepared to appeal to the republican gallery while in opposition but when taoiseach (1979–81, 1982, and again from 1987) has tended to adopt a more cautious, if still ideologically narrow, approach. Garret FitzGerald, taoiseach 1981–2 and 1982–7 and leader of Fine Gael between 1977 and 1987, spoke much of 'pluralism', 'reality', and the need to comprehend all 'traditions' in Irish life and even launched a 'crusade' in 1981 to remove from the republic's constitution many of those sectarian items repugnant to Protestants. But it soon became apparent that, however sincere the intentions behind them, such words amounted to little more than eirenical loquacity. Indeed, the 'crusade' sank rapidly beneath the waves as the republic's electorate moved briskly in the opposite direction by delivering decisive referendum majorities to place a clause against abortion into the constitution and to retain the constitutional prohibition of divorce. Again, the report issued in May 1984 by the New Ireland Forum (a government-sponsored body which included the major political parties of the South as well as the SDLP), by clothing the old nationalist verities in more sophisticated linguistic apparel, persuaded many that some kind of important advance had been made – until Haughey's insistence that the Forum's call for a unitary state 'was not an option but a conclusion' showed that the emperor had been naked all along (O'Halloran 1987: 197). Even so, FitzGerald was visibly shocked when, six months later, the British prime minister, Margaret Thatcher, emerged from an Anglo-Irish summit with the machine-gun declaration that 'I have made it quite clear . . . that a unified Ireland was one solution. That is out. A second solution was confederation of the two States. That is out. A third solution was joint authority. That is out. That is a derogation of sovereignty' (Girvin 1986b: 157). Yet, within a year the two leaders were able to conclude the Hillsborough or Anglo-Irish Agreement, which, by setting up an 'intergovernmental conference', gave the republic some input into the administration of the North – though what exactly this will amount to still remains to be seen (Kenny 1986).

For their part most unionists have felt ignored and betrayed and have not hesitated to give vent to anger and rage. If as yet they have proved unable to undermine the Agreement, they are more fearful than ever before. The British government finds it exceedingly difficult to combine the maintenance of law and order with the search for a political settlement. In the face of serious economic difficulties the republic, when not indulging in linguistic gymnastics, concerns itself largely with the 'real' stuff of politics: 'local concerns, local problems', or, as its politicians would have it, 'national' concerns, 'national' problems, 'such as rates, jobs, employment, prices and the managing of . . . resources' (Boyce 1982: 369). Repeated opinion polls have demonstrated a wish for unity on the cheap – without any kind of psychological, cultural, or, indeed, financial payment – and sometimes not even much of a wish at all (Gallagher 1985b: 53; Carty 1983: 125; Bowman 1982: 335). Britain, it is blithely believed – not least by those who argue that if only London ceased to interfere all would be sunshine and flowers – can be made to pick up the financial costs of unification by eternally underwriting Northern Ireland's tottering economy (O'Malley 1983: 89–90), and if not a guilty Britain then a wealthy America. As yet, however, the United States has shown only a modest willingness to unlock its coffers despite (or perhaps because of) the presence of a traditionally active Irish-American community, some of whose members have long provided, not only guns to the IRA and its forerunners, but striking proof that distance and ignorance can lend enchantment even to the politics of death.

The North has seen many critical changes and adjustments over the last twenty years. Discrimination has been tackled with vigour, though not with complete success, for ultimately discrimination lies in the individual human heart. The once proud and powerful Unionist Party has splintered into a congeries of lesser fragments. Paramilitary groups have emerged to make manifest the cruel and violent populism long present in Protestant politics (Nelson 1984). On the Catholic side the SDLP has, not without difficulty, succeeded in maintaining a central position. The republican movement too has experienced profound change. Most of the Officials have turned to electoral and community politics along left-wing lines, although some broke away in 1976 to set up the Irish National Liberation Army, which, behind a mask of 'socialism', eventually began to occupy itself with bloody internecine feuds of mafia-like complexity. The Provisionals – now far more independent of control from Dublin headquarters – have pursued a policy which has wavered in everything but its dedication to violence: now the gun only, now hunger strikes, now the armalite in one hand and the ballot paper in the other. Although the Alliance Party founded in 1970 has had only a modest success, opinion polls have discovered that a majority of nationalists 'would accept the continuation of Northern Ireland within the United Kingdom if the position of the minority could be improved' (Girvin 1986a: 132) – a finding more opaque and less simple than it seems because, of course, one man's 'improvement' remains another's political poison. Yet, in various ways, there has been an atmosphere of adjustment and change in the North, not always perhaps for the better, but certainly indicative of a world painfully freeing itself from some at least of its traditional preconceptions.

No comparable movement has been evident in the republic apart from the recent formation of the Progressive Democrat Party, which, though initially made up largely of former Fianna Fail deputies, seems, at the general election of 1987 (an election remarkable for the inward-looking quality of its political discourse) to have taken most of its support from Fine Gael. For the mass of the people in the South the North of Ireland might as well, in every context but that of words, be a thousand miles away. But still the rhetoric continues, and to such effect that, by the very repetitiveness of its assertions, it has become transformed into something as hard and as tangible as stone.

It is not surprising that Ulster's recent experience has attracted the attentions of students of conflict from all over the world. Indeed, added to the greater horrors of life in the ghettos of Belfast has been the lesser one of endless questionnaires and interviews on the part of sociologists, anthropologists, experts in 'peace studies', and other academic birds of passage. Such 'explanations' as have emerged from all this activity reflect the presuppositions of the investigators as much as the realities of the situation itself (Whyte 1978). Perhaps in the end, one looks most fruitfully to geography and to history, not for a solution (for there may be none), but for a context.

The border did not create, though it did render more naked, that asymmetry by which Catholics are a minority in Northern Ireland while Protestants are a minority in Ireland as a whole. And because this is something with long seventeenth-century colonial roots it is precisely the length of time during which it has been so that has prevented the creation of a shared sense of identity in the counties of the North-East (Moody 1974; Harris 1972; Rose 1971). As unionists and nationalists simply do not trust one another so each 'invokes majority rule in an attempt to dominate the other' (Girvin 1986a: 131), with the result that all those ingenious mechanisms of balance used in other countries with religious or linguistic cleavages (such as Switzerland, Holland, and Belgium) have proved incapable of meeting the Irish case.

Of course all nationalism asserts the interior unity of the nation and finds it difficult to incorporate groups which insist on standing apart. In Ireland the particular intensity of the tension between ideal and reality has resulted, in large measure, from geographical accident – the fact that Ireland is an island. Irish nationalists have, therefore, found it even more difficult than their counterparts elsewhere to avoid assuming that the whole island *must* constitute a single political unity and many British politicians and administrators, from Gladstone to Wilson, 'have taken the same instinctive view' (Townshend 1987). It is, however, an assumption which lies at the heart of the present difficulties. All sorts of changes will of course have to be made on all sides. But until Irish nationalists can rethink their definition of the nation so as to remove its traditional implications of territorial and cultural imperialism, the border in both its physical and mental forms and the sense of failure and fragmentation which has flowed from its existence will remain. There is precious little evidence that any such painful process is under way.

CHAPTER 8
Society
Stagnation, Boom, Slump

In social and economic matters, as in so many others, partition proved a more comfortable phenomenon than all but a handful of heretics has ever been willing to admit. Trade between North and South had long been modest and (despite the heroic efforts of the smuggling fraternity) merely became more modest still (Johnson 1974 and 1979). Although neither part of Ireland could escape a broadly common economic and geographical heritage, in those spheres where human decisions are not without influence the border made it locally possible to pursue the politics of both bread and circuses in new and exciting ways. From the start the Ulster unionists could revel in their industrial 'superiority' and their success in matching at least some of contemporary Britain's social security achievements. Many southern nationalists found it an equally congenial experience to live in an agrarian (and authentically 'Celtic') economy now happily separated from the alien intrusions of Belfast. And once both Britain and the Free State had moved towards protectionism in the early 1930s, the North could also congratulate itself upon remaining able to send livestock and linen to England duty-free, while de Valera, for his part, found it possible to pursue a policy of self-sufficiency that would never even have got off the ground in a political entity incorporating the industrial North-East.

I

Given that a continuation of the state of things before 1921 was no longer acceptable, partition provided economic benefits all round.

204

Northern Ireland received (at first modest) subsidies towards its agriculture and social security system, obtained services such as defence and diplomatic representation on the cheap, and remained unaffected by rising British tariffs. The Free State, in turn, was able to adopt the economic appurtenances of independence while being liberated from having to help support the North's unemployed or make any contribution towards the United Kingdom's national debt (Johnson 1981 and 1985a: 7). To the border's significance as a political and cultural divide were, therefore, added, not only a new economic dimension as protectionism replaced free trade, but also a social dimension which became especially apparent with the advent of a British Labour government after the Second World War. Indeed, so dramatic were the fissures which this latter development opened up, that, had the South matched Ulster's social service standards in, for example, 1969–70, its current relevant expenditure would have doubled, while, had it in addition shouldered the cost of British payments to Northern Ireland, 'the effect would have been to raise the level of taxation by 60 per cent' (Buckland 1981: 103).

That for all these partitioned 'advantages' there was a price to pay was at first disguised by Cumann na nGaedheal's decision to apply in the Free State many of the economically conservative policies forced upon Belfast by the Government of Ireland Act of 1920. For Ulster, indeed, the price was economic impotence: no control over trade, almost none over taxation, precious little even over expenditure (Buckland 1979: 81–129). But because Northern ministers did what they could with the very modest powers at their disposal and Cosgrave rarely chose to do much more, economic management in the 1920s diverged less notably between the six and the twenty-six counties than might have been supposed. As regards agriculture Dublin's Land Purchase Act of 1923 was echoed by Belfast two years later, with the result that soon virtually all Irish farms were owned by their occupiers (Rumpf and Hepburn 1977: 227; Johnson 1985a: 11). In both jurisdictions 'economic' criteria were allowed their head and extensive cattle rather than intensive tillage farming was encouraged, a policy which tended to favour large ranchers and thus reopened many old wounds. Perhaps most remarkable of all is that, even after de Valera's introduction of a new 'independent' economic policy in 1932, the South in the mid-1930s should have continued to send as high a proportion of its exports to Britain (over 90 per cent) as did the North, which, as part of the United Kingdom, was not of course technically 'exporting' at all (Isles and Cuthbert 1957: 88–103; Rumpf and Hepburn 1977: 117).

The impotence of Craig's administrations was revealed, above all, in their inability to arrest the rundown of those industries, which, together with agriculture, underpinned the local economy – linen and shipbuilding. While Ulster's agriculture did better during the depression than that of the South because it could sell freely within the United Kingdom and benefit from British price support, its industries fared worse (Cullen 1972: 180). Linen entered a period of almost unrelieved decline after 1920 as demand faded away, while shipbuilding, however hard it tried, could not avoid severe recession in the face of post-war overcapacity. Given such a context, both sectors did well enough in retaining their market shares. But because the international cake was rapidly shrinking Ulster's share became absolutely smaller as time went on (Johnson 1985b: 190–6). With 30 per cent of employed males engaged in agriculture and almost 53 per cent of those covered by the 1924 census of production working in textiles, shipbuilding, and engineering (Buckland 1979: 52), such developments inevitably led to serious hardship. From the mid-1920s until the Second World War Northern Ireland's unemployment rate rarely fell below 20 and in 1932 reached 27.2 per cent (Harkness 1983: 188). Although the slum dwellers of Belfast protested loudly and with much justice about their lot, things were perhaps even worse in the countryside. There in 1930 the average wages of agricultural labourers were actually below the thirty shillings (£1.50) a week unemployment benefit paid to married men elsewhere (Johnson 1985b: 199).

While Northern Ireland's economic experience at this time was no worse than that of many other regions in the United Kingdom (Johnson 1985a: 34–5 and 1985b: 199), there can be little doubt that British governments between the wars relegated Ulster's needs to a comparatively invisible level of priority. During the negotiations between London and Dublin which led to the Anglo-Irish agreements of 1938 Northern Ireland's demands for consideration were brusquely rejected. Senior Treasury civil servants were especially hostile, their chief going so far as to declare that 'Blackmail and bluff (oddly enough called "loyalty") have for many years been the accepted methods of Northern Ireland' (Johnson 1980: 155). In the end only the palpable impracticalities of the Government of Ireland Act's financial provisions and the necessity of stopping backwoods Conservatives from rallying to Ulster's defence persuaded successive British administrations to keep Northern Ireland afloat by means of a series of fudges, dodges, and more or less outright bribes (Harkness 1983: 55–6). Although real incomes per head in the six counties fell even further behind the United Kingdom average between the wars, an absolute increase of between 10 and 15 per cent was, nonetheless, achieved. And in contrast to the feebleness of the advances recorded in housing and health (common enough throughout the United Kingdom and the Free State), in other fields of social welfare, notably unemployment benefit, conditions were very much better than in the South (Buckland 1979: 150–75).

During the Second World War the North's economy, though not without its continuing difficulties, experienced the nearest thing to take-off it was ever to enjoy. Demand for most of Ulster's products increased dramatically. National income in real terms rose by 84 per cent between 1938 and 1947 compared to 47 per cent in the United Kingdom as a whole and incomes per head of the population moved from 55 per cent of the United Kingdom average to nearly 70 per cent. This was a rate of growth far beyond that experienced in the South (Johnson 1985a: 43). And as further reward for such already well-rewarded political loyalty a series of agreements between 1945 and 1951 ensured that the full measure of Britain's new welfarism was extended to Ulster and underwritten by the imperial government. It was, therefore, largely as a *rentier* of Britain that Northern Ireland emerged into the post-war world: by 1968–9 London was handing over no less than £72 million a year while the 'imperial contribution' had fallen below a sixth of that amount (Lyons 1971: 730; Buckland 1981: 103). All of this represented a 'progressive deinsulation' of the Ulster economy and effectively foreshadowed later developments in the field of politics (Bew, Gibbon and Patterson 1979: 103). Of course other parts of the United Kingdom also received high levels of assistance. But in the case of Northern Ireland the adjustments made necessary by metamorphosis from pauper mendicant to shabby genteel remittance man involved psychological shifts of a peculiarly intense kind. By the time direct rule was introduced in 1972 the links between Ulster and the British administrative and financial system had become so close that few significant changes in social and economic policies still needed to be made (Daly 1981a: 218).

Within the narrow fiscal fishbowl still under local control post-war governments in Belfast could do little more than attempt to smooth out the waves. In one respect, that of attracting new industries, some success was achieved and achieved well before the South had woken up to the importance of such things. But even though some 50,000 new jobs were 'created' in the period 1945–63 the continued decline of Ulster's traditional staples meant that growth was painfully slow and often not perceptible at all. And even if unemployment remained much lower than it had been in the 1930s it now also remained much higher than in, for example, Scotland, Wales, or Merseyside (Bew, Gibbon and Patterson 1979: 133–50). In addition, while the average individual share of gross domestic product rose in Northern Ireland after the war in comparison with Britain, it still in 1972 stood over a quarter lower in real terms, though higher than in the South (Spencer and Harrison 1977: 8). Progress, therefore, was tangible if fairly unimpressive and was sustained by hand-outs from a Britain itself falling seriously behind in the international economic steeplechase of the time.

As in the Republic 'planning' became a modish term in official circles and especially so during the prime ministership of Terence O'Neill (1963–9). Whether it amounted to much in either part of Ireland remains open to doubt. Certainly in the North few objective gains ensued (Bew, Gibbon and Patterson 1979: 152–7; Buckland 1981: 111–14) and not even the psychological uplift which the South experienced in the 1960s could take root in a divided society soon to be overwhelmed by new bouts of violence, bitterness, and distrust.

By the mid-1980s a congeries of different circumstances, including disorder in Ulster and a general fondness for the notion that two and two can be persuaded to make five, had rendered the economies of both North and South feebler still. Both were marked by slow growth and high unemployment and both were spending much more than they earned. 'The difference was that the North was being bankrolled by *ex gratia* payments from the British Exchequer whereas the Republic was accumulating debt which would eventually have to be serviced from taxation' (McAleese 1986a: 27–8). More than ever before Britain is having to pay a high price – in treasure, men, and reputation – for its long and continuing Irish entanglements.

II

Knowing this as we do it is curious to recall how slavishly the Free State at first followed British models in economics and finance.

Fears, understandable if exaggerated, that anything repugnant to the banking sector, the British Treasury, or wealthier elements in the community might plunge a delicate society into chaos, together with a degree of instinctive caution among Cumann na nGaedheal leaders, combined to create a policy in which rectitude, balanced budgets, and 'realism' constituted the touchstones of both action and thought (Daly 1981a: 138–9). The currency was tied to sterling at par so that Britain's tergiversations with regard to the gold standard (which it re-adopted in 1925 and abandoned again six years later) and the consequent overvaluation of the pound were followed with limpet fidelity. In a fit of artistically significant but financially unimportant independence a distinctive coinage was introduced in 1928 based on animal designs by Percy Metcalfe, an Englishman chosen by a committee under the chairmanship of W. B. Yeats, twin sins in the eyes of many Gaelic chauvinists. Happily the committee's recommendations were accepted and Ireland was not only given the most beautiful coins in the world but saved from having to contemplate an alternative design featuring 'a kneeling angel pouring money from a sack' (Meenan 1970: 218), however appropriate an icon that might have been of continuing failures to identify rather than merely assert the economic benefits which would 'inevitably' flow from the ending of colonial rule.

If it remains to the lasting credit of Cumann na nGaedheal that the Free State did not, like so many other countries, resort to printing money when times got hard, there can be no doubt that its patrician disdain for the social consequences of policy was neither attractive nor, in the end, politically remunerative. The frugal hand of the Department of Finance (a powerful limb controlled by able men) was allowed to slap down any doubts ministers occasionally entertained regarding the advantages to be derived from an unrelieved diet of parsimony. Only the impressive scheme to build a hydroelectric power station on the Shannon in the mid-1920s survived Finance's assaults. Although at the time quite untypical this lone exception did at least foreshadow the pragmatic extension by subsequent administrations of what later became known as the state-sponsored or semi-state sector which eventually – in a country notable for its resistance to socialism – came to encompass a vast range of activities from sugar production to greyhound breeding. It also showed that ministerial willpower could always, if energetically enough deployed, defeat the objections of the civil service mind (Fanning 1978: 178–86; Lyons 1971: 605–9). But as regards industrial policy in general Cosgrave's ministers

209

moved with extreme caution. When rising unemployment led them to introduce some limited protection a Tariff Commission was set up in 1926 under the chairmanship of one of the chief bureaucratic guardians of the holy grail, J. J. McElligott, himself a future Secretary of the Department of Finance. It issued three reports during the first two years of its existence: one rejected duties on flour, the others granted them on margarine and on that key constituent of Irish industrial enterprise – rosary beads (Daly 1981a: 143–4).

True to the traditions of Sinn Fein before 1921 the Free State paid no more than lip service to making provision for the poor. The 'Democratic Programme' adopted by the Dail in 1919 was more remarkable for the fact that all of half an hour had been devoted to its discussion than for its ringing declarations about making 'provision for the physical, mental and spiritual well-being' of the helpless and deprived (Lynch 1966). Indeed, long before independence, Sinn Fein had effectively constituted itself an 'establishment-in-waiting' (Laffan 1985: 219) and Cumann na nGaedheal saw no reason to behave differently once the waiting had come to an end. Thus, while income tax was substantially reduced and tax levels in general were kept low by international standards (Daniel 1976: 59–60), health services remained entirely Victorian, old-age pensions were cut, and proposals to extend the unemployment insurance scheme were doggedly resisted. Ernest Blythe (finance minister from 1923 to 1932), no doubt anxious to dispel any lingering hopes the newly liberated poor might still have entertained, actually declared himself willing to look into 'the possibility of doing away with the national health insurance and labour exchanges' on the grounds that neither 'seemed necessary in the Free State' (Fanning 1983: 64–5, 72; Barrington 1987: 96–100). Nonetheless, despite the collapse of agricultural prices after 1920, the decade was comparatively buoyant in general economic terms. The slump of 1929 took some time to reach Ireland, with the result that average real incomes per head may have risen by as much as 14 per cent between 1926 and 1931 or from 55 to 61 per cent of British incomes. Though not dramatic in a world context, this was well ahead of the 2 per cent achieved during the depressed period 1931–9 at the end of which Irish incomes had actually fallen to only half the level of those in Britain (Crotty 1966: 131, 156; Johnson 1985a: 39).

Such advances as were made were, however, spread very unevenly throughout society as a whole and proved insufficient to prevent

an electoral victory for de Valera and Fianna Fail in 1932 based
on the populist trinity of welfare, tariff protection, and a better
deal for the small farmer. If in all these spheres progress was to
prove modest in comparison with promises then this was largely
the result of a downturn in the world economy, though some of
de Valera's own actions were hardly designed to improve matters.
While, therefore, Irish historians (for reasons of social background,
ideology, and academic fashion) have tended to be less willing to
extend the benefit of the doubt to the early Fianna Fail administrations than to those which had gone before, the record itself is
more ambiguous and speaks of energetic self-mutilation in some
areas but also of limited improvement in others. Between 1932
and 1944 unemployment provisions were enhanced and extended
to include small farmers, agricultural labourers (though these were
not fully incorporated until 1952) and many casual workers of all
kinds. Old-age pensions were increased and widows' and orphans'
pensions and a very modest children's allowance introduced. While
less than 2400 houses a year had been built with state aid under
Cosgrave this rose dramatically to almost 9000 a year between
1933 and 1939 (Daly 1981a: 173–82, 192). However, despite
some rationalization of hospital administration, health provision
for those unable to pay still differed only superficially from the
poor-law practices of former times (Barrington 1987: 135–7;
Lyons 1971: 649). Education too saw few changes apart from
an increased emphasis upon compulsory Irish language teaching.
Indeed, despite Fianna Fail's limited achievements, Irish welfare
services remained, as late as the 1950s, very much like those of
Britain immediately after the end of the First World War.

As regards trade and industry Fianna Fail had long proclaimed
the virtues of self-sufficiency and the importance of protection.
It, therefore, briskly accelerated the hesitant gestures Cumann na
nGaedheal had made in that direction, with the result that throughout the inter-war period as a whole the Free State moved altogether
with the economic tendencies of the time. Because, however, in
Ireland's case the whole business became hopelessly entangled with
de Valera's refusal to continue handing over to London the annuity
payments made by Irish farmers for earlier land purchase loans
and with the 'Economic War' that ensued, Irish tariffs were raised
well beyond even the high levels prevailing elsewhere. Agriculture
(which now faced heavy British import duties) was especially badly
hit and expansion in the manufacturing sector was neither as
significant nor as rapid as the flawed statistics of the time suggest

(Johnson 1985a: 23, 29–30). Although de Valera's lieutenant, Sean Lemass, then the very epitome of self-sufficiency or 'autarkism', had insisted in 1928 that 'Ireland can be made a selfcontained unit, providing all the necessities of life in adequate quantities' (Meenan 1967: 74), the experience of the 1930s, despite valiant attempts to grow tobacco in the South-East, proved otherwise. Certainly a number of new industries appeared as average nominal tariffs were cranked up from 9 per cent in 1931 to no less than 35 per cent in 1938 and highly restrictive import quotas were introduced as well (McAleese 1986b: 90). By their very nature, however, such industries were uncompetitive. They supplied the minuscule domestic market. Having done so they ceased to grow and simply ticked over to the admitted benefit of their workers and even more so to that of their owners many of whom were in fact English. Thus the footwear industry, half of whose employees worked in 'English' factories, though it produced about £19 million worth of goods between 1933 and 1938, only managed to send abroad the derisory average of 117 pairs of boots and shoes a year (Press 1986). While, therefore, net industrial output rose from £25.6 million in 1931 to £36 million in 1938 and industrial employment may even have gone up by 50 per cent, industrial exports declined to bathetic levels (£600,000 in 1935), cattle exports collapsed from £12.7 million in 1931 to a miserable £4.3 million three years later, and non-food imports actually increased (Lyons 1971: 590–1, 609–10; Johnson 1985a: 16–17).

As time went on reality kept breaking through. Legislative attempts in 1932 and 1934 to preserve Irish industry in Irish hands were not pursued with any extremity of zeal and amounted to little more than a device for disguising private infringements beneath public declarations of sea-green economic chauvinism (Daly 1984b). As early as 1935 a series of so-called coal–cattle pacts with Britain was inaugurated in order to permit a strictly equal interchange of the named commodities despite the general restrictions then still in force. By 1938 the British prime minister, Neville Chamberlain, had become convinced (on *political* grounds) that something more sensible was required and de Valera was ready enough to accept the generous terms available: virtually duty-free entry into Britain for Irish goods subject to certain quotas (in return for much less substantial reciprocations in the other direction), the payment by Dublin of £10 million in final settlement of the land annuities (one of the bargains of the century), plus more strictly political concessions such as the return of the Treaty ports (Buckland 1979: 111).

While the whole affair had proved economically foolish, that had never been the main consideration, for, as Sir Horace Plunkett once remarked, in Ireland the term political economy was invariably spelled with a big 'P' and a small 'e' (Meenan 1970: xxvii). Protection would of course have been on any sensible government's menu in the 1930s. But the gay abandon with which tariffs were imposed on crucial raw materials like coal and cement, the additional complications caused by the land annuities and the unrealistic hankerings for autarky, all made things far more complicated than they need have been. At the same time, however, Fianna Fail undoubtedly delivered some real gains in social welfare, while its encouragement of local industries was by no means without positive advantages.

More generally, de Valera's first years in power saw a substantial growth in the state's participation in economic and social affairs. Taxes were increased. The imposition of tariffs, quotas, and minimum agricultural prices required more civil servants and their number grew from 21,522 in 1934 to 25,387 in 1940 (Chubb 1982: 256). Inevitably, total central government expenditure also rose – from an annual average of £29.2 million in 1926–30 to £40 million in 1936–40 (Mitchell 1981: 737) – and did so not only absolutely but as a proportion of gross national product, in which respect it moved from 23.6 per cent in 1926/7 to no less than 29.7 per cent in 1938/9, a rate of increase not far short of double that recorded by the United Kingdom over the same period (O'Hagan 1980). Although these percentages fell during the Second World War, the state's overall profile developed yet further with the advent of rationing, wage controls, and a greater direction of economic activity in general and agriculture in particular.

The third main plank of Fianna Fail's pre-war programme related to agrarian matters. Because agriculture was also closely tied up with the Economic War and with autarkism in general it inevitably experienced profound short-term shocks, though whether the events of the 1930s did much to divert broad long-term tendencies from the paths they would have followed in any case is very questionable. Many separate issues were involved. In particular, Fianna Fail had consistently promised to do more for those small farmers who, especially in the West, had given it enthusiastic electoral support (Rumpf and Hepburn 1977: 100–107). And, indeed, the Land Commission did receive additional powers in 1933 and for a few years the tempo of redistribution increased substantially (Ó Tuathaigh 1982: 183). The problem of course was that, with virtually no real landlords left, the only way in which more land could now be found was by taking it away from the more substantial farmers, among whom ranchers were especially prominent. However, during the 1920s, Cumann na nGaedheal, pursuing strictly 'economic' policies (O'Brien 1936), had favoured the extensive cattle farming practised by such men, a collaboration which, in terms of exports and output, had yielded abundant fruit (Meenan 1970: 52–6, 75). While, however, de Valera was of course emotionally opposed to such an approach, his encouragement of further redistribution proved a very temporary affair. Already by the late 1930s hostility to ranchers had become 'more rhetorical than anything else'. And it was not long before a Fianna Fail minister could be heard telling the Dail that there were 'enough' people on the land and explaining so Pauline a conversion with the recollection that 'I, as a boy, disagreed with the Bible. I could never see why the poor should always be with us and I could never understand the phrase "to him that hath shall be given". But those old boys who wrote the Bible were wiser than I' (Bew and Patterson 1982: 21–8). No wonder, therefore, that the small farmers of the West rapidly lost patience and were soon deserting de Valera in favour of their own sectional political party, Clann na Talmhan.

There can be no doubt that cattle farmers (not all of them ranchers by any means) suffered badly during the Economic War. The volume of livestock and livestock products fell by 6 per cent between 1929/30 and 1934/5. Because prices were also falling dramatically the value of gross agricultural output collapsed from £61.4 million in 1929/30 to £38.8 million in 1934/5 and the value of agricultural exports was *halved* in the period 1929/30–1937/8 (Crotty 1966: 140, 155; Meenan 1970: 52). The government desperately provided subsidies, unsuccessfully sought alternative export markets, and encouraged tillage in an attempt to increase self-sufficiency. In anything but the shortest of runs little of this had much significant effect. Wheat acreage – perhaps partly in response to the *Catholic Bulletin*'s article citing thirteenth-century decrees by Pope Celestine IV on compulsory tillage in the Papal States (Meenan 1980: 135) – rose impressively but did so largely at the expense of other crops; although the war of course brought about a further temporary expansion (Daly 1981a: 149). While cattle farmers received little direct help from a government initially unsympathetic to their aspirations, livestock prices recovered in 1938 and things began to improve. Even if some observers took a distinctly pessimistic view of what had happened (Johnston 1951), by the late 1940s it was almost becoming possible to imagine that the events of the previous decade had exercised comparatively little impact upon the long-term patterns of Irish agricultural development as a whole.

In practice, therefore, de Valera's agrarian activities before the war constituted no more than a brief entr'acte. Not only was the main play soon resumed, but soon too it could count among the cast actors who had once been loudest in denouncing the growing gap between nationalist aspirations and the realities of rural life. As late as 1942 a senior official of the Land Commission was still telling the cabinet that every true Irishman 'wants to see settled in the land as many families as possible, on holdings large enough to secure them a fair measure of frugal comfort, but not large enough to secure them a livelihood independent of their labour' (Bew 1982: 87). But, though his sentiments echoed, almost to the word, the views of nineteenth-century nationalists like Bishop Nulty (Chapter 6) and actually foreshadowed those contained in de Valera's St Patrick's Day address of 1943 (Chapter 7), they had long represented a bogus prospectus, the bogusness of which had become (the mid-1930s apart) more and more obvious as the years passed by. The original rustic vision of a re-gaelicized Ireland faded away as the proportion of the population living in towns (of 1500 and more inhabitants) grew steadily until it reached a clear preponderance at the Republic's census of 1971. The number of people engaged in agriculture fell from 670,000 in 1926 to 393,000 in 1961 and has continued to move downwards ever since (Meenan 1970: 112). That of those farming between one and fifty acres dropped from 163,709 in 1926 to 111,576 in 1966. By contrast, farmers with larger holdings actually grew in number from 53,360 to 65,115 over the same period (Kennedy 1973: 101; Weinz 1986: 89). Even if to all but the wildest of optimists this should not have come as much of a surprise, it did, of course, run directly counter to the programme upon which agrarian nationalism had first been floated as a serious political force.

Relentlessly the scale of farming operations increased. The percentage of holdings above fifty acres rose from 23.5 in 1931 to 29.0 in 1960 and 33.2 in 1980. Even the Land Commission (supposedly the great engine of redistribution) repeatedly pumped up the acreage which it regarded as necessary for comfort and efficiency (Gillmor 1985: 173–6; Commins 1985). What had, in the late-nineteenth century, seemed something of a paradox, namely, that in a country of small farmers the bulk of the land was actually included in relatively large holdings, now became so glaringly obvious that it remained paradoxical no more. By 1960, therefore, when almost 11.2 million acres were under crops or pasture, only 4 million belonged to farms of fifty acres or less (Meenan 1970: 109). And the measure of de Valera's brief dash for tillage can be gauged by the further fact that 85 per cent of this land was then under grass, a proportion which has recently increased further still (Meenan 1971: 50–1; Gillmor 1985: 169). Indeed, there is no longer any pretence about such things: small farms are now seen as the enemy of progress and progress is what matters most. Thus the Second Programme for Economic Expansion called in 1963 for the 'creation of viable family farm units with minimum disturbance of the population', while a decade later a Common Market-inspired Farm Modernization Scheme simply divided holdings into three groups – 'commercial', 'development', and 'transitional' or 'other' – and proposed that those farmers in the last and largest category be 'encouraged' to retire. That these should have included men with as much as forty-five acres constitutes a deeply ironic conclusion to what had supposedly been the main thrust of agrarian agitation in Ireland for a century and more (Meenan 1971: 52; Scheper-Hughes 1979: 42–3; Sheehy 1984: 90–2).

Landless labourers, who had never enjoyed even the romantic prominence accorded the small farmer, received shorter shrift still. In the early 1920s their attempts to obtain better than starvation conditions by joining the Irish Transport and General Workers Union were crushed by militant farmers (who in Waterford formed themselves into a 'White Guard') and overwhelmed by the open hostility of Cosgrave's government which seems, more or less openly, to have adhered to the proposition that 'labourers' right is farmers' wrong' (O'Connor 1980). Although Fianna Fail set up an Agricultural Wages Board in 1936 to fix minimum pay, the years immediately after the 'Emergency' saw renewed attempts on the part of labourers to improve their lot through trade union organization. These were again met by fierce farmer opposition and denounced in the Catholic press as evidence of rural Communism and unbelief (Bradley 1986). Soon, however, the problem disappeared, blown away by that grim liquidator of post-Famine difficulties – demographic annihilation. The whole shape of rural society underwent profound change; and amidst the overall decline in the agrarian population between 1926 and 1966 the number of hired workers shrank from 122,000 to 46,200 and of 'relatives assisting' from 264,000 to 83,300, by, in other words, about two-thirds in each case. Farmers, on the other hand, only lost a quarter of their number and thus came to dominate the countryside as never before (Meenan 1970: 112; Kennedy 1973: 103). But if, on the surface, this might seem to represent the completion of the Irish farmers' long post-Famine quest for agrarian supremacy, for all but a handful of highly commercialized operators (and despite an EEC-inspired Indian Summer in the 1970s) the triumph has proved more symbolic than real. Especially in the poorer areas of the West many farmers are still what they have always been – objectively little different from labourers. And now that the latter have given up the ghost, the men who remain with only a handful of acres of unproductive land find themselves unequivocally dumped at the very bottom of the agrarian heap.

III

In general terms the decade and a half which followed 1945 constituted a depressing entrance into the post-war world. Both Fianna Fail and inter-party governments shovelled money into agriculture, with no very obvious signs of a return. Diversification ground rapidly to a halt. Cattle alone moved ahead and by 1960 accounted for 70 per cent of all agricultural exports as compared to 50 per cent before the war (Daly 1981a: 160). The Republic's gross agricultural production by volume limped feebly along and recorded an increase of 8 per cent at a time (1947/8 to 1959/60) when western Europe as a whole was able to achieve a rise of no less than two-thirds (Crotty 1966: 161). While industry experienced a boom as wartime restraint came to an end this proved a transient phenomenon and was, in any case, largely confined to satisfying the demands of the domestic market alone (Lynch 1969: 189; Cullen 1972: 181–2).

Inflation and balance of payments crises represented Ireland's chief economic preoccupations in the 1950s. Every increase in wages seemed to lead to falling exports and rising imports. Finance ministers reacted by sternly closing the tap and rendering the country even less capable of sustaining the bulk of its citizens in conditions of anything other than penury and despair. Unemployment rose, but with inadequate social benefits it was emigration rather than the dole which absorbed most of the resultant misery. Independence itself had done little to alter the demographic patterns of the immediate past. As before, the birthrate (in both parts of Ireland) remained fairly close to the European average by means of an unusual combination of late marriage age, widespread celibacy, and high marital fertility (Johnson 1985a: 36–7). But while in the North the population rose slowly from the 1920s onwards, in the South emigration continued to drain away the large families which had become a characteristic feature of domestic life. When, in the 1930s, Britain rather than the United States became the emigrants' main destination, ease of movement was added to all the other things which helped to make departure the best of the bad choices available.

After the war a widening gap between employment opportunities in Britain and Ireland meant that average annual emigration per thousand inhabitants in the 1950s rose to more than twice what it had been before 1945: 1926–36 = 5.6; 1936–46 = 6.3; 1946–51 = 8.2; 1951–6 = 13.4; 1956–61 = 14.8 (Vaughan and Fitzpatrick 1978: 266). Between 1922 and 1961 about 900,000 people abandoned the twenty-six counties (Drudy 1986: 109). 'The ranks of the young were particularly diminished: of the 502,000 persons aged 10 to 19 in 1951, only 303,000 remained in the country by 1961' (Rottman and O'Connell 1982: 78). Those leaving were predominantly from the agricultural sector (labourers and the sons and daughters of small farmers) or from unskilled and semi-skilled families in the towns. The monochrome dejection experienced by many men and women outside the prosperous classes at this time is difficult to recapture, though John Montague's lines of 1953 (Montague 1977: 32) preserve something of the unhappiness of 'the white-faced children'

> Deprived of sun, scurrying with sharp laughter
> From point to point of shelter,
> And arched over all, the indifferent deadening rain.

The story of how such things were for a time banished is one which Irish historians have become so accustomed to telling that, like all oft-repeated tales, it has acquired something of the character of myth. In its most usual form the role of modern St Patrick expelling the snakes of depression with a wave of his Keynesian crozier has been divided between two dynamic innovators, namely, T. K. Whitaker, Secretary of the Department of Finance between 1956 and 1969, and Sean Lemass, who in 1959 succeeded de Valera as prime minister (Lee 1979c; Lyons 1971: 618–23; Brown 1981: 241–66). In 1958 Whitaker produced a report entitled *Economic*

Development in which he openly acknowledged the lassitude of the times and recommended policies for renewal. These, in a somewhat transmogrified form, were then embodied in the First Programme for Economic Expansion issued by de Valera's last government in the same year.

Both addressed themselves to the fact that, ever since the Second World War, the Irish economy had been decoupled from international developments to an extent previously unknown. Employers, labour, and governments had all clung to protectionism while the rest of the world was marching briskly back towards free trade. In an effort to wake Ireland up from this Rip Van Winkle torpidity Whitaker put forward a three-pronged strategy: more planning, fewer tariffs, and greater emphasis upon 'productive' investment. Because things undoubtedly improved almost immediately – national output jumped by nearly a quarter between 1958 and 1963, the purchasing power of wages rose by a fifth, unemployment fell by a third, emigration too declined rapidly (Murphy 1975: 144) – it soon became universally accepted, not only that the First Programme had been entirely responsible for all this, but that its prescriptions were both completely novel and capable of unlocking riches beyond the dreams of avarice. In truth, Whitaker had not appeared on the scene without herald or forerunner, nor did subsequent growth flow exclusively from his proposals if only because in one important respect these were never actually carried out. More generally still, the economic horse that eventually ran proved to be rather different from the horse that was in 1958 being entered on the card.

Already well before the publication of *Economic Development* views had been expressed that over-rigid adherence to the rules of classical economics – balanced budgets, low government expenditure, importing no more than one earned abroad – was simply failing to produce acceptable results. During the war the importance of planning had impressed itself upon certain political minds. Lemass, in particular, as more or less permanent Minister for Industry and Commerce since 1932 and Minister of Supplies during the 'Emergency', was beginning to have doubts about the view put to the cabinet by the Department of Finance in 1945 that Keynes, with his belief that not all public spending was a mark of the Beast, was simply another colourful representative of what the department chose to call the 'escapist school of economics' (Raymond 1983: 128). And though Lemass's subsequent intellectual Odyssey was to include many recantations and opportunistic denunciations of planning, state spending, free trade, foreign capital, and all the other pillars with which he was later to support his economic policies (Bew and Patterson 1982), by the mid-1950s he had undoubtedly emerged as the most significant political exponent of a new approach.

However, the fact that most of the others who were expressing similar dissatisfactions constituted a remarkably variegated body of opinion lent a high degree of ambivalence to the enterprise as a whole. Indeed, between 1948 and 1951 Keynesianism, in so far as it gained any significant following in Ireland, did so within the inter-party government rather than the Fianna Fail opposition of the time. Thus Sean MacBride, the leader of Clann na Poblachta, even advocated 'planning' (hitherto a very dirty word in holy Ireland), while his followers, with a mixture of old-world nationalism and new-style economics, denounced the link with sterling as the chief cause of all the nation's woes (Lynch 1969). It was also this government which established the Industrial Development Authority to attract foreign manufacturers and its coalition successor which in 1956 at last provided the powers and resources required for such a task. In that year also an official Capital Advisory Committee argued strongly that capital spending be directed more towards 'productive' purposes, something which had in fact already been hinted at four years earlier by other outside experts in a report which had suggested that the amount of investment in areas like housing was too great in relation to national output as a whole (Daly 1981a: 164–6; Rumpf and Hepburn 1977: 128).

Amidst all the subsequent hosannas heaped upon Lemass and Whitaker it is often forgotten that in the late 1950s neither was proposing that Ireland should simply spend its way out of recession. In some respects the very opposite was the case. Whitaker, in particular, should be regarded, not as some genial magician conjuring largesse out of thin air, but as the stern exponent of 'productive' investment he has always in fact remained. Indeed, some of his remarks at the time were reminiscent of nothing so much as earlier Cumann na nGaedheal attitudes and like them might have evoked a hollow laugh from the poor. 'A slowing down in housing and certain other forms of social investment', he bleakly predicted in *Economic Development*, 'will occur from now on because needs are virtually satisfied over wide areas of the state' (Blackwell 1982: 52). However, as it turned out, Whitaker's prescriptions in this regard were simply ignored and eventually ignored to such an heroic extent that the economy was brought to ruin. Not the least reason for this was the general intellectual confusion among those favouring a new departure. Few were prepared to follow Whitaker in his unwelcome insistence that states, like individuals, cannot easily have both this *and* that at the same time. Many, indeed, believed that conditions had become so bad that caution should be thrown to the winds and a resounding affirmative given to James Dillon (Minister for Agriculture in Costello's inter-party administration) when he asked 'Do we mean to house the people, provide hospital beds for the sick, or do we not? I think we do, and prophesying woe and dislocation . . . cuts no ice at all, because whatever the economic consequences . . . [of] providing hospital beds and evacuating verminous tenement rooms, they cannot be worse than letting TB patients cough their lungs out in the family kitchen' (Fanning 1983: 170).

Of course in some important respects the emphasis upon 'productive' investment was not entirely ignored. In particular a good deal was done to attract foreign enterprises through tax concessions and other benefits. By 1969 more than 350 new foreign-owned companies had come to the Republic, though many of the existing firms showed few signs of abandoning the lethargic practices of yesteryear (Walsh 1979). However, despite all such efforts, the share of jobs provided by manufacturing rose by a mere 5 percentage points between 1961 and 1984 and it was left to the growing services sector to mop up most of those who could no longer find a living on the land (Table 8.1). Agriculture had in fact featured prominently in the First and the more detailed Second Programme for Economic Expansion drawn up in 1958 and 1963 respectively. In both cases, however, it entirely failed to live up to expectations and proved a serious disappointment.

Table 8.1 Employment by sectors in the twenty-six counties, 1926–84 (in percentages)

	Agriculture etc.	Manufacturing etc.	Services
1926	53.6	12.8	33.6
1936	49.9	16.1	34.0
1946	47.1	16.6	36.3
1951	41.5	22.1	36.4
1961	36.9	23.5	39.6
1971	26.9	29.6	43.5
1981	17.4	30.8	51.8
1984	16.7	28.7	54.6

(Source: Gillmor 1985: 31)

221

In the event the whole planning enterprise ran rapidly into the sands. Not only did agriculture fail to perform as predicted, but Whitaker's hopes of lower taxation and much reduced public spending were never fulfilled (Walsh 1986). Indeed, the very plans designed to produce a fiscal policy for sustained economic growth seem, instead, to have heralded high levels of government expenditure on social welfare payments of all kinds. They did this not because there was any logical connection between the two things, but because the increased prosperity which undoubtedly occurred in the 1960s lulled politicians and public alike into a belief that all things were now possible in the best of all possible worlds. That in truth the growth achieved was not at all remarkable by international standards mattered less than the feeling that stagnation had at last been overcome. Comparisons had traditionally always been made with the United Kingdom and here at least it seemed as if Ireland could now glow with pride. Unfortunately Britain had for some time been the sick man of Europe, so that progress in this respect merely served to demonstrate that in the regions of the blind even the one-eyed man could be king. Thus, while per capita gross national product in the Republic grew from 55 per cent of the United Kingdom's in 1960 to 65 per cent in 1973, with respect to other European countries as different as France, West Germany, Belgium, Denmark, Italy, Greece, and Holland the move was actually in the opposite direction and sometimes substantially so (Bairoch 1976: 307). And much the same continued to be the case after 1973, with the result that by 1985 Ireland's per capita gross domestic product stood at 59 per cent of the European Community average – lower, that is, than it had been a quarter of a century before (Blackwell 1982; Weinz 1986: 87).

IV

By at last beginning after 1958 to plug itself into the world economy and by cutting tariffs throughout the 1960s, both unilaterally and through the bilateral provisions of the Anglo-Irish Trade Agreement of 1965, the Republic was able to benefit from buoyant international trends while still temporarily maintaining a considerable (if reducing) degree of protection for its own industries (McAleese 1982: 285). It would, in any case, have required monstrous incompetence not to make *some* progress at this time and to continue to do so until the first oil price crisis erupted in 1973. While, therefore, domestic decisions have never been unimportant, the comparatively modest Hibernian boomlet of the 1960s 'was less a consequence of planning than of the remarkably high level of world activity in this period', and also, it must be allowed, 'of the move in Irish policy from a closed economic system to a more open one' (Cullen 1972: 184). In other words, the real significance of the events of 1958 lies in the area of policy rather than planning. And, given that this is so, it is hardly surprising that many previous writers on the matter, after asserting the high importance of *Economic Development* and the First Programme, have often found it difficult to identify the mechanisms by which many of the plans therein contained are actually supposed to have affected the world of hard knocks. Some, indeed, have gone on to conclude that perhaps the most important success achieved by Whitaker and Lemass was a psychological one: they simply persuaded people into optimism (Walsh 1979: 36; Brown 1981: 241; Daly 1981a: 167; Gillmor 1985: 10). Yet, significant as shifts in popular temper can be, it does, nonetheless, seem a very Nietzschean view to assign quite so vital a role in the creation of material prosperity to something as intangible as a mighty triumph of the will.

With the economy accelerating in the 1960s government expenditure began to mount even in relation to an increasing gross national product: from less than 21 per cent in 1960/1 to more than 28 per cent in 1968. As part of this total the cost of social security, education, and housing rose from 7.5 to 9.5 per cent and then to 10.7 per cent in 1981, by which time real expenditure in these fields had grown by a factor of three (Meenan 1970: 251; McCashin 1982: 209). When in 1973 the first oil crisis called a halt to global expansion Irish policy makers, remembering what had happened before 1958 but forgetting that history never repeats itself, deliberately chose to assume that life could go on as before. By 1979, the year of the second rise in oil prices, they had evidently become incapable of breaking the spell of their own self-enchantment. Already in 1972 the convention of not running a current budget deficit had been abandoned. This proved a disastrous decision for (to return briefly to the realm of economic psychology) it seems to have removed those inhibitions which had previously allowed Keynesianism to function in a context of moderation and restraint. Governments of all persuasions began to behave as if prosperity no longer needed to be earned. In particular, borrowing rose to new heights, despite the fact that an economy now heavily dependent on foreign trade and no longer enjoying the strong credit balances abroad which had been a feature of earlier crises, had, in the justifiable pursuit of growth, inevitably rendered itself more vulnerable than before.

Like all profligates the Republic enjoyed a brief vision of fairyland. Already in the 1960s the population had started to rise for the first time since the Famine. In the following decade emigrants actually began to return (though some also continued to leave) and dramatic increases were recorded at successive censuses: from a low point of 2,818,000 in 1961 to no less than 3,537,000 a quarter of a century later. At the same time demographic patterns became less idiosyncratic: the age of marriage fell, as did marital fertility, though in many rural areas celibacy remained common enough (Walsh 1985; Drudy 1986). Yet the legacy of earlier departures meant that the population's age distribution now became idiosyncratic in turn, with, by 1979, no less than 31 per cent under 15 years of age and 11 per cent over 65. As a result, the fruits of the real prosperity of the 1960s and the false prosperity thereafter have consisted, in part at least, of having to find jobs for teenagers and provide care for the elderly to an extent beyond that required elsewhere in Europe and well beyond that which Ireland itself had ever known.

Substantial welfare improvements were undoubtedly introduced during the decades after 1958. The number covered by state insurance schemes rose from 69 to 85 per cent of the labour force between 1966 and 1979. The real value of benefits increased in the 1970s and provision became far more generally (sometimes universally) available, especially in the fields of education and health. Already by the late 1960s public expenditure on health had roughly doubled in real terms over the previous ten years, while in 1972 those receiving free medical treatment were at long last able to enjoy a 'choice of doctors' (McCashin 1982; Hensey 1982; Barrington 1987: 265). Yet much poverty remained and, despite all the advances, Ireland continued to be a laggard in the European welfare league.

Although some warning voices were raised after 1973, among them that of Whitaker himself, the consequences of what was going on were disguised, in part by public myopia, in part by the initial bonanza which Ireland, and especially Irish agriculture, experienced on joining the European Economic Community in January of that year. For Irish industry entry constituted another important stage in the pursuit of those outward-looking policies first introduced in the late 1950s. While most indigenous industries continued to fall back, the substantial influx of foreign firms produced what was by European standards a strong overall performance. But while the benefits were tangible enough, the dangers were at first less visible. These have, however, in recent years become more obvious, flowing as they do from the fact that the type of foreign business attracted to Ireland 'lacks strong ties with any particular economic environment and is thus sufficiently mobile to choose the lowest cost site suitable for its purposes' (Blackwell and O'Malley 1984: 135). However, the agricultural sector, which in the 1960s had experienced a bitter campaign of mass protest against government policies (Manning 1979), entered a five-year period of unalloyed well-being, largely at the expense of consumers elsewhere in the Common Market. By 1978 the EEC was handing over £447.1 million to Ireland (almost nine-tenths of it relating to agriculture) while receiving a mere £42 million in return: by 1983 net receipts had climbed to £522.4 million (Weinz 1986: 92). Price support, which had provided about 15 per cent of agricultural income in 1957, rose so enormously after entry to the Common Market that by 1977 it was furnishing roughly a half (Matthews 1982: 259). Family farm incomes rose rapidly in relation to average industrial earnings: from 75 per cent in 1971 to 106 per cent in 1977 (Cox and Kearney 1983: 172), though the bulk of the benefits of price support went to the wealthiest farmers with the largest sales (Commins 1985). Indeed, because the burden of more expensive food falls disproportionately upon the most indigent sections of society, it is highly probable that agricultural price policy has actually redistributed 'income from the relatively poor to the relatively well-off' (Matthews 1982: 264).

Already in the 1960s the larger towns had led the way in presenting a new appearance to the world: more cars, better clothes, the spread of plastic into lounge bars, new buildings, more electrical goods, more TV sets to receive programmes transmitted from Britain and by the national television service established in 1961. A decade later the countryside followed suit with an orgy of destruction as old farmsteads were torn down and replaced by curiously suburban bungalows or even at times by Hibernicized versions of what increasingly affluent farmers had seen on their holidays along the Costa del Sol.

It was not to last. By the end of the 1970s even the Common Market had begun to realize that agriculture might prove a bottomless pit. A sharp drop in prices occurred and aggregate farm incomes fell by 40 per cent between 1978 and 1980 while the relationship of family farm income to average industrial earnings collapsed from 104 to 53 per cent (Cox and Kearney 1983: 172; Sheehy 1984: 89). As agriculture entered into severe depression the veil of self-delusion proved progressively less and less capable of hiding the economic problems which had been allowed to develop. Gradually it began to dawn on people that the bird that had come home to roost was the albatross (Lee 1986: 153). The increase in living standards over the previous ten years had been financed by borrowing on both the domestic and the international markets. The current spending of public authorities had grown from 24 per cent of gross national product in 1958 to 42 per cent in 1978 and no less than 50 per cent in 1985: if capital spending is added the proportions become higher still. By 1986 total public-sector debt stood at one and a half times gross national product (McDowell 1982: 184; *Sunday Tribune* [Dublin]: 8 Feb. 1987). The large rise in the number of civil servants from 36,388 in 1968 to 60,463 in 1980 (Chubb 1982: 246), the fact that while total employment had only gone up by 26,000 between 1957 and 1980 public employment had risen from 117,600 to no less than 214,300 (Blackwell 1982: 49), the many expensive improvements in social services, had all of them to a large extent been paid for with borrowed money.

With the economy showing virtually no growth at all in the 1980s unsympathetic critics have begun to employ phrases like 'banana republic' and – according to some (though only some) league tables – not without cause. Ireland has the fourth largest foreign debt per person in the world (after Kuwait, the United Arab Emirates, and Israel). By the more revealing measure of the ratio of debt to gross national product it ranks eighth, behind Chile but ahead of Mexico (*Financial Times*: 24 Sept. 1987). The easier methods of escape have all been tried and have all failed. Relatively huge capital investment by both the public and the private sectors yielded extremely disappointing results (Barrington 1982: 92; McDowell 1982: 185–6). Massive rises in personal taxation (especially for employees) proved quite unable to furnish the amounts required. Entry into the European Monetary System in 1979 and the consequent break with sterling created more troubles than it solved, in large part because Britain unobligingly failed to join as well (McAleese 1986b: 98–101). By the mid-1980s harsher measures were so obviously necessary that even weak governments relying on a myriad of irresponsible pressure groups began to tackle a few of the many problems which had for long been allowed to fester unchecked. Inflation was brought down dramatically and the balance of payments situation greatly improved. But the first signs of a wider attack did not start to appear until the budget of March 1987 when a new Fianna Fail government under Charles Haughey put forward proposals designed to reduce the budget deficit and get annual government borrowing down from 13 to 8 per cent of gross national product, a level at which the overall ratio of total debt to GNP would at least be stabilized (*Financial Times*: 24 Sept. 1987). Though these are modest enough plans and while, coming as they do from a source previously dedicated to markedly less thrifty policies, one wonders whether all the necessary and highly painful cuts will in the end be made, it does look as if someone has at last begun to take Whitaker's warning to heart, that, as he recently put it, 'Adults should not believe in Santa Claus' (*Irish Times*: 23 Feb. 1987).

In the long run Ireland's economic performance has been unimpressive. 'No other economy in the whole of Europe appears to have experienced remotely so slow a growth of its total gross national product'. If things 'do not look quite so forlorn in terms of per capita income', that is because the population has grown less rapidly than elsewhere; yet, even by this measure, Ireland has fallen behind every other nation in Europe (save Britain) that was ahead of it sixty-five years ago (Lee 1986: 153–4). More recently, although recession has been a general phenomenon, the Republic has again performed less well than most other countries. Net emigration has resurfaced to reach 31,000 (or 8.8 per thousand population) in the twelve months ending in April 1986. Unemployment stood at almost 20 per cent in the following year. Rural life in the western regions – though much less so in other areas (Kennedy 1985b) – is riddled with alienation, depression, and poverty, though whether this marks a change from conditions before the Second War remains a matter of dispute (Arensberg and Kimball 1968; Brody 1973; Scheper-Hughes 1979; Hannan 1982; Gibbon 1973). Metropolitan Dublin, with about a third of the total population, exhibits all the signs of economic recession cohabiting with headlong growth. It is the epicentre, not only of an over-centralized bureaucracy, but of rising crime rates, which now, in certain respects, exceed those of urban Britain. Drugs too have become a widespread problem and provide a sphere of aggrandizement for 'political' as well as for merely criminal operators (Rottman 1986).

Perhaps the most striking aspect of Ireland's social and economic environment since independence is how rigid have remained the relativities within society as a whole. It is not simply that, hidden behind a general increase in living standards, there were in 1986

227

some 811,000 people trying to exist on welfare payments where the basic single adult rate was less than fifty Irish pounds a week (*Sunday Tribune*: 8 Feb. 1987), but that mobility between classes and redistribution between rich and poor have remained, for all but a lucky few, mere dreams. Of course there has been a good deal of social change – agricultural decline and other developments have, for example, greatly reduced the number of self-employed persons (Rottman and O'Connell 1982: 69–71) – but all of this has amounted to little more than rearranging the old furniture. The prosperous – large farmers, professional people, captains of industry – have all proved tenaciously successful in retaining their slice of whatever cake was being baked.

To say this is not to accept the nostalgic views of those who contrast a new harshness with the 'old easy-going, tolerant, egalitarian ways' of yesteryear (Brown 1981: 265 citing assistant editor of *Irish Times*), for such attitudes do no more than create a past that never was. Rather it is to emphasize how little has changed as regards the manner in which men and women find themselves placed upon the ladder of life. Social mobility in Ireland has been more restricted than in countries like England, Sweden or France. The degree of inequality of opportunity 'is high by international standards' (Whelan 1986: 83). During the boom of the 1970s the Republic was far less prepared to redistribute income through its tax and benefits system than was the United Kingdom (O'Connell 1982). Indeed, it is quite probable that in relative terms there was actually a shift from the poor to those at the top of the economic scale (Blackwell 1982: 45). And nowhere has the special pleading of the privileged proved more successful than in the field of education. Here the massive increase in state expenditure which began in the 1960s has merely had the effect of reinforcing the existing allocation of advantages: the many support the few and demands can even be heard that the few who benefit most should be given more (McCashin 1982: 216). Above all, therefore, the education system has served to keep the rich man in his castle and the poor men at the gate and it has done so with an efficiency and to a degree rarely found elsewhere in Europe. Overall, indeed, 'the same families, by and large, have continued to occupy the most advantaged positions . . . [and] large scale property-holdings or professional qualifications in the 1950s were able to secure a comparable level of advantage for the children born to such families in the 1960s and 1970s, either through inheritance or through disproportionate shares in the educational credentials that had the greatest market value' (Rottman and O'Connell 1982: 75).

The fact that the Republic has failed to fulfil the pledges of the 1916 Declaration of Independence, the Democratic Programme of 1919, and Article 45 of the Constitution of 1937 to cherish all the children of the nation equally and provide for their physical, mental, and spiritual well-being is hardly surprising. Subsequent realities rarely match initial promises. But that so little relative progress has been made, that the handicap weights carried by individuals have been redistributed hardly at all, that, by western standards, Ireland remains not only a highly unequal society but one in which inequality is generally apportioned by accident rather than ability, adds up to at best a poignant and at worst a melancholy commentary upon almost seven decades of self-rule.

CHAPTER 9
Religion
Piety and its Spoils

If by the 1920s religion had come to mean different things in the different parts of a now formally divided island a recognition of its importance was, nonetheless, at once universal and ill-defined. In the North denominational affiliation continued to be used as a measuring rod with which to calculate the relative superiorities and inferiorities of a provincial society. In the South Catholicism had become so powerful a force for cultural homogeneity that Protestants needed little excuse for seeking a means of escape – either abroad or into a species of make-believe internal exile where clocks stood still and life went on 'much as before' (Inglis 1962). While the Free State adopted, almost without protest, the legislative appurtenances of 'Catholic' ethics, the North pursued a no less sectarian or, indeed, clericalist path. Of course the six counties, as part of the United Kingdom, were occasionally obliged to compromise with the forces of darkness in the shape of easier divorce, the availability of contraceptive devices, and so on. Yet, in many important respects, their Unionist leaders proved willing enough to sustain a Protestant version of that ecclesiastical triumphalism established over large areas of southern life in the decades after 1921. This was all the more remarkable in the light of the fact that, while Catholics dominated the twenty-six counties by ten to one (and eventually by more than twenty to one), Protestants constituted less than two-thirds of Northern Ireland's population and were in addition divided between the Church of Ireland, mainstream Presbyterianism, and many lesser sects besides.

I

In the South the Catholic Church had already achieved so much that few worlds remained for it to conquer. As an institution it continued to expand. On a thirty-two county basis the ratio of parochial clergy to laity increased from 1 to 1149 in 1901 to 1 to 861 in 1961 and that of all priests (including members of religious orders) from 1 to 963 to no less than 1 to 558 (Newman 1962: 6). In addition, there were nuns and brothers belonging to teaching orders, many of whom – like many Irish priests – worked abroad. Indeed, taking all these elements into account, a recent estimate – made *after* vocations had already begun to decline – suggests that Ireland's religious personnel in 1981 amounted to 21,026 at home and 6044 overseas, a total of 27,070 in all (Inglis 1987: 47). Although the actual number of churches was not greatly increased after 1921, many were extended or demolished and replaced by grander buildings. In the Dublin area alone thirty-two substantial churches were put up during a dozen years after the end of the Second World War (Blanchard 1963: 54) and significant investment in seminaries, monasteries, convents, and the like also took place.

The clergy continued to depend upon the offerings of the faithful. They also continued to come from the same social backgrounds as before. A survey of a western diocese in the 1950s showed that almost half the seminarians belonged to the 'rural classes' and more than a quarter were the sons of 'traders'. This was concrete evidence of the survival of that alliance between farmers and shopkeepers which had long dominated the outlook of the church and was now to prove so powerful in shaping the 'political, social and cultural moulds of the independent state' (Blanchard 1963: 106; Brown 1981: 26). According to a leading clerical sociologist (himself appointed Bishop of Limerick in 1974), all this was of simply 'immeasurable . . . pastoral advantage', for it meant that 'parish clergy, farmers, rural businessmen and white-collar workers speak the same language, as it were, or, to put it differently, are on the same wavelength' (Fahy 1971: 10). Small wonder, therefore, that many people continued to be excluded from this closed circle of shared understanding. With agricultural labourers no longer worth discriminating against, the urban working class – though singularly pious (Humphreys 1966: 37–8) – took their place. Thus, for example, while Archbishop McQuaid of Dublin (1940–72) may well have been one of the few members of the hierarchy to display much energy in the field of social welfare (Corish 1985: 248), he also, for much of his episcopate, presided over a diocese in which many churches were physically divided between superior areas where a sixpenny offering was solicited and inferior ones at the back where only threepence was required.

Just as independent Ireland was entering a fuller democracy so the church moved smartly in the opposite direction. Ever since the 1820s parish priests had played a formal role in the selection of bishops. And even on those occasions when Rome had decided to reject their choice the very publicity surrounding the business had at least made secret wire pulling more embarrassing than it might otherwise have been. From 1925 onwards, however, all this changed (Keogh 1986: 230–1). The views of priests were, indeed, still to be 'ascertained', but in no very precise or ordered fashion. In effect, the episcopate (apart from occasional hiccups when the Vatican wished to assert higher priorities) was now virtually allowed to become a self-selecting oligarchy at once changeless and – in all save personal eccentricities – conventional.

During the 1920s a good deal of political nimbleness was displayed on all sides, even if at first much of the footwork was hidden from the public's gaze. Throughout the years immediately before and during the Civil War the bishops – singly and in unison – poured the oils of legitimacy over the pro-Treaty party. In April 1922 a joint pronouncement actually echoed Collins's own words when it urged the people to accept the Treaty and 'make the most of the freedom it undoubtedly brings' (Younger 1970: 277). The following October a pastoral letter declared the killing of 'national' soldiers 'murder' and barred all those who persevered 'in such evil courses' from being absolved in confession or admitted to holy communion (Keogh 1986: 95–6; Whyte 1980: 10–11). De Valera, though deeply upset, took as little practical notice of all this as the later IRA was to do when it too was formally condemned in 1931, 1956, and on numerous occasions more recently (Fanning 1983: 104; Whyte 1980: 320–1). Not only could sympathetic priests always be found but keeping one's fingers crossed behind one's spiritual back had become something of a revolutionary art form in itself.

Less public were the efforts in the 1920s of some bishops, notably Byrne of Dublin, to persuade Cosgrave's government to take a less intransigent line over reprisals and executions generally. And at the Irish College in Rome a number of senior churchmen who disapproved strongly of what they saw as the episcopate's habit of condemning 'every forward movement of Irish nationality' kept alternative lines of communication open and proved an important influence in encouraging de Valera to enter constitutional politics in 1926. The bishops themselves made no secret of their opposition to renewed efforts by the Vatican to intervene in nationalist quarrels and virtually boycotted an unfortunate delegate sent by Pius XI to Ireland in 1923 (Keogh 1986: 102–21, 87). They had never much liked the papacy's previous attempts to deal directly with Irish matters and were now – as they had not been in the 1880s – confident enough to make this absolutely plain from the start. Indeed, however things may at times have looked, the local church authorities remained comparatively faithful throughout the 1920s to their traditional policy of not putting all their eggs into a single basket. And by following such a course they not only allowed de Valera's instinctive devotionalism to rise above the waves but ensured that no significant element in the South's political life would, in the foreseeable future, seek to espouse principles deeply unpalatable to ecclesiastical minds.

If from the perspective of the early 1920s the future of the church's influence was thus – partly by accident partly by instinctual design – assured, the present also furnished rewards at once significant and gratifying. Rising illegitimacy rates, an international preoccupation with decadence, worries about the large number of unmarried people in rural areas all helped to render the period a time of high moral nervousness. Bishops and priests encouraged such feelings and were themselves simultaneously swept along by vociferous elements among the laity. Then as later a mutual discourse of encouragement between clergy and lay activists helped to inflate eternal moral fears into occasional bursts of intense and unusual anxiety. As independence had at last made possible the creation of a Catholic state, so it is not surprising that the opening decades of that state's existence should have been marked by formal manoeuvres designed to align secular law to ecclesiastical imperatives. And, given the manner in which the church had long worked out its priorities, such alignments were inevitably concerned, above all, with matters of sexual morality broadly interpreted.

A succession of statutes marks out the pace and extent of the processes involved. In 1923 film censorship was introduced under the control of a paid official with extensive powers. Six years later a long campaign by the Irish Vigilance Association, the Catholic Truth Society, and the Priests' Social Guild, together with the labours of a Committee on Evil Literature set up by the government, resulted in the Censorship of Publications Act. Five unpaid censors under priestly chairmanship were soon briskly banning real pornography, real literature, and pamphlets advocating 'artificial' birth control with, so far as one can see, indiscriminate enthusiasm. Not, however, until the 1940s were sustained protests mounted on the side of those who thought all this too severe. Until then the opposite had, if anything, been the case (Adams 1968). Again, in 1924 and 1927 restrictions were placed upon the sale of intoxicating liquor – perhaps the prime example of the state's deference to extreme 'Catholic' norms (Whyte 1980: 36). And, although nineteenth-century British divorce reforms had never been extended to Ireland in the first place, Cosgrave's government, after consultations with the hierarchy, so arranged matters in 1925 that even the existing cumbersome procedure of bringing private divorce bills to the legislature was rendered impossible. In effect, the Free State simply refused to countenance divorce, a prohibition made stronger still when it was written into de Valera's new constitution of 1937 (Fanning 1983: 54–6; Fitzpatrick 1987).

The religious triumphalism of the Cumann na nGaedheal years reached its public apogee with the celebration in 1929 of the centenary of Catholic Emancipation. Half a million people attended mass in Phoenix Park outside Dublin. A papal envoy gratifyingly declared it was 'pious, it was good, it was Irish' and newspapers dug out their largest type to proclaim 'FAITH OF OUR FATHERS TRIUMPHANT, THE NATION'S ACT OF THANKSGIVING' (Keogh 1986: 153). Three years later another, more international, festival was held in the shape of a Eucharistic Congress. Though planned by Cosgrave's administration, the results of the general election held in February 1932 meant that it was de Valera who was allowed to bask in the fervour and enthusiasm generated. Again there were enormous crowds. Again the whole country was *en fête*. Again a papal envoy perambulated the land. Government ministers, lord mayors, and members of the Dail joined huge open-air congregations to 'renounce the devil: and all his works and pomps'. In particular, the affair showed that the arrival of Fianna Fail was destined to cause only the smallest of ripples upon the calm surface of relations between church and state. Indeed, the new ministers' most dramatic initial innovation consisted of their willingness to offend the pope's legate by wearing lounge suits rather than formal dress (Keogh 1986: 188–96).

As a parliamentary opposition Fianna Fail had already gone out of its way to beat the Catholic drum and out-Cosgrave the pious Cosgrave himself (Fanning 1983: 129; Keogh 1986: 160–2). And this remained the policy after de Valera came to power in 1932. Admittedly there was now a rather greater determination to draw a line beyond which the church's wishes ceased to carry automatic authority. But all the frequently-catalogued acts of machismo by de Valera in 'standing up' to the church amounted in reality to little enough. He rejected episcopal attacks on the Economic War, moved more slowly against the IRA than bishops would have liked, and refused to become sufficiently agitated over the republican lurch to the left in the early 1930s. Above all he declined to follow the hierarchy in its vociferous demands for immediate recognition of the Franco government and for some kind of 'intervention' in the Spanish Civil War (Whyte 1980: 89–93). But while none of this was without a certain significance, it scarcely marked a dramatic new departure. Things continued more or less as before. The church remained by far the most important institution in the state. And the state remained as much under the control of laymen as it had been from the start.

Fianna Fail smoothly extended the litany of moral reforms initiated by its predecessor. In 1933 a tax was placed upon imported newspapers, something the bishops had long desired. Two years later the sale of contraceptive devices (or instruments of 'race suicide' as they were widely called) was made a criminal offence. Also in 1935 a long clerical campaign against immodest deportment and 'company-keeping' was crowned by a Dance Halls Act which (not very successfully) regulated the licensing and management of such places. From the early 1920s pastoral letters had grieved that morally uplifting Irish dances were being discarded in favour of foreign importations which, 'according to all accounts, lent themselves not so much to rhythm as to loose sensuality' (Akenson 1975: 138; Whyte 1980: 25). Bishop O'Doherty of Galway urged fathers to 'lay the lash' upon the backs of disobedient daughters, while his colleagues generally identified the 'Evil One' as working, above all, through 'the dance hall, the bad book, the indecent paper, the motion picture, the immodest fashion in female dress – all of which tend to destroy the virtues characteristic of our race' (Whyte 1980: 26–7).

If the activities of Limerick's Mary Immaculate Modest Dress and Deportment Crusade and fears of what took place between unmarried couples on 'the dark way home' from dance halls were firmly in line with post-Famine norms, a more modish note was struck by the concurrent battle against 'jazz music' and decadent motoring. Cars (invariably referred to as 'roadsters') were

235

denounced as little more than mobile occasions of sin enabling 'evil minded roysterers' to cover vast distances in an unceasing quest for immorality. Jazz, it was claimed, excited the passions, either because of its 'nigger' (Archbishop Gilmartin of Tuam) or 'Ethiopian' (Mr Casey of Westmeath) origins or possibly – as was readily apparent from the 'masochistic melancholy of the average foxtrot' – because the Jews were behind it all (*The Irish Rosary*). Doctors of medicine published articles on 'Eliminating Sex Incitements: The Dance'. The Gaelic League accused one government minister of 'jazzing every night of the week' – perhaps a hitherto unnoticed aspect of Fianna Fail's secularizing thrust. In Wexford a county councillor, neatly killing two birds with a single stone, thought jazz simply 'dancing gone Bolshevik' (Kennedy 1985c).

Not the least striking aspect of such manifestations was the fact that priests and bishops were far from alone in the tightness of their moral attitudes. The anti-dancing campaign represented little more than a Hibernian version of contemporary global obsessions, while on divorce priests were merely expressing the necessary requirements of a special kind of rural society (Fitzpatrick 1987: 196). Already for years the church's stress upon sexual purity had 'dovetailed perfectly with the people's social and economic patterns. In his sermons the local curate articulated as moral virtues a code of sexual mores to which the people were committed through social usage' (Akenson 1975: 139). The advent of political independence simply made it possible to add legislative weapons to an already powerful armoury of moral control.

Those who thought that this was not enough were, however, far from satisfied. If Rev. Denis Fahey of the Holy Ghost Fathers presented an unusual *combination* of views when denouncing freemasonry (responsible for, among other things, the French and Russian Revolutions), international Jewry, 'usury', and processed white bread (Whyte 1980: 72–3) there were many who knew that smoke could never be produced without fire. And the sustained invective against liberalism and Protestantism of the *Catholic Bulletin* (whose editor earned obituary recognition for his 'heroic intolerance') showed the lengths to which a remorseless logic could drive contemporary Catholic attitudes.

Yet, in the end, a sense of reality never entirely deserted those in control of the state. While enthusiasm for corporatism was aroused by a papal encyclical in 1931 and certain clerics and academics began to talk in a jew jargon about 'vocational organization' and 'subsidiary function' (Whyte 1980: 66–72), de Valera felt confident enough to disguise his boredom with no more than the merest figleafs of concession. His new constitution, sometimes mistakenly hailed as a vehicle for corporatist thinking, was in reality a clear and unambiguous statement of Irish Catholicism at its most 'traditional'. What, indeed, de Valera was doing in 1937 was merely putting into effect many of those things Cumann na nGaedheal ministers would almost certainly have liked to do fifteen years earlier had they not been committed to Treaty restraints imposed upon them by the British government of the time.

It has become something of a cliché to emphasize the liberal, even secular, nature of the constitution of 1922 (Whyte 1980: 14). What is often forgotten is that, while Cosgrave's administration had little freedom of manoeuvre on the matter, it was still able to smuggle in, as it were, some earnests of Catholic intent. Most notable among these was the qualification that 'freedom of conscience' be granted only 'subject to public order and morality', a phrase quite consciously directed against 'Mormonism and things of that sort' – 'Mormonism' being a 'contemporary code-word for remarriage following civil divorce' (Fitzpatrick 1987: 188; Nolan 1975). Of course de Valera's constitution represented a genuine shift of tone, with its recognition of the 'special position' of the Catholic Church, its emphasis upon the 'natural' rights of the family, its prohibition of divorce, its making blasphemy a *constitutional* offence. But, however distasteful Protestants and a handful of liberal Catholics may have found the language and however many hostages were undoubtedly being given to unionists in the North, certain bishops would have liked a good deal more (Keogh 1986: 207–20). One idiosyncratic judge, Mr Justice Gavan Duffy, admittedly used the constitution to introduce some dubious sectarian innovations into the law. But none of his colleagues were moved to follow suit, so that, in the end, the document proved a disappointment to those who had hoped that it might help to bring about a greater and more formal integration between the ecclesiastical and the secular worlds.

Overall, indeed, the cultural experience of the inter-war years proved somewhat less negative than is often supposed. Of course the values which the church helped to sustain were relatively narrow and reflected almost a hundred years of struggle to render Ireland a special kind of religious society. That, after all, was what a great deal of recent Irish nationalism had been about. Yet, despite the complaints of the intelligentsia about the difficulty of reading world literature in the Free State and notwithstanding the petty-mindedness of the times, not all would think Ireland's failure to plug into the febrile and modish commercialisms so evident elsewhere an unmitigated disaster. Resistance to pornography, to siren calls for 'adult' standards in morality, to the drumbeats of global integration did not amount to an entirely despicable enterprise however diminished it may have been by a lack of social awareness and a debilitating atmosphere of self-congratulation all round.

II

Although an ubiquitous strain of anti-English feeling ran through much of the Catholic moralism of the Free State, the very extent to which religion had become the central symbol of nationality helped to torpedo the more strictly cultural and linguistic aspirations which had formed the other prominent strand in revolutionary thought. Whereas, therefore, in the case of Catholicism, the people both genuflected and believed, in that of Gaelicism genuflection was all the great majority proved willing to supply (Hutchinson 1987: 309–10).

Once the bishops had been persuaded that the church's entrenched position as regards schooling would become stronger still the whole issue of education and Irish language revival moved from the realms of power politics into those of symbol and illusion. Primary schools remained under the control of 'managers' – a few of them Protestant ministers, the rest Catholic priests – while the state paid almost all of the costs. At the secondary level private (mostly ecclesiastical) enterprise was modestly augmented by government grants and the newly-independent state proved more than willing to abandon the official attempts made just before 1921 to improve the lot of lay teachers. These, therefore, continued to be exploited, underpaid, and undervalued by church and state alike (Ó Cuív 1966; Daly 1981a: 186–7). Indeed, between 1932 and 1945 the number of lay primary teachers fell from 12,480 to 10,820 while that of those in religious life actually rose by almost a tenth (Titley 1983: 110–35). Yet, because, once again, the church was moving with, rather than against, the grain of public opinion, it experienced few difficulties in extending the system of clerical control inherited from the days of British rule.

Influential educational conferences in the early 1920s concluded that the nation's 'fibre' could best be strengthened by 'giving the language, history, music and traditions of Ireland their natural place in the life of the schools' (Bowen 1983b: 156). The ubiquitous Father Timothy Corcoran, professor of education at University College Dublin until shortly before his death in the mid-1940s, exercised a stridently chauvinistic influence over what was taught in all but Protestant establishments. School history, in the Corcoranian view, was to be firmly 'national rather than international' (Akenson 1975: 194). In the South, therefore, British history was simply ignored save as a demonology of wickedness and folly. In Ulster's Protestant schools the very opposite occurred: Britain was made the embodiment of all excellence, so that the past became, in the strictest sense, 'another country' where things had been done not only differently but admirably as well (Murray 1985: 56–7).

Corcoran, who had the disconcerting habit of 'dropping in' on the Department of Education, wrote copiously against the Reformation, the Enlightenment, 'soft pedagogy', and foreign literature (Titley 1983: 94–100). Although not himself a speaker of Irish he was enthusiastically dictatorial about the benefits children would derive from its compulsory exposition. The mixture of absolutism and insularity which characterized his approach was forcefully echoed by the *Catholic Bulletin* (to which he was a frequent anonymous contributor) when it insisted that 'the Irish nation is the Gaelic nation; its language and literature is the Gaelic language; its history is the history of the Gael. All other elements have no place in Irish national life, literature and tradition, save as far as they are assimilated into the very substance of Gaelic speech, life and thought' (Brown 1981: 63).

Even if not all concerned could match Corcoran's steeliness of vision, almost all agreed that the church should dominate both primary and secondary education and that, in consequence, its spiritual values and cultural aims should be allowed a privileged access to the young. Successive ministers of education were entirely sympathetic, for, as one of them declared in 1950, the state was 'determined to see that such facilities as Ecclesiastical Authorities consider proper shall be provided' (Mescal 1957: 137).

Only with regard to the universities did the hierarchy feel it necessary to express a repeated sense of unease. What this amounted to was simple enough: a determination that Catholics should go to the colleges of the National University established in 1908 and not to Trinity College Dublin with its Protestant origins and traditions. In 1927 Catholics were strongly dissuaded from going to Trinity;

in 1944 Archbishop McQuaid forbade those in the archdiocese of Dublin from enrolling without his permission; and in 1956 an outright ban was extended to the country as a whole (Whyte 1980: 305–8). Curiously, therefore, the church's view of Trinity reached a state of arctic frigidity just as the climate elsewhere was beginning to show signs of approaching spring.

In large measure this was because McQuaid (who did not retire until 1972) felt very strongly about the matter which he repeatedly discussed in pastoral letters read out to congregations among whom only a tiny minority can have aspired to higher education of any sort. 'There is a notion', he characteristically grieved in 1961, 'that a university is a school in which youth is expected to think for itself.' This, of course, was not so. Guidance of the strictest kind was essential. Fortunately the National University, adorned as it was by the 'personal and professional dignity of the body of [its] professors' and widely admired for standards 'certified by the fraternal supervision of scholars from other seats of learning', was thoroughly acceptable to the Catholic authorities. Trinity, on the other hand, was the nursemaid of 'liberalism, so wrongly named' (McQuaid 1961). In other words, it was really nineteenth-century continental liberalism, with its intimations of free-thinking and anti-clericalism, which men like McQuaid still feared, despite all the success the church had enjoyed in inoculating the Irish people against what had, by 1961, become a distinctly moth-eaten intellectual bacterium. Eventually, however, his episcopal colleagues called a halt and in 1970 the 'ban' was suddenly removed.

III

Neither the pronouncements of the Catholic hierarchy concerning university education nor the policies of government regarding the Irish language did anything to make southern Protestants feel inclined to come out of the well-padded laagers they had retreated to in 1921. Compulsion in primary schools (where infant teaching was supposed to be entirely through the medium of Irish), an insistence that no pupil could obtain a leaving certificate unless an examination in Irish had been passed, and the requirement that language competence be demonstrated before entry could be obtained to the civil service or to certain professions were, none of them, 'ecumenical' acts. But, while there was much excess and hypocrisy on the part of nationalists (clerics prominent among them) and while mistakes were undoubtedly made, Protestant reactions tended to be patronizing, ostrich-like, and banal. Certainly comments like those in 1926 of Rev. A. A. Luce, Church of Ireland minister and academic, to the effect that the whole enterprise was merely 'eye wash, political window dressing, dope for republicans' (Bowen 1983b: 59) yielded nothing in offensiveness to the diatribes of the *Catholic Bulletin* at the other extreme.

The language revival proved a failure because not enough people saw any urgent reason to learn Irish as a living tongue. The so-called 'native' speakers faded almost entirely away, while even official publications now admit that, for example, the 1981 census total of just over a million speakers 'is a gross figure which fails to make many necessary distinctions in regard to degrees of competence' (*Facts about Ireland* 1985: 81). Given that nationalism had succeeded in finding quite enough popular sustenance from religion, the Irish language became for most people merely an optional extra. Such things were not, however, blindingly obvious in the early years of the Free State.

The tragedy of southern Protestantism lies in the fact that, by the time it had developed enough confidence to accept changed circumstances, it had virtually ceased to exist. In 1911 more than a tenth of the people in the twenty-six counties were Protestants. By 1926 this had fallen to 8 per cent, by 1961 to 5 per cent, and by 1981 to little more than 3 per cent. Obviously the events of 1919–23 drove many into exile. But high rates of Protestant emigration continued for decades thereafter (Kennedy 1973: 110–19), while Rome's insistence that the children of so-called 'mixed' marriages be brought up as Catholics encouraged further leakage as well as much understandable disgust (Bowen 1983b: 40–6; Lee 1985b).

In strictly formal terms Protestants were treated well, sometimes exceedingly well, from the very beginning. As regards education both the state and the Catholic authorities realized that perfect financial equality for so tiny a community would prove the simplest way of safeguarding their own sectarian requirements. Among the professions and the higher reaches of commerce Protestants for long continued to be heavily over-represented, largely because they were an overwhelmingly (though not an exclusively) middle- and upper-class group (Bowen 1983b: 85–94, 134–65). All this, of course, helped to ensure that separateness was maintained rather than diminished – something which suited all sides and meant that all concerned could lay claim to a species of painless goodwill.

241

Protestants belonged to their 'own' clubs, joined the Freemasons and in some cases the Orangemen, even maintained minute distinctions between members of the dominant Church of Ireland and those who adhered to Presbyterianism, Methodism, Congregationalism, or the Society of Friends, all of which, together with many other denominations, maintained small followings in the South (White 1975).

Because they were rich Protestants could support a numerous clergy and thus provide a relatively large army of professionals to patrol sectarian divides. Indeed, the Church of Ireland, with in 1961 one minister to every 201 parishioners was, in this respect, considerably more 'priest-ridden' than even the best-supplied of Catholic dioceses (Bowen 1983b: 118–19). What, however, the Protestant community so long fatally lacked was a sense of confidence. Its early leaders yearned for times gone by and maintained a bizarre faith in Britain as the trustee of 'Christianity in a pagan world' (O'Callaghan 1984: 233). Many of its spokesmen oscillated between private alienation and public expressions of gratitude for not having been driven out of the country entirely. Not until the late 1960s did Protestant clerics feel confident enough to complain sensibly to the government on an issue of real importance when they insisted that new educational reforms, however theoretically even-handed, in fact took little account of their community's peculiar demographic circumstances (Akenson 1975: 110–11, 143–56). By then, however, it was much too late. A combination of external pressure and internal caution had brought things well beyond the boundaries of viability. Indeed, the 100,000 or so Protestants who remain are barely enough to supply the balanced forces required for those ecumenical events which have become so fashionable at more or less the precise moment when participation in them has ceased to require any real sacrifice from either side.

IV

Among the most notorious, if also one of the most potentially misleading, episodes in the history of church–state relations in the twenty-six counties was that concerning the so-called 'mother and child' scheme of 1950–1. This has often been hailed as a prime example of the Catholic Church interfering in political matters and doing so even to the extent of securing the resignation of a cabinet minister. The real story is more complicated.

When the first inter-party government came into office in 1948 the young Dr Noel Browne of Clann na Poblachta was appointed minister for health. He proved energetic, arrogant, and efficient. He hoped to crown his efforts with a plan for providing better medical treatment for children and their mothers. What he did not know was that some few years previously the hierarchy had protested privately to de Valera's government about a related piece of health legislation on the grounds that it gave the state excessive authority over the 'rights' of the family and over those of medical practitioners also (Whyte 1980: 143). Although then operating in a 'vocational' intellectual atmosphere critical of anything likely to increase the centralizing tendencies of contemporary government, it is clear that, from the start, the bishops were more concerned with hardnosed practicalities than with ideological persiflage. Indeed, they had objected to the earlier legislation because it seemed to interfere with the independence of the powerful Catholic secondary school sector (by requiring compulsory medical examination of pupils) rather than because they entertained any wish 'to unsettle the comfortable equanimity' of their relations with the state in pursuit of any recent development in the church's 'social teaching' (McKee 1986: 168).

Much the same was true of the mother and child affair, although the Byzantine complexities which marked its political progress – or rather lack of progress – were caused as much by confusion all round as by ruthless devotion on anyone's part to the exercise of power and authority. Browne's support for universal free medical treatment only emerged late in the day (Barrington 1987: 195–221). But when it did it aroused the medical profession (whose members feared that their private fee incomes would gurgle down the drain) to steadily increasing bouts of protest and rage. When the bishops got to hear of Browne's proposals they objected both to the powers of compulsion given to the Department of Health and to the debilitating effects free treatment for all would have upon the self-reliance of those who could afford to pay. Browne quickly made concessions on the former matter, but, in the erroneous belief that the cabinet was fully behind him, refused to accept the hierarchy's view that moral decline would inevitably flow from giving all mothers and children medical attention without charge. He managed, nonetheless, to persuade himself that he had 'squared' the bishops and was astounded when, months later, the prime minister revealed that this was not in fact the case.

Matters were rendered more complex still by tensions between

Browne and the leader of Clann na Poblachta, Sean MacBride. Eventually Browne was forced to resign and caused a sensation by publishing as much of the relevant correspondence as he possessed. It was this action which at once gave the case its unique status among Ireland's administrative and political disputes and made it seem as if a pioneering minister had been laid low by traditional ecclesiastical power lords acting secretly through spineless secular auxiliaries. But while the published letters contain some wonderful invective from Browne – who on one occasion had written to MacBride (a former IRA chief of staff) that 'your references to a conflict between the spiritual and temporal authorities will occasion a smile among the many people who remember the earlier version of your kaleidoscopic self' (O'Clery 1986: 111–12) – they disguise as much as they reveal. Certainly the bishops played an important role. Equally certainly they experienced little difficulty in persuading the cabinet to take a 'Catholic' line, for most ministers were only too ready to find an excuse for ditching their troublesome colleague. But in the end no one, not even Browne himself, ever denied that the bishops had a perfect right to pronounce on such matters and that loyal Catholics were obliged to take account of their views.

Above all, however, the whole business showed how very dangerous it was for Irish governments to tangle with entrenched interests of any kind. Many ministers disliked Browne's scheme because they sympathized with their school friends and acquaintances in the medical profession. And the doctors proved doubly lucky in finding yet another powerful group – the hierarchy – to fight on their behalf. The true clash had, in any case, always been between the wishes of a reforming minister (and his department) and the self-interested conservatism of the Irish Medical Association. When the latter proved able to persuade the bishops that the survival of private practitioners in the field of public health was crucial to the safeguarding of Catholic morality a specious cloak of principle was very effectively thrown over what had, from the start, been essentially a fight over cash and the privileges cash can buy (Whyte 1980: 120–272; Fanning 1983: 181–7; McKee 1986).

V

The 1950s was the last decade in which ecclesiastics like Bishop Lucey of Cork could still think it unremarkable to insist that the hierarchy was the final arbiter 'of right and wrong even in political matters' (Whyte 1980: 312). In 1957 priests in County Wexford, and some bishops also, happily supported a boycott of Protestants in the village of Fethard over a case involving the religious upbringing of children. Although de Valera as prime minister issued a firm condemnation, the affair left a nasty taste in the mouth (Whyte 1980: 322–5). Yet, over the next twenty years, a considerable change became evident as the church seemed to be making a conscious attempt to render itself – in the fashionable phrase of the day – more 'relevant to modern times'. The Second Vatican Council (1962–5), though regarded with undisguised suspicion by many bishops, made a modest amount of internal adjustment difficult to avoid. Externally too it became possible to liberalize the censorship of films in 1964 and of books three years later despite public objections from certain prominent churchmen. In 1972 few, however, even objected when a referendum gave decisive backing to the deletion from the constitution of the clause proclaiming Catholicism's 'special position' in the state – to date the Republic's only (and painless) constitutional concession to unionist opinion in the North.

With attendances at mass remaining buoyant – in the early 1970s more than 90 per cent of Catholics declared they went at least once a week (Inglis 1987: 26) – it was easy to believe that the ecclesiastical ship was negotiating the seas of change with confidence and success. Yet there were signs that younger Catholics were becoming noticeably less constant than their elders and that university students in particular were beginning to make it plain that adherence to church norms did 'not extend to the personal moral area' (Brown 1981: 302; Inglis 1980). Such forms of compartmentalization had of course always been practised by those pious usurers and exploiters of the poor without whom Irish society in general and religious society in particular might well have ground to a halt. But, while these had confined their lack of moral consistency to the clerically uncontroversial domain of the cash nexus, the young were now moving noisily into the far more 'dangerous' realms of sexual behaviour and social analysis.

As regards one particular question, that of contraception, a failure to follow the church's official teaching has not been confined to students. The papal encyclical *Humanae Vitae* of 1968 condemning 'artificial' birth control has produced for church leaders a new situation in which, despite their best efforts, many Catholics find it perfectly possible to practise both contraception and their faith without consciousness of sin.

The embarrassment involved in publicly recognizing such a state of things also accounts for the crab-like movement of secular legislation on the matter. In 1974 a government bill to permit the strictly limited sale of contraceptive materials was condemned by the bishops and by such as Father Healy SJ who had the good fortune of knowing many 'happy couples . . . who have abstained from sexual intercourse for over twenty years'. It was also rejected by several parliamentary representatives of the party in office, among them none other than the prime minister, Liam Cosgrave, and, less surprisingly, that evergreen crusader against moral laxity, Oliver Flanagan, who took the opportunity to proclaim his belief that 'coupled with the chaotic drinking we have, the singing bars, the side-shows and all-night shows', the availability of condoms 'would bring the country to its knees' (O'Clery 1986: 153–61). Five years later a Fianna Fail government successfully enacted legislation which allowed contraceptives to be sold by chemists on prescription and (it was firmly asserted though not actually written into the act) to married couples alone. This grudging acceptance of reality was memorably described by its chief proponent, Charles Haughey, as 'an Irish solution to an Irish problem' (Whyte 1980: 414–16; Bowen 1983b: 75). By 1985, however, the contradictions involved in this complicated piece of politico-religious gymnastics had become so great that parliament, not without another round of denunciations, eventually legalized the sale of contraceptive devices to all those aged eighteen and over, whether married or not.

The problems associated with the debate over birth control helped to create a 'liberal' constituency composed in the main of middle-class Catholics prepared to question episcopal authority. They also, however, persuaded the hierarchy to reconsider its recent policy of flexibility and respond to the complaints of an increasingly vocal and influential 'backlash' group among their lay followers. At times, indeed, it had almost begun to look as if the clergy was in danger of being left behind by the fervour of the Republic's 'moral majority'. But as the 1980s unrolled so the bishops have undoubtedly moved back, with what private satisfactions or regrets it is difficult to judge, towards the stricter ways of former times.

When in 1983, after much pressure from lay activists, a referendum was held on a proposal to enshrine a clause against abortion (which had never been legal in the Republic but could have been rendered so by simple act of parliament) into the constitution, the bishops delivered themselves of far more than mere advice (Girvin 1986c). Again, in 1986, when another referendum was held on whether divorce (which *was* constitutionally forbidden) should be allowed, the hierarchy, while declaring it did not ask for Catholic doctrine 'as such' to be 'enshrined in law', left individual bishops free to insist that the view of those favouring change 'finds no warrant, no justification in the teaching we have given. It finds no basis in Catholic social and moral doctrine' (Inglis 1987: 87).

In both cases the 'new conservatives' won decisively. As regards abortion, few were surprised. As regards divorce, many were disappointed. Dublin City proved least, rural Connacht most, loyal to traditional values. The fact that turn-out was low – in 1983 it was less than 55 per cent – suggests that many may have been repelled by the stridency which accompanied the respective debates. How far the results reflect a direct response to religious influences is difficult to assess. It does, however, remain the case that large numbers of people voted against the church's declared wishes and, if those who stayed at home are taken into account, only a minority was prepared to come out actively on the side of the angels.

The recrudescence, after only the briefest of intermissions in the 1960s and 1970s, of traditionalist values among significant sections of the laity has been accompanied by something of an upswing in popular religious practices. Not that Irish Catholics had ever, for example, lost their love of going on pilgrimage (Inglis 1987: 21). Nor had the public furniture of everyday life ceased to be impregnated with religious imagery. But in 1985 there occurred an unusually intense revival of popular devotion to the Virgin Mary. Between February and September at least thirty-three separate accounts spoke of statues in churchyards and wayside grottos appearing to move, shimmer, smile, shed blood, and even speak. At Ballinspittle in County Cork up to 20,000 people gathered each night to await further signs. Although the hierarchy remained officially aloof, Bishop Murphy of Cork had no hesitation in declaring that the increase in piety which the sightings had brought about 'was no bad thing' (*The Times*, 28 Sept. 1985).

Yet much of this is capable of being read in two ways. According to one interpretation it marks a welcome return to old-style norms and attitudes. According to another it represents instead the instinctive reactions of threatened groups to the inevitable and painful processes of change. For the moment it certainly looks as if the church leadership has decided to withdraw to the fortresses of yesteryear, with the result that, only when some quite unavoidable *force majeure* appears on the scene can the abandonment of territory now even be contemplated. In the 1960s and 1970s modest concessions were voluntarily made to meet the spread of free education into the secondary sector while fully safeguarding the continuance of effective clerical domination (Whyte 1980: 337–41, 389–95). More recently, however, it has been only developments seemingly outside the hierarchy's control, in particular the dramatic drop in vocations (Inglis 1987: 48–9), which have been able to persuade the authorities to consider the unthinkable, namely, co-education, giving more power to lay staff, even appointing lay head teachers to schools owned by religious orders (*Times Educational Supplement*, 29 Sept. 1986). Yet the very fact that bishops and clergy now feel obliged to engage in public argument and to use their authority in a public and controversial manner suggests that the former implicit and automatic alliance between church and state may be beginning to break down.

VI

To Protestant unionists in Ulster these developments have proved welcome grist to the polemical mill. But, while in many respects the religious history of the six counties has, indeed, followed a distinct pattern of its own – not least because the minority there constitutes a third of the population – in many others it has come to represent nothing so much as a kind of inverted equivalent of what has taken place in the South.

Partly out of a general disgruntlement and partly because of the violent attacks upon them in the 1920s and 1930s (Harkness 1983: 76–8; Hickey 1984: 21–2; Munck 1985: 246–9), northern Catholics soon settled back into the separate sectarian world they had long inhabited and did so with an increased sense of outrage and inferiority. Discrimination against them, though neither quite so vicious as nationalists nor so trivial as unionists have liked to pretend, was an undoubted fact (Aunger 1975; Boyle 1977; Whyte 1983a). Social contact between Catholics and Protestants, already reduced to the level of conventional pleasantries, became more strained than ever. 'Forced back on their own resources Catholic men and women found outlets for their abilities in the service of their neighbours in the fellowship of the church' (Kennedy 1967: 148).

Introspection all round led to the deepening of grotesque misunderstandings and prejudices. Among town dwellers the existence
of virtual ghettos encouraged such tendencies. In the countryside
the most important factor was endogamy or the practice of only
marrying those within one's own 'group', for kinship alone might
have allowed an intermingling of what had become hermetically
separated worlds (Harris 1972). As one observer reported in
1948, 'the Ulster community is a dual community . . . almost
every association exists in duplicate'. Even different trades had
distinct sectarian orientations: publicans tended to be Catholics,
hardware and drapers' shops to be owned by Protestants, while
grocers and butchers maintained a more equal religious division
of labour (Mogey 1948: 85–7 and 1947: 198–200.

The clergy rarely exchanged even the time of day. Indeed, the
recollections of a Methodist minister provide an insight into more
complex divisions still.

> When I commenced my ministry in Belfast just before the outbreak
> of World War Two, there was no contact whatever between Romans
> and Protestants. Indeed I have often said that in those days when
> parish clergy did their work on foot or on a bicycle, a Presbyterian
> and Methodist would stop and talk, if they met in the street. Should
> either meet a Church of Ireland clergyman, they would feel that all
> proprieties had been met adequately, if he nodded to them in passing.
> And should they see a Catholic priest bearing down on them, or should
> he see them, it was remarkable how one or other found a street to
> cross, a door to knock or a shop window to inspect (Gallagher 1983:
> 272).

Priests were and remained ruggedly nationalist and looked entirely
to the kind of culture and politics being developed in the South –
more strongly so, in fact, than did their parishioners, some of whom
maintained more ambiguous perceptions of identity (Rose 1971:
208, 251; Fahy 1971; Hickey 1984: 131). For their part Protestant
clerics, especially those of an evangelical disposition, were ready
enough to hurl scriptural condemnations against popery, while
in 1931 Cardinal MacRory, like some unsmiling conjurer pulling
an ace from his sleeve, crushingly announced that the 'Protestant
Church in Ireland' was, quite simply, not 'a part of the Church of
Christ' at all (Akenson 1973: 141).

The one overarching point on which the clergymen of both sides
were in agreement was the importance of making certain that no
cracks should ever be allowed to appear in the walls which divided
their communities. More specifically, they all possessed a strong
vested interest in ensuring that schools in Northern Ireland should

continue to operate along strictly denominational lines. Indeed, the history of education in the six counties after 1920 demonstrates, not only the importance of this point, but also how Ulster's Protestant clerics had nothing to learn from Catholic bishops in their ability to get what they wanted from the civil authorities.

By pretending in the early 1920s that Northern Ireland did not actually exist Catholic churchmen missed a crucial opportunity for influencing events (Harkness 1983: 33–4; Akenson 1973: 52). While their insistence that 'the only satisfactory system of education for Catholics is one wherein Catholic children are taught in Catholic schools by Catholic teachers under Catholic management' (Farren 1986: 20) was not contradicted by the government, the freedom to carry on in such a manner was soon to be accompanied by a certain degree of financial disadvantage. In effect the Education Act of 1923 set up three different types of school. Schools of the first type were entirely financed from official funds and were, in theory at least, entirely under local authority control. Those of the second came under a committee of four nominees of the previous (clerical) manager and two of the education authority and were obliged to find a small proportion of their maintenance costs. Those in the last and 'independent' category could more or less do as they pleased while receiving full reimbursement of teachers' salaries, partial maintenance, but nothing at all towards their capital costs (Akenson 1973: 61–2).

While Catholic schools, almost without exception, adopted the 'independent' path and thus secured a less well funded level of support, many Protestant clergymen were, nonetheless, angry that certain provisions in the act rendered those schools paid for entirely by the taxpayer (the first type) less than completely ideal from their own point of view. What of course they wanted was fully Protestant schools at state expense. That this was not immediately on offer was due largely to the exotic personality of Craig's first minister of education, the seventh Marquess of Londonderry. A figure from another age – he wore a high black stock over his collar and a tightly fitting frock coat – the marquess was wealthy, able, amusing, and anything but parochial. Above all he nurtured an unusual desire to 'be fair to the Catholics' (Akenson 1973: 41, 64). But, although himself a keen rider to hounds, Londonderry was soon to find that in this particular hunt it was he who was destined to adopt the role of fox. Three Protestant clergymen under the dynamic leadership of Rev. William Corkey, a Presbyterian, established a United Education Committee, agitated on public platforms (especially just as general elections were about to take place), involved the Orange Order, and called forth amending legislation in 1925 and 1930 which effectively granted all their demands. The result was that 'state' schools did, indeed, become Protestant in all but name, both as regards effective control and the sort of religious instruction they were allowed to provide.

Protestant champions blandly declared they could see no reason why Catholics should not transfer their own schools to the fully-funded category. But of course the kind of bible instruction permitted in such schools made this quite impossible. And once Londonderry's initial approach had been so heavily compromised Unionist governments embarked upon what was to become a familiar policy, namely, that of more or less 'matching' every concession to Protestants of the Corkey variety with an increase of grant to Catholic schools – as happened in 1930, 1947, and 1968. Catholics took the money but still felt aggrieved. Though they were being more generously treated than their co-religionists in England, they knew that Protestants were being treated much better still. More generally, however, the continuing reinforcement of denominationalism in education – which also applied to second-ary schools and teacher training colleges – suited both sides well enough, while the provision of more resources allowed Unionists to pose as heroes of generosity all round.

In many respects educational provision, especially after the Second World War, was 'better' in Northern Ireland than in the Republic. In some respects too the southern system was not quite as denominationally fair as its supporters always claimed. Everywhere, however, division along religious lines had an effect upon schools of virtually all kinds. Studies have shown how in the six counties, for example, not only the general atmosphere but even specific rituals, attitudes, and implicit patterns of behaviour differ markedly between 'state' (Protestant) and Catholic schools (Murray 1985). Over the years, indeed, such things have become so entrenched and so set within the contours of a divided society that, in the North at any rate, well-intentioned suggestions for 'integrated' schooling as a solution to all sorts of problems simply ignore the difficulties which any such approach would now necessarily involve.

Priests and ministers thus collaborated in achieving something which they – and probably most of the people of Ireland – had long equally desired: internal unanimity within the tribe. And in pursuing this end they have found themselves engaged in the same kind of enterprise, that of bringing pressure to bear. 'Before partition, the Protestant Ulsterman had often denounced the Catholic "priest in politics", but no band of Catholic priests . . . had [ever] engaged in politics with the energy and the efficacy of the Protestant clerics who led the United Education Committee of the Protestant Churches' (Akenson 1973: 88).

The divisions within Northern Ireland are in many crucial respects quite literally *religious* ones and it is a mistake (tempting above all for intellectuals with no religion themselves) to seek to explain this away. Of course there are many aspects to the matter. But religion must be central to any analysis. Catholics and Protestants adhere to separate views of life and its destinies based, in the end, upon different notions of freedom, discipline, and (for the more devout) salvation itself (Hickey 1984: 72–3). Though Northern Ireland remains a far more God-fearing and church-going society than any other in the United Kingdom, a particular history has, in addition, charged such ideas with so special a resonance that they influence even those to whom formal religious practices mean comparatively little.

While, therefore, Protestants and Catholics in Ulster may often express mutual antagonisms in curiously similar ways, they, nonetheless, inhabit very different mental worlds. Catholics, when denouncing Protestant political claims can, however unrealistically, look to the South and cling to a belief that, if only the *change* they desire – a united Ireland – were brought into existence, all would be sweetness and light. And it is precisely this which has enabled them to avoid wandering into that labyrinth of 'psychological fears' which the Protestant community – with its heavy investment in immobility – has long inhabited (Heskin 1980: 43–4). Not only that, but Ulster Protestants usually perceive themselves to be both vulnerable and friendless, the more so because from the very beginning, British support has always seemed – and in recent years has clearly become – at once indispensable and unreliable.

At the same time Protestants do not belong to a single church and have, as a result, been much exercised by fears of impotence and disunity in comparison with papist homogeneity and power. Thus the notion of 'freedom', which lies at the heart of Ulster's Protestant ethic (Rose 1971: 255–6), has simultaneously provided a focus of cohesive identity and a justification for factionalist sectarianism.

Out of this paradox has stepped a long line of evangelical preachers – at once prophets of Protestant unity and often themselves the founders of new, purer, more authentically scriptural denominations. Ian Paisley, whose Free Presbyterian Church now numbers about 12,000 active members, is merely the latest, though far from the least gifted, representative of this now-hallowed tradition. His combination of vituperation and warmth, of rhetorical power and political dexterity, of dedication, hard work, and personal magnetism speaks to large sections of opinion well beyond the confines of his own sect in a manner which any time-travelling contemporary of Hugh Hanna in the nineteenth century or William Nicholson, who conducted revivals in Ulster in the 1920s, would instantly recognize (Bruce 1986).

It is the peculiar circumstances of Northern Ireland since the 1960s which have allowed Paisley to use his considerable talents to play a more central role in politics than most (but not all) of his predecessors were able to do. His career, successes, and failures illuminate the restraints within which Ulster – indeed to some extent all Irish – politicians and churchmen necessarily operate. On many 'moral' issues Paisley and his supporters take a view very close to that of the most conservative elements within Irish Catholicism. But while many fundamentalists in America's 'moral majority' have concluded that only an alliance with the hated Catholic Church can now provide them with sufficiently large battalions, the 'constitutional issue so overrides everything else in Northern Ireland' that there is no expectation or need for Paisley to follow a similar course. Though many Catholics supported his campaign in the early 1980s to 'Save Ulster from Sodomy' (that is, prevent the extension to Northern Ireland of British laws concerning adult male homosexual activity) Paisley would not work with Catholic organizations or with officials of the Catholic Church because of the dangers that might pose for the integrity of 'his separatist witness' (Bruce 1986: 149–51).

While Ulster Catholics maintain a comparatively secure sense of *national* identity which can be placed within a context encompassing the whole of Ireland, Ulster Protestants lack a national sense and seem, as a result, to constitute no more than an 'ethnic group'. Because of this unionist loyalism, so otherwise alone in a friendless world, depends in a peculiarly intense manner upon its religious base and does so even for those who no longer ardently practise their beliefs.

The recent 'troubles' have pushed both sides back towards their traditional redoubts. The effect has been to make more explicit than ever before the deep antagonisms of Ulster society. Indeed, the whole business is best seen, not under its usual guise of a 'Problem', but instead precisely as a *'Conflict'*. Unlike 'problems' conflicts have 'outcomes, not solutions. Somebody wins and somebody loses' (Bruce 1986: 268). If this seems too pessimistic a view, it remains the case that no one has yet discovered a formula to square this long-revolving circle of enmity and distrust and grant to the antagonists that aspiration which marks the strongest common link between so many of them – to gain everything while giving nothing at all away.

Postscript

It is important when assessing the course of Irish history since 1800 to examine more than the mere surface of events. It is equally important to realize that the very language historians are obliged to use – made up as it is in large measure of terms such as 'development', 'progress', and 'change' – inevitably tends to produce a picture in which flux is painted in brighter colours than immobility. The result can be distortion, not because untruths are told or errors propagated, but because often unconscious forms of selectivity have been allowed to emphasize some truths at the expense of others. Quite apart, therefore, from those writers about Ireland who have quite deliberately used the past as a vehicle for polemics, less partisan interpreters have also found it difficult to avoid assuming that the journey between yesterday and today has always been a purposive one undertaken only by travellers with both the ability and the inclination to turn the world upside down.

Of course in certain obvious ways contemporary Ireland differs greatly from the Irelands of Catholic Emancipation, the Land War, or the Easter Rising. Yet, perhaps more strikingly than in most places, many of the underlying realities have remained largely intact. The deep divisions splintering Irish society along religious lines are not only an inheritance from the past but are still expressed in a grammar and clothed in attitudes which owe almost everything to ground rules laid down some two hundred years ago or more. The manner in which Irish politicians of all kinds still follow their trade is entirely consistent with norms established in the middle of the nineteenth century, if not before. Nor has Ireland yet experienced those fundamental social changes which certain at least of its revolutionaries held close to their hearts. Thus, for example, the elimination of the Anglo-Irish landowners, though it aroused intimations of dangerous radicalism in contemporary Britain, proved in the end a profoundly conservative phenomenon.

Indeed, notwithstanding occasional lurches towards modernization, twentieth-century Ireland remains, in religious, social, and political terms, a remarkably conservative country. Its most characteristic values and modes of procedure constitute, above all, a faithful epitome of past experiences, triumphs, and wrongs. But because in the Irish case conservatism of this very general kind has seldom existed merely as a generator of quiescence, its continuing survival has been entirely consistent with the survival also of disorder, violence, and unrest. On the one hand, it has ensured that the physical manifestations of discontent have tended to follow a precise and increasingly traditional choreography. On the other, it has guaranteed that even the greatest upheavals have, more often than not, eventually dissolved themselves into comforting reconstructions of a seemingly essential *status quo*.

As, therefore, the long Irish dialectic between conflict and conformity continues, the strength of the latter remains no less potent than before. Not for nothing did Kevin O'Higgins boast in the 1920s that he and his colleagues in Cosgrave's government were the most conservative revolutionaries who had ever lived, for, in doing so, he was articulating, not merely a set of personal preferences, but something very like a definitive statement of Ireland's singular capacity in modern times for standing still while persuading itself and others that it is actually running very fast indeed.

Bibliography

Section A Some General Books
Section B Works cited in the Text

Note Occasional references in the text to manuscripts, newspapers, and parliamentary debates are self-explanatory and need no detailed listing here.

A

Although the items noted in Section B below constitute at least the beginnings of a sensible bibliography of Irish history since 1800 it may be useful to refer separately to some of the more interesting *general* works on the subject (not all of which have been specifically cited in the text).

Those anxious to start with brief single-volume accounts of Irish history as a whole will find that J. C. Beckett's *A Short History of Ireland* (London, 1952; 6th ed. 1979) is showing its age. More up to date are K. S. Bottigheimer, *Ireland and the Irish: A Short History* (New York, 1982), J. O'Beirne Ranelagh, *A Short History of Ireland* (Cambridge, 1983), and L. de Paor, *The Peoples of Ireland from Prehistory to Modern Times* (London, 1986). *The Course of Irish History* edited by T. W. Moody and F. X. Martin (Cork, 1967) is a collection of essays dealing chronologically with the period from the earliest times until 1966. Over the middle distance J. C. Beckett's *The Making of Modern Ireland 1603–1923* (London, 1966;

with revised bibliography 1981) has been augmented by R. F. Foster's *Modern Ireland 1600–1972* (London, 1988).

The only book which tackles the whole of the period since 1800 – E. Norman's *A History of Modern Ireland* (London, 1971) – is breezily idiosyncratic. R. Kee's *The Green Flag: A History of Irish Nationalism* (London, 1972) is precisely what its title suggests, though *The Evolution of Irish Nationalist Politics* by T. Garvin (Dublin, 1981) and *Nationalism in Ireland* by D. G. Boyce (London, 1982) have more analytic bite.

In a class of its own is F. S. L. Lyons's *Ireland Since the Famine* (London, 1971; new ed. 1973), a splendid, if sometimes overcautious, work of insight and synthesis which set new standards and remains a monument to its author and to the more optimistic times in which most of it was written.

Two multi-volume series have produced some interesting books dealing with the years since 1800. The 'Gill History of Ireland' is complete and offers G. Ó Tuathaigh's sensible *Ireland before the Famine 1798–1848* (Dublin, 1972), J. Lee's spritely *ballon d'essai The Modernisation of Irish Society 1848–1918* (Dublin, 1973), and J. A. Murphy's useful *Ireland in the Twentieth Century* (Dublin, 1975). The still unfinished 'Helicon History of Ireland' gives its authors more space and three relevant works are already available: D. McCartney's *The Dawning of Democracy: Ireland 1800–1870* (Dublin, 1987), which reflects recent interest in agrarianism, R. Fanning's *Independent Ireland* (Dublin, 1983), which – unusually for a general book of this kind – contains much original research, and D. Harkness's detailed and valuable *Northern Ireland since 1920* (Dublin, 1983).

Two writers have, in their very different ways, offered important insights into particular aspects of modern Irish history. P. O'Farrell, in *Ireland's English Question: Anglo-Irish Relations 1534–1970* (London, 1971) and *England and Ireland since 1800* (London, 1975), explores the religious and secular sides of a long cohabitation. O. MacDonagh exhibits both epigrammatic dexterity and an ability to see old things in new ways in his allusive yet powerful *Ireland: The Union and its Aftermath* (London, 1977) and *States of Mind: A Study of Anglo-Irish Conflict 1780–1980* (London, 1983).

On social and economic developments L. Cullen's *Life in Ireland* (London, 1968) is useful and deals with medieval as well as modern times. Mary E. Daly's *Social and Economic History of Ireland since 1800* (Dublin, 1981) is straightforward and up to date, while *An Economic History of Ulster, 1820–1940* edited by L. Kennedy and P. Ollerenshaw (Manchester, 1985) is more analytic in approach.

The most readily available collection of maps is that in Ruth D. Edwards, *An Atlas of Irish History* (London, 1973; 2nd ed. 1981). Those with access to a well-stocked library should also consult Volumes VIII and IX of *A New History of Ireland* edited by T. W. Moody, F. X. Martin, F. J. Byrne and others (Oxford, 1982 and 1984); the former provides an invaluable 'Chronology of Irish History to 1976' while the latter contains excellent maps, lists of office holders, and electoral data.

Photographic images can often succeed in impressing the mind in peculiarly compelling ways. Among the more useful collections that have appeared are B. M. Walker, *Faces of the Past; A photographic and literary record of Ulster life 1880–1915* (Belfast, 1974), A. Byrne and S. McMahon, *Faces of the West 1875–1925* (Belfast, 1976), K. Hickey, *The Light of Other Days: Irish Life at the turn of the century in the photographs of Robert French* (London, 1973), and G. Morrison, *An Irish Camera* (London, 1979).

Two extremely useful critical bibliographies are available, namely, *Irish Historiography 1936–70* edited by T. W. Moody (Dublin, 1971) and *Irish Historiography 1970–79* edited by J. Lee (Cork, 1981). The periodical *Irish Historical Studies* (1936–) has published annual bibliographies (in various forms, including microfiche), while the annual issues of *Irish Economic and Social History* (1974–) include lists of relevant publications.

B

Adams, M., 1968. *Censorship: The Irish Experience*. Dublin.

Adams, W. F., 1932. *Ireland and Irish Emigration to the New World from 1815 to the Famine*. New Haven.

Akenson, D. H., 1970. *The Irish Education Experiment: The National System of Education in the Nineteenth Century*. London.

Akenson, D. H., 1971. *The Church of Ireland: Ecclesiastical Reform and Revolution, 1800–1885*. New Haven.

Akenson, D. H., 1973. *Education and Enmity: The Control of Schooling in Northern Ireland 1920–50*. Newton Abbot.

Akenson, D. H., 1975. *A Mirror to Kathleen's Face: Education in Independent Ireland 1922–1960*. Montreal.

Akenson, D. H., 1981. *A Protestant in Purgatory: Richard Whately, Archbishop of Dublin*. Hamden (Conn.).

Arensberg, C. M. and Kimball, S. T., 1968. *Family and Community in Ireland*, 2nd ed. Cambridge (Mass.).

Aunger, E. A., 1975. 'Religion and Occupational Class in Northern Ireland', *Economic and Social Review*, vii, 1–18.

Bairoch, P., 1976. 'Europe's Gross National Product: 1800–1975', *Journal of European Economic History*, v, 273–340.

Baker, Sybil E., 1973. 'Orange and Green: Belfast, 1832–1912' in H. J. Dyos and M. Wolff (eds.), *The Victorian City: Images and Realities*, 2 vols., ii, 789–814. London.

Barrington, Ruth, 1987. *Health, Medicine and Politics in Ireland 1900–1970*. Dublin.

Barrington, T., 1927. 'A Review of Irish Agricultural Prices', *Journal of the Statistical and Social Inquiry Society of Ireland*, xv, 249–80.

Barrington, T. J., 1967. 'Public Administration 1927–1936' in F. MacManus (ed.), *The Years of the Great Test*, pp. 80–91. Cork.

Barrington, T. J., 1982. 'Whatever happened to Irish Government?' in F. Litton (ed.), *Unequal Achievement: The Irish Experience 1957–1982*, pp. 89–112. Dublin.

Barry, Ann and Hoppen, K. T., 1978–9. 'Borough Politics in O'Connellite Ireland: The Youghal Poll Books of 1835 and 1837', *Journal of the Cork Historical and Archaeological Society*, Two Parts, lxxxiii, 106–46, and lxxxiv, 15–43.

Bax, M., 1976. *Harpstrings and Confessions: Machine-Style Politics in the Irish Republic*. Assen/Amsterdam.

Beames, M., 1975. 'Cottiers and Conacre in pre-Famine Ireland', *Journal of Peasant Studies*, ii, 352–4.

Beames, M., 1978. 'Rural Conflict in pre-Famine Ireland: Peasant Assassinations in Tipperary 1837–1847', *Past & Present*, No. 81, 75–91.

Beames, M., 1982. 'The Ribbon Societies: Lower-Class Nationalism in pre-Famine Ireland', *Past & Present*, No. 97, 128–43.

Beames, M., 1983. *Peasants and Power: The Whiteboy Movements and their Control in pre-Famine Ireland*. Brighton.

Bell, P. M. H., 1969. *Disestablishment in Ireland and Wales*. London.

Bew, P., 1978. *Land and the National Question in Ireland 1858–82.* Dublin.

Bew, P., 1980. *C. S. Parnell.* Dublin.

Bew, P., 1982. 'The Land League Ideal: Achievements and Contradictions' in P. J. Drudy (ed.), *Ireland: Land, Politics and People: Irish Studies 2*, pp. 77–92. Cambridge.

Bew, P., 1987. *Conflict and Conciliation in Ireland 1890–1910: Parnellites and Radical Agrarians.* Oxford.

Bew, P., 1988. 'Sinn Fein, Agrarian Radicalism and the War of Independence, 1919–1921' in D. G. Boyce (ed.), *The Revolution in Ireland, 1879–1923*, pp. 217–34 and 265–7. London.

Bew, P., Gibbon, P. and Patterson, H., 1979. *The State in Northern Ireland 1921–72: Political Forces and Social Classes.* Manchester.

Bew, P. and Patterson, H., 1982. *Sean Lemass and the Making of Modern Ireland 1945–66.* Dublin.

Bicheno, J. E., 1830. *Ireland and its Economy; being the result of observations made in a tour through the country in the Autumn of 1829.* London.

Bishop, P. and Mallie, E., 1987. *The Provisional IRA.* London.

Blackwell, J., 1982. 'Government, Economy and Society' in F. Litton (ed.), *Unequal Achievement: The Irish Experience 1957–1982*, pp. 43–60. Dublin.

Blackwell, J. and O'Malley, E., 1984. 'The Impact of EEC Membership on Irish Industry' in P. J. Drudy and D. McAleese (eds.), *Ireland and the European Community: Irish Studies 3*, pp. 107–44. Cambridge.

Blanchard, J., 1963. *The Church in Contemporary Ireland.* Dublin.

Bourke, P. M. A., 1965. 'The Agricultural Statistics of the 1841 Census of Ireland: A Critical Review', *Economic History Review*, 2nd Series, xviii, 376–91.

Bowen, D., 1970. *Souperism: Myth or Reality: A Study in Souperism.* Cork.

Bowen, D., 1978. *The Protestant Crusade in Ireland, 1800–70: A Study of Protestant–Catholic Relations between the Act of Union and Disestablishment.* Dublin.

Bowen, D., 1983a. *Paul Cullen and the Shaping of Modern Irish Catholicism.* Dublin.

Bowen, K., 1983b. *Protestants in a Catholic State: Ireland's Privileged Minority.* Dublin.

Bowley, A. L., 1899. 'The statistics of wages in the United Kingdom during the last hundred years (Part III) Agricultural Wages – Ireland', *Journal of the Royal Statistical Society*, lxii, 395–404.

Bowley, A. L., 1900. *Wages in the United Kingdom in the Nineteenth Century*. Cambridge.

Bowman, J., 1982. *De Valera and the Ulster Question 1917–1973*. Oxford.

Bowyer Bell, J., 1970. *The Secret Army: A History of the IRA, 1916–1970*. London.

Boyce, D. G., 1972. *Englishmen and Irish Troubles: British Public Opinion and the Making of Irish Policy 1918–22*. London.

Boyce, D. G., 1982. *Nationalism in Ireland*. London.

Boyle, J. F., 1977. 'Educational Attainment, Occupational Achievement and Religion in Northern Ireland', *Economic and Social Review*, viii, 79–100.

Boyle, J. W., 1962. 'The Protestant Association and the Independent Orange Order, 1901–10', *Irish Historical Studies*, xiii, 117–52.

Boyle, J. W., 1983. 'A Marginal Figure: The Irish Rural Labourer' in S. Clark and J. S. Donnelly, Jr. (eds), *Irish Peasants: Violence and Political Unrest 1780–1914*, pp. 311–38. Manchester.

Bradley, D. G., 1986. 'Speeding the Plough: The Formation of the Federation of Rural Workers, 1944–1948', *Saothar: Journal of the Irish Labour History Society*, xi, 39–53.

Bric, M. J., 1983. 'Priests, Parsons and Politics: The Rightboy Protest in County Cork 1785–1788', *Past & Present*, No. 100, 100–23.

Broderick, J. F., 1951. *The Holy See and the Irish Movement for the Repeal of the Union with England 1829–1847*. Rome.

Brody, H., 1973. *Inishkillane: Change and Decline in the West of Ireland*. London.

Brown, T., 1981. *Ireland: A Social and Cultural History 1922–79*. London.

Brown, T. N., 1953. 'Nationalism and the Irish Peasant, 1800–1848', *Review of Politics*, xv, 403–45.

Bruce, S., 1986. *God Save Ulster: The Religion and Politics of Paisleyism*. Oxford.

Buckland, P., 1972. *The Anglo-Irish and the New Ireland 1885–1922*. Dublin.

Buckland, P., 1973. *Ulster Unionism and the Origins of Northern Ireland 1886–1922*. Dublin.

Buckland, P., 1979. *The Factory of Grievances: Devolved Government in Northern Ireland 1921–39*. Dublin.

Buckland, P., 1980. *James Craig, Lord Craigavon*. Dublin.

Buckland, P., 1981. *A History of Northern Ireland*. Dublin.

Budge, I. and O'Leary, C., 1973. *Belfast: Approach to Crisis: A Study of Belfast Politics 1613–1970*. London.

Bull, P. J., 1972. 'The Reconstruction of the Irish Parliamentary Movement, 1895–1903: An Analysis with special reference to William O'Brien' (University of Cambridge, Ph.D. Thesis).

Cahill, G. A., 1957. 'The Protestant Association and the anti-Maynooth Agitation of 1845', *Catholic Historical Review*, xliii, 273–308.

Campbell, J. J., 1967. 'Between the Wars' in J. C. Beckett and R. E. Glasscock (eds.), *Belfast: The Origin and Growth of an Industrial City*, pp. 144–56. London.

Canning, P., 1985. *British Policy towards Ireland 1921–1941*. Oxford.

Cannon, S., 1979. *Irish Episcopal Meetings, 1788–1882: A Juridico-Historical Study*. Rome.

Carbery, Mary, 1973. *The Farm by Lough Gur: The Story of Mary Fogarty*. Cork.

Carney, F. J., 1975. 'Pre-Famine Irish Population: The Evidence from the Trinity College Estates', *Irish Economic and Social History*, iii, 35–45.

Carroll, J. T., 1975. *Ireland in the War Years*. Newton Abbot.

Carson, J. T., 1958. *God's River in Spate: The story of the religious awakening of Ulster in 1859*. Belfast.

Carty, R. K., 1983. *Electoral Politics in Ireland: Party and Parish Pump*. Dingle.

Chubb, B., 1963. 'Going about persecuting Civil Servants: The Role of the Irish Parliamentary Representative', *Political Studies*, xi, 272–86.

Chubb, B., 1982. *The Government and Politics of Ireland*. 2nd ed. London.

Clark, S., 1971. 'The Social Composition of the Land League', *Irish Historical Studies*, xvii, 447–69.

Clark, S., 1979. *Social Origins of the Irish Land War*. Princeton.

Clear, Catriona, 1987. *Nuns in Nineteenth-Century Ireland*. Dublin.

Coldrey, B. M., 1988. *Faith and Fatherland: The Christian Brothers and the Development of Irish Nationalism 1838–1921*. Dublin.

Collins, C. A., 1985. 'Clientelism and Careerism in Irish Local Government: the persecution of civil servants revisited', *Economic and Social Review*, xvi, 273–86.

Comerford, R. V., 1979. *Charles J. Kickham: A Study in Irish Nationalism and Literature*. Dublin.

Comerford, R. V., 1981. 'Patriotism as pastime: the appeal of Fenianism in the mid-1860s', *Irish Historical Studies*, xxii, 239–50.

Comerford, R. V., 1985. *The Fenians in Context: Irish Politics and Society 1848–82*. Dublin.

Commins, P., 1985. 'Continuity and Change on the Land', *Studies*, lxxiv, 252–66.

Connell, K. H., 1950. *The Population of Ireland 1750–1845*. Oxford.

Connell, K. H., 1962. 'The Potato in Ireland', *Past & Present*, No. 23, 57–71.

Connell, K. H., 1968. *Irish Peasant Society: Four Historical Essays*. Oxford.

Connolly, S. J., 1979. 'Illegitimacy and pre-Nuptial Pregnancy in Ireland before 1864: The Evidence of some Catholic Parish Registers', *Irish Economic and Social History*, vi, 5–23.

Connolly, S. J., 1981. 'Catholicism in Ulster, 1800–50' in P. Roebuck (ed.), *Plantation to Partition: Essays in Ulster History in Honour of J. L. McCracken*, pp. 157–71 and 273–5. Belfast.

Connolly, S. J., 1982. *Priests and People in pre-Famine Ireland 1780–1845*. Dublin.

Connolly, S. J., 1983a. 'The "blessed turf": Cholera and Popular Panic in Ireland, June 1832', *Irish Historical Studies*, xxiii, 214–32.

Connolly, S. J., 1983b. 'Religion, Work-Discipline and Economic Attitudes: The Case of Ireland' in T. M. Devine and D. Dickson (eds.), *Ireland and Scotland 1600–1850: Parallels and Contrasts in Economic and Social Development*, pp. 235–45. Edinburgh.

Connolly, S. J., 1985a. 'Marriage in pre-Famine Ireland' in A. Cosgrove (ed.), *Marriage in Ireland*, pp. 78–98. Dublin.

Connolly, S. J., 1985b. *Religion and Society in Nineteenth-Century Ireland*. Dublin.

Coogan, T. P., 1970. *The IRA*. London.

Coogan, T. P., 1987. *Disillusioned Decades: Ireland 1966–87*. Dublin.

Cooke, A. B. and Vincent, J., 1974. *The Governing Passion: Cabinet Government and Party Politics in Britain 1885–86*. Brighton.

Corish, P. J., 1962. 'Cardinal Cullen and the National Association of Ireland', *Reportorium Novum: Dublin Diocesan Historical Record*, iii, 13–61.

Corish, P. J., 1967. 'Political Problems 1860–1878' in P. J. Corish (ed.), *A History of Irish Catholicism*, V, Fascicule 3. Dublin.

Corish, P. J., 1979. 'Gallicanism at Maynooth: Archbishop Cullen and the Royal Visitation of 1853' in A. Cosgrove and D. McCartney (eds.), *Studies in Irish History presented to R. Dudley Edwards*, pp. 176–89. Dublin.

Corish, P. J., 1985. *The Irish Catholic Experience: A Historical Survey.* Dublin.

Cox, P. G. and Kearney, B., 1983. 'The Impact of the Common Agricultural Policy' in D. Coombes (ed.), *Ireland and the European Communities: Ten Years of Membership*, pp. 158–82. Dublin.

Crawford, E. Margaret, 1981. 'Indian Meal and Pellagra in Nineteenth-Century Ireland' in J. M. Goldstrom and L. A. Clarkson (eds.), *Irish Population, Economy, and Society: Essays in Honour of the late K. H. Connell*, pp. 113–33. Oxford.

Crotty, R. D., 1966. *Irish Agricultural Production: Its Volume and Structure.* Cork.

Cuddy, M. and Curtin, C., 1983. 'Commercialisation in West of Ireland Agriculture in the 1890s', *Economic and Social Review*, xiv, 173–84.

Cullen, L. M., 1968. 'Irish History without the Potato', *Past & Present*, No. 40, 72–83.

Cullen, L. M., 1972. *An Economic History of Ireland since 1660.* London.

Cullen, L. M., 1981. *The Emergence of Modern Ireland 1600–1900.* London.

Cullen, L. M., 1985. 'The 1798 Rebellion in its Eighteenth-Century Context' in P. J. Corish (ed.), *Radicals, Rebels and Establishments: Historical Studies XV*, pp. 91–113. Belfast.

Cunningham, P., 1960. 'The Catholic Directory for 1821', *Reportorium Novum: Dublin Diocesan Historical Record*, ii, 324–63.

Curran, J. M., 1980. *The Birth of the Irish Free State 1921–1923.* University (Alabama).

Curtin, Nancy J., 1985. 'The Transformation of the Society of United Irishmen into a Mass-Based Revolutionary Organization, 1794–6', *Irish Historical Studies*, xxiv, 463–92.

Curtis, Jr., L. P., 1963. *Coercion and Conciliation in Ireland 1880–1892.* Princeton.

Curtis, Jr., L. P., 1968. *Anglo-Saxons and Celts: A Study of anti-Irish Prejudice in Victorian England.* Bridgeport (Conn.).

Curtis, Jr., L. P., 1970. 'The Anglo-Irish Predicament', *Twentieth Century*, No. 4, 37–63.

Curtis, Jr., L. P., 1971. *Apes and Angels: The Irishman in Victorian Caricature.* Newton Abbot.

Curtis, Jr., L. P., 1980. 'Incumbered Wealth: Landed Indebtedness in post-Famine Ireland', *American Historical Review*, lxxxv, 332–67.

Curtis, Jr., L. P., 1987. 'Stopping the Hunt, 1881–1882: An Aspect of the Irish Land War' in C. H. E. Philpin (ed.), *Nationalism and Popular Protest in Ireland*, pp. 349–402. Cambridge.

d'Alton, I., 1973. 'Southern Irish Unionism: A Study of Cork Unionists, 1884–1914', *Transactions of the Royal Historical Society*, 5th Series, xxiii, 71–88.

d'Alton, I., 1975. 'Cork Unionism: Its Role in Parliamentary and Local Elections, 1885–1914', *Studia Hibernica*, No. 15, 143–61.

d'Alton, I., 1978. 'A Contrast in Crises: Southern Irish Protestantism, 1820–43 and 1885–1910' in A. C. Hepburn (ed.), *Minorities in History: Historical Studies XII*, pp. 70–83. London.

d'Alton, I., 1980. *Protestant Society and Politics in Cork 1812–1844*. Cork.

Daly, Mary E., 1979. 'The Development of the National School System, 1831–40' in A. Cosgrove and D. McCartney (eds.), *Studies in Irish History presented to R. Dudley Edwards*, pp. 150–63. Dublin.

Daly, Mary E., 1981a. *Social and Economic History of Ireland since 1800*. Dublin.

Daly, Mary E., 1981b. 'Late Nineteenth and Early Twentieth Century Dublin' in D. Harkness and Mary O'Dowd (eds.), *The Town in Ireland: Historical Studies XIII*, pp. 221–52. Belfast.

Daly, Mary E., 1982. 'Social Structure of the Dublin Working Class, 1871–1911', *Irish Historical Studies*, xxiii, 121–33.

Daly, Mary E., 1984a. *Dublin: The Deposed Capital: A Social and Economic History 1860–1914*. Cork.

Daly, Mary E., 1984b. 'An Irish-Ireland for Business?: The Control of Manufacturers Acts, 1932 and 1934', *Irish Historical Studies*, xxiv, 246–72.

Daly, Mary E., 1986. *The Famine in Ireland*. Dublin.

Daniel, T. K., 1976. 'Griffith on his Noble Head: The Determinants of Cumann na nGaedheal Economic Policy, 1922–32', *Irish Economic and Social History*, iii, 55–65.

Darby, J., 1976. *Conflict in Northern Ireland: The Development of a Polarised Community*. Dublin.

D'Arcy, F. A., 1970. 'The Artisans of Dublin and Daniel O'Connell, 1830–47: An Unquiet Liaison', *Irish Historical Studies*, xvii, 221–43.

Davis, R., 1974. *Arthur Griffith and Non-Violent Sinn Fein*. Dublin.

Davis, R., 1987. *The Young Ireland Movement*, Dublin.

Deane, Phyllis and Cole, W. A., 1967. *British Economic Growth 1688–1959: Trends and Structure*. 2nd ed. Cambridge.

De Vere White, T., 1946. *The Road of Excess* [A biography of Isaac Butt]. Dublin.

Dewar, M. W., Brown, J. and Long, S. E., 1967. *Orangeism: A New Historical Appreciation*. Belfast.

Dickson, D., 1979. 'Middlemen' in T. Bartlett and D. W. Hayton (eds.), *Penal Era and Golden Age: Essays in Irish History, 1690–1800*, pp. 162–85. Belfast.

Dickson, D., 1987. *New Foundations: Ireland 1660–1800*. Dublin.

Donnelly, Jr., J. S., 1973. *Landlord and Tenant in Nineteenth-Century Ireland*. Dublin.

Donnelly, Jr., J. S., 1975. *The Land and the People of Nineteenth-Century Cork: The Rural Economy and the Land Question*. London.

Donnelly, Jr., J. S., 1976. 'The Irish Agricultural Depression of 1859–64', *Irish Economic and Social History*, iii, 33–54.

Donnelly, Jr., J. S., 1977–8. 'The Rightboy Movement 1785–8', *Studia Hibernica*, No. 17/18, 120–202.

Donnelly, Jr., J. S., 1978. 'The Whiteboy Movement 1761–5', *Irish Historical Studies*, xxi, 20–54.

Donnelly, Jr., J. S., 1981. 'Hearts of Oak, Hearts of Steel', *Studia Hibernica*, No. 21, 7–73.

Donnelly, Jr., J. S., 1983a. 'Irish Agrarian Rebellion: The Whiteboys of 1769–76', *Proceedings of the Royal Irish Academy*, Section C, lxxxiii, 293–331.

Donnelly, Jr., J. S., 1983b. 'Pastorini and Captain Rock: Millenarianism and Sectarianism in the Rockite Movement of 1821–4' in S. Clark and J. S. Donnelly, Jr. (eds.), *Irish Peasants: Violence and Political Unrest 1780–1914*, pp. 102–39. Manchester.

Donnelly, Jr., J. S., 1985. 'The Social Composition of Agrarian Rebellions in early Nineteenth-Century Ireland: The Case of the Carders and Caravats, 1813–16' in P. J. Corish (ed.), *Radicals, Rebels and Establishments: Historical Studies XV*, pp. 151–69. Belfast.

Donnelly, Jr., J. S., 1986. 'The Terry Alt Movement of 1829–31' (Typescript).

Drake, M., 1963. 'Marriage and Population Growth in Ireland, 1750–1845', *Economic History Review*, 2nd Series, xvi, 301–13.

Drudy, P. J., 1986. 'Migration between Ireland and Britain since Independence' in P. J. Drudy (ed.), *Ireland and Britain since 1922: Irish Studies 5*, pp. 107–23. Cambridge.

Dunne, T., 1986. 'Murder as Metaphor: Griffin's Portrayal of Ireland in the year of Catholic Emancipation' in O. MacDonagh and W. F. Mandle (eds.), *Ireland and Irish–Australia: Studies in Cultural and Political History*, pp. 64–80. London.

Edwards, R. D. and Williams, T. D. (eds.), 1956. *The Great Famine: Studies in Irish History 1845–52*. Dublin.

Edwards, Ruth D., 1977. *Patrick Pearse: The Triumph of Failure*. London.

Egan, P. K., 1960. *The Parish of Ballinasloe*. Dublin.

Elliott, Marianne, 1982. *Partners in Revolution: The United Irishmen and France*. New Haven.

Ervine, St J., 1949. *Craigavon: Ulsterman*. London.

Facts About Ireland, 6th ed. 1985. Dublin.

Fahy, P. A., 1971. 'Some Political Behaviour Patterns and Attitudes of Roman Catholic Priests in a Rural Part of Northern Ireland', *Economic and Social Review*, iii, 1–24.

Fanning, R., 1978. *The Irish Department of Finance 1922–58*. Dublin.

Fanning, R., 1982a. 'The Response of the London and Belfast Governments to the Declaration of the Republic of Ireland, 1948–49', *International Affairs*, lviii, 95–114.

Fanning, R., 1982b. 'The United States and Irish Participation in NATO: The Debate of 1950', *Irish Studies in International Affairs*, i, 38–48.

Fanning, R., 1983. *Independent Ireland*. Dublin.

Fanning, R., 1986a. ' "The Great Enchantment": Uses and Abuses of Modern Irish History' in J. Dooge (ed.), *Ireland in the Contemporary World: Essays in Honour of Garret FitzGerald*, pp. 131–47. Dublin.

Fanning, R., 1986b. 'Britain's Legacy: Government and Administration' in P. J. Drudy (ed.), *Ireland and Britain since 1922: Irish Studies 5*, pp. 45–64. Cambridge.

Farrell, B., 1971. *The Founding of Dail Eireann: Parliament and Nation Building*. Dublin.

Farrell, B., 1985. 'Ireland: From Friends and Neighbours to Clients and Partisans: Some Dimensions of Parliamentary Representation under PR-STV' in V. Bogdanor (ed.), *Representatives of the People? Parliamentarians and Constituents in Western Democracies*, pp. 237–64. Aldershot.

Farren, S., 1986. 'Nationalist Catholic Reaction to Educational Reform in Northern Ireland, 1920–30', *History of Education*, xv, 19–30.

Feingold, W. L., 1975. 'The Tenants' Movement to Capture the Irish Poor Law Boards, 1877–1886', *Albion*, vii, 216–31.

Feingold, W. L., 1984. *The Revolt of the Tenantry: The Transformation of Local Government in Ireland, 1872–1886*. Boston.

Fergusson, J., 1964. *The Curragh Incident*. London.

Fisk, R., 1983. *In Time of War: Ireland, Ulster and the Price of Neutrality 1939–45*. London.

Fitzpatrick, D., 1977. *Politics and Irish Life 1913–1921: Provincial Experience of War and Revolution*. Dublin.

Fitzpatrick, D., 1978. 'The Geography of Irish Nationalism 1910–1921', *Past & Present*, No. 78, 113–44.

Fitzpatrick, D., 1980a. 'The Disappearance of the Irish Agricultural Labourer, 1841–1912', *Irish Economic and Social History*, vii, 66–92.

Fitzpatrick, D., 1980b. 'Irish Emigration in the Later Nineteenth Century', *Irish Historical Studies*, xxii, 126–43.

Fitzpatrick, D., 1982. 'Class, Family and Rural Unrest in Nineteenth-Century Ireland' in P. J. Drudy (ed.), *Ireland: Land, Politics and People: Irish Studies 2*, pp. 37–75. Cambridge.

Fitzpatrick, D., 1984. *Irish Emigration 1801–1921*. Dublin.

Fitzpatrick, D., 1985a. 'Unrest in Rural Ireland', *Irish Social and Economic History*, xii, 98–105.

Fitzpatrick, D., 1985b. 'Marriage in post-Famine Ireland' in A. Cosgrove (ed.), *Marriage in Ireland*, pp. 116–31. Dublin.

Fitzpatrick, D., 1987. 'Divorce and Separation in Modern Irish History', *Past & Present*, No. 114, 172–96.

Flanagan, K., 1978. 'The Godless and the Burlesque: Newman and the other Irish Universities' in J. D. Bastable (ed.), *Newman and Gladstone: Centennial Essays*, pp. 239–77. Dublin.

Fogarty, L., 1918. *James Fintan Lalor: Patriot and Political Essayist (1807–1849)*. Dublin.

Forester, Margery, 1971. *Michael Collins: The Lost Leader*. London.

Foster, R. F., 1976. *Charles Stewart Parnell: The Man and his Family*. Hassocks.

Foster, R. F., 1980. 'To the Northern Counties Station: Lord Randolph Churchill and the prelude to the Orange Card' in F. S. L. Lyons and R. A. J. Hawkins (eds.), *Ireland under the Union: Varieties of Tension: Essays in Honour of T. W. Moody*, pp. 237–87. Oxford.

Foster, R. F., 1983. 'History and the Irish Question', *Transactions of the Royal Historical Society*, 5th Series, xxxiii, 169–92.

Freeman, T. W., 1977. 'Irish Towns in the Eighteenth and Nineteenth Centuries' in R. A. Butlin (ed.), *The Development of the Irish Town*, pp. 101–38. London.

Gailey, A., 1987. *Ireland and the Death of Kindness: The Experience of Constructive Unionism 1890–1905*. Cork.

Gallagher, E., 1983. 'The Irish Churches 1968–1983', *The Month*, ccxlv, 271–9.

Gallagher, M., 1978. 'Party Solidarity, Exclusivity and Inter-Party Relationships in Ireland, 1922–1977: The Evidence of Transfers', *Economic and Social Review*, x, 1–22.

Gallagher, M., 1979. 'The Pact General Election of 1922', *Irish Historical Studies*, xxi, 404–21.

Gallagher, M., 1985a. *Political Parties in the Republic of Ireland.* Manchester.

Gallagher, T., 1985b. 'Fianna Fail and Partition, 1926–1984', *Eire-Ireland*, xx, 28–57.

Garvin, T., 1972. Continuity and Change in Irish Electoral Politics, 1923–1969', *Economic and Social Review*, iii, 359–72.

Garvin, T., 1980. 'Decolonisation, Nationalism, and Electoral Politics in Ireland 1832–1945' in O. Büsch (ed.), *Wählerbewegung in der Europäischen Geschichte*, pp. 259–80. Berlin.

Garvin, T., 1981. *The Evolution of Irish Nationalist Politics.* Dublin.

Garvin, T., 1982. 'Defenders, Ribbonmen and Others: Underground Political Networks in pre-Famine Ireland', *Past & Present*, No. 96, 133–55.

Garvin, T., 1986a. 'Priests and Patriots: Irish Separatism and Fear of the Modern, 1890–1914', *Irish Historical Studies*, xxv, 67–81.

Garvin, T., 1986b. 'The Anatomy of a Nationalist Revolution: Ireland, 1858–1928', *Comparative Studies in Society and History*, xxviii, 468–501.

Garvin, T., 1987. *Nationalist Revolutionaries in Ireland 1858–1928.* Oxford.

Gavan Duffy, C., 1884. *Young Ireland: A Fragment of Irish History 1840–1845.* Dublin.

Gavan Duffy, C., 1886. *The League of North and South: An Episode in Irish History 1850–1854.* London.

Geary, L., 1986. *The Plan of Campaign 1886–91.* Cork.

Gibbon, P., 1973. 'Arensberg and Kimball Revisited', *Economy and Society*, ii, 479–98.

Gibbon, P., 1975. *The Origins of Ulster Unionism: The Formation of Popular Protestant Politics and Ideology in Nineteenth-Century Ireland.* Manchester.

Gilley, S., 1984. 'The Catholic Church and Revolution in Nineteenth Century Ireland' in Yonah Alexander and A. O'Day (eds.), *Terrorism in Ireland*, pp. 121–45. London.

Gilley, S., 1988. 'The Catholic Church and Revolution' in D. G.

Boyce (ed.), *The Revolution in Ireland, 1879–1923*, pp. 157–72 and 258–62. London.

Gillmor, D. A., 1985. *Economic Activities in the Republic of Ireland: A Geographical Perspective*. Dublin.

Girvin, B., 1986a. 'National Identity and Conflict in Northern Ireland' in B. Girvin and R. Sturm (eds.), *Politics and Society in Contemporary Ireland*, pp. 105–34. Aldershot.

Girvin, B., 1986b. 'The Anglo-Irish Agreement 1985' in B. Girvin and R. Sturm (eds.), *Politics and Society in Contemporary Ireland*, pp. 150–65. Aldershot.

Girvin, B., 1986c. 'Social Change and Moral Politics: The Irish Constitutional Referendum 1983', *Political Studies*, xxxiv, 61–81.

Goldring, M., 1982. *Faith of our Fathers: The Formation of Irish Nationalist Ideology 1890–1920*. Dublin.

Goldstrom, J. M., 1981. 'Irish Agriculture and the Great Famine' in J. M. Goldstrom and L. A. Clarkson (eds.), *Irish Population, Economy, and Society: Essays in Honour of the late K. H. Connell*, pp. 155–71. Oxford.

Graham, A. H., 1961. 'The Lichfield House Compact, 1835', *Irish Historical Studies*, xii, 209–25.

Greene, D., 1960. 'Michael Cusack and the Rise of the GAA' in C. C. O'Brien (ed.), *The Shaping of Modern Ireland*, pp. 74–84. London.

Grogan, V., 1967. 'Towards the New Constitution' in F. MacManus (ed.), *The Years of the Great Test*, pp. 161–72. Cork.

Hannan, D. F., 1982. 'Peasant Models and the Understanding of Social and Cultural Change in Rural Ireland' in P. J. Drudy (ed.), *Ireland: Land, Politics and People: Irish Studies 2*, pp. 141–65. Cambridge.

Harkness, D., 1969. *The Restless Dominion: The Irish Free State and the British Commonwealth of Nations, 1921–31*. London.

Harkness, D., 1983. *Northern Ireland since 1920*. Dublin.

Harris, Rosemary, 1972. *Prejudice and Tolerance in Ulster: A Study of Neighbours and 'Strangers' in a Border Community*. Manchester.

Hayden, Mary and Moonan, G. A., 1921. *A Short History of the Irish People*. Dublin.

Hempton, D. N., 1980. 'The Methodist Crusade in Ireland 1795–1845', *Irish Historical Studies*, xxii, 33–48.

Hempton, D. N., 1986. 'Methodism in Irish Society, 1770–1830', *Transactions of the Royal Historical Society*, 5th Series, xxxvi, 117–42.

Hensey, B., 1982. 'The Health Services and their Administration' in F. Litton (ed.), *Unequal Achievement: The Irish Experience 1957–1982*, pp. 147–64. Dublin.

Hepburn, A. C., 1978. 'Catholics in the North of Ireland, 1850–1921: The Urbanization of a Minority' in A. C. Hepburn (ed.), *Minorities in History: Historical Studies XII*, pp. 84–101. London.

Hepburn, A. C. (ed.), 1980. *The Conflict of Nationality in Modern Ireland*. London.

Heskin, K., 1980. *Northern Ireland: A Psychological Analysis*. Dublin.

Heslinga, M. W., 1962. *The Irish Border as a Cultural Divide: A Contribution to the Study of Regionalism in the British Isles*. Assen (Netherlands).

Hickey, J., 1984. *Religion and the Northern Ireland Problem*. Dublin.

Higgins, M. D. and Gibbons, J. P., 1982. 'Shopkeeper-Graziers and Land Agitation in Ireland, 1895–1900' in P. J. Drudy (ed.), *Ireland: Land, Politics and People: Irish Studies 2*, pp. 93–118. Cambridge.

Hill, Jacqueline, 1980. 'The Protestant Response to Repeal: The Case of the Dublin Working Class' in T. W. Moody and R. A. J. Hawkins (eds.), *Ireland under the Union: Varieties of Tension: Essays in Honour of T. W. Moody*, pp. 35–68. Oxford.

Hill, Jacqueline, 1988. 'Popery and Protestantism, Civil and Religious Liberty: The Disputed Lessons of Irish History 1690–1812', *Past & Present*, No. 118, 96–129.

Hogan, J., 1873. 'Patron Days and Holy Wells in Ossory', *Journal of the Royal Society of Antiquaries of Ireland*, xii, 261–81.

Holmes, F., 1981. *Henry Cooke*. Belfast.

Holmes, F., 1982. 'Ulster Presbyterianism and Irish Nationalism' in S. Mews (ed.), *Religion and National Identity: Studies in Church History 18*, pp. 535–55. Oxford.

Holt, E., 1960. *Protest in Arms: The Irish Troubles 1916–1923*. London.

Hoppen, K. T., 1970. 'Tories, Catholics, and the General Election of 1859', *Historical Journal*, xiii, 48–67.

Hoppen, K. T., 1977a. 'Landlords, Society, and Electoral Politics in mid-Nineteenth Century Ireland', *Past & Present*, No. 75, 62–93; also in C. H. E. Philpin (ed.), *Nationalism and Popular Protest in Ireland*, pp. 284–319. Cambridge, 1987.

Hoppen, K. T., 1977b. 'Politics, the Law, and the Nature of the Irish Electorate 1832–1850', *English Historical Review*, xcii, 746–76.

Hoppen, K. T., 1979. 'National Politics and Local Realities in mid-Nineteenth Century Ireland' in A. Cosgrove and D.

McCartney (eds.), *Studies in Irish History presented to R. Dudley Edwards*, pp. 190–227. Dublin.

Hoppen, K. T., 1984. *Elections, Politics, and Society in Ireland 1832–1885*. Oxford.

Hoppen, K. T., 1985. 'The Franchise and Electoral Politics in England and Ireland 1832–1885', *History*, lxx, 202–17.

Humphreys, A. J., 1966. *New Dubliners: Urbanization and the Irish Family*. London.

Hutchinson, J., 1987. *The Dynamics of Cultural Nationalism: The Gaelic Revival and the Creation of the Irish Nation State*. London.

Huttman, J. P., 1970. 'Institutional Factors in the Development of Irish Agriculture, 1850–1915' (University of London, Ph.D. Thesis).

Hynes, E., 1978. 'The Great Hunger and Irish Catholicism', *Societas*, viii, 137–56.

Inglis, B., 1962. *West Briton*. London.

Inglis, H. D., 1838. *A Journey throughout Ireland, during the Spring, Summer, and Autumn of 1834*, 5th ed. London.

Inglis, T., 1980. 'Dimensions of Irish Students' Religiosity', *Economic and Social Review*, xi, 237–56.

Inglis, T., 1987. *Moral Monopoly: The Catholic Church in Modern Irish Society*. Dublin.

Isles, J. S. and Cuthbert, N., 1957. *An Economic Survey of Northern Ireland*. Belfast.

Jalland, Patricia, 1980. *The Liberals and Ireland: The Ulster Question in British Politics to 1914*. Brighton.

Jenkins, R. P., 1977. 'Witches and Fairies: Supernatural Aggression and Deviance among the Irish Peasantry', *Ulster Folklife*, xxiii, 33–56.

Johnson, D. S., 1974. 'The Economic History of Ireland between the Wars', *Irish Social and Economic History*, i, 49–61.

Johnson, D. S., 1979, 'Cattle Smuggling on the Irish Border 1932–38', *Irish Economic and Social History*, vi, 41–63.

Johnson, D. S., 1980. 'Northern Ireland as a Problem in the Economic War 1932–1938', *Irish Historical Studies*, xxii, 144–61.

Johnson, D. S., 1981. 'Partition and Cross-Border Trade in the 1920s' in P. Roebuck (ed.), *Plantation to Partition: Essays in Ulster History in Honour of J. L. McCracken*, pp. 229–46 and 280–3. Belfast.

Johnson, D. S., 1985a. *The Interwar Economy in Ireland*. Dublin.

Johnson, D. S., 1985b. 'The Northern Ireland Economy, 1914–39' in

L. Kennedy and P. Ollerenshaw (eds.), *An Economic History of Ulster, 1820–1940*, pp. 184–223. Manchester.

Johnston, J., 1951. *Irish Agriculture in Transition*. Dublin.

Jones, D. S., 1983. 'The Cleavage between Graziers and Peasants in the Land Struggle, 1890–1910' in S. Clark and J. S. Donnelly, Jr. (eds.), *Irish Peasants: Violence and Political Unrest 1780–1914*, pp. 374–417. Manchester.

Jones, E., 1967. 'Late Victorian Belfast: 1850–1900' in J. C. Beckett and R. E. Glasscock (eds.), *Belfast: The Origin and Growth of an Industrial City*, pp. 109–19. London.

Jordan, D., 1986. 'John O'Connor Power, Charles Stewart Parnell and the Centralisation of Popular Politics in Ireland', *Irish Historical Studies*, xxv, 46–66.

Jordan, D., 1987. 'Merchants, "Strong Farmers" and Fenians: The post-Famine Political Elite and the Irish Land War' in C. H. E. Philpin (ed.), *Nationalism and Popular Protest in Ireland*, pp. 320–48. Cambridge.

Jupp, P. J., 1967. 'Irish Parliamentary Elections and the Influence of the Catholic Vote, 1801–20', *Historical Journal*, x, 183–96.

Kearney, H. F., 1979. 'Fr. Mathew: Apostle of Modernisation' in A. Cosgrove and D. McCartney (eds.), *Studies in Irish History presented to R. Dudley Edwards*, pp. 164–75. Dublin.

Keatinge, P., 1973. *The Formulation of Irish Foreign Policy*. Dublin.

Kee, R., 1972. *The Green Flag: A History of Irish Nationalism*. London.

Keenan, D. J., 1983. *The Catholic Church in Nineteenth-Century Ireland*. Dublin.

Kelly, T. F., 1970. 'Education' in M. Hurley (ed.), *Irish Anglicanism 1869–1969*, pp. 51–64. Dublin.

Kennedy, A. M., 1985c. 'The Dance Hall and Jazz Music in Ireland 1925–1935' (University College Dublin, M.A. Thesis).

Kennedy, D., 1967. 'Catholics in Northern Ireland' in F. MacManus (ed.), *The Years of the Great Test*, pp. 138–49. Cork.

Kennedy, L., 1977. 'A Sceptical View on the Reincarnation of the Irish "Gombeenman" ', *Economic and Social Review*, viii, 213–22.

Kennedy, L., 1978a. 'The Early Response of the Irish Catholic Clergy to the Co-operative Movement', *Irish Historical Studies*, xxi, 55–74.

Kennedy, L., 1978b. 'The Roman Catholic Church and Economic Growth in Nineteenth-Century Ireland', *Economic and Social Review*, x, 45–59.

Kennedy, L., 1979a. 'Profane Images in the Irish Popular Consciousness', *Oral History*, vii, 42–7.

Kennedy, L., 1979b. 'Traders in the Irish Rural Economy, 1880–1914', *Economic History Review*, 2nd Series, xxxii, 201–10.

Kennedy, L., 1981. 'Regional Specialization, Railway Development, and Irish Agriculture in the Nineteenth Century' in J. M. Goldstrom and L. A. Clarkson (eds.), *Irish Population, Economy, and Society: Essays in Honour of the late K. H. Connell*, pp. 173–93. Oxford.

Kennedy, L., 1983a. 'Studies in Irish Econometric History', *Irish Historical Studies*, xxiii, 193–213.

Kennedy, L., 1983b. 'Farmers, Traders, and Agricultural Politics in pre-Independence Ireland' in S. Clark and J. S. Donnelly, Jr. (eds.), *Irish Peasants: Violence and Political Unrest 1780–1914*, pp. 339–73. Manchester.

Kennedy, L., 1984. 'Why One Million Starved: An Open Verdict', *Irish Economic and Social History*, xi, 101–6 [review article on Mokyr 1983].

Kennedy, L., 1985a. 'The Rural Economy, 1820–1914' in L. Kennedy and P. Ollerenshaw (eds.), *An Economic History of Ulster, 1820–1940*, pp. 1-61. Manchester.

Kennedy, L., 1985b. 'Social Change in Middle Ireland', *Studies*, lxxiv, 242–51.

Kennedy, Jr., R. E., 1973. *The Irish: Emigration, Marriage, and Fertility*. Berkeley.

Kennedy, T. P., 1970. 'Church Building' in P. J. Corish (ed.), *A History of Irish Catholicism*, V, Fascicule 8. Dublin.

Kenny, A., 1986. *The Road to Hillsborough: The Shaping of the Anglo-Irish Agreement*. Oxford.

Keogh, D., 1986. *The Vatican, the Bishops and Irish Politics 1919–39*. Cambridge.

Kerr, D., 1981. 'Peel and the Political Involvement of the Priests', *Archivium Hibernicum*, xxxvi, 16–25.

Kerr, D., 1982. *Peel, Priests and Politics: Sir Robert Peel's Administration and the Roman Catholic Church in Ireland, 1841–1846*. Oxford.

Kirkpatrick, R. W., 1980. 'Origins and Development of the Land War in Mid-Ulster, 1879–85' in F. S. L. Lyons and R. A. J. Hawkins (eds.), *Ireland under the Union: Varieties of Tension: Essays in Honour of T. W. Moody*, pp. 201–35. Oxford.

Komito, L., 1984. 'Irish Clientelism: A Reappraisal', *Economic and Social Review*, xv, 173–94.

Laffan, M., 1971. 'The Unification of Sinn Fein', *Irish Historical Studies*, xvii, 353–79.

Laffan, M., 1983. *The Partition of Ireland 1911–1925*. Dundalk.

Laffan, M., 1985. '"Labour Must Wait": Ireland's Conservative Revolution' in P. J. Corish (ed.), *Radicals, Rebels and Establishments: Historical Studies XV*, pp. 203–22. Belfast.

Lane, P. G., 1972–3. 'On the General Impact of the Encumbered Estates Act of 1849 on Counties Galway and Mayo', *Journal of the Galway Archaeological and Historical Society*, xxxii, 44–74.

Lane, P. G., 1981–2. 'The Impact of the Encumbered Estates Court upon the Landlords of Galway and Mayo', *Journal of the Galway Archaeological and Historical Society*, xxxviii, 45–58.

Larkin, E., 1962. 'Church and State in Ireland in the Nineteenth Century', *Church History*, xxxi, 294–306.

Larkin, E., 1964. 'Socialism and Catholicism in Ireland', *Church History*, xxxiii, 462–83.

Larkin, E., 1965. *James Larkin: Irish Labour Leader 1876–1947*. London.

Larkin, E., 1967. 'Economic Growth, Capital Investment, and the Roman Catholic Church in Nineteenth-Century Ireland', *American Historical Review*, lxxii, 852–84.

Larkin, E., 1972. 'The Devotional Revolution in Ireland, 1850–75', *American Historical Review*, lxxvii, 625–52.

Larkin, E., 1975a. *The Roman Catholic Church and the Creation of the Modern Irish State 1878–1886*. Dublin.

Larkin, E., 1975b. 'Church, State, and Nation in Modern Ireland', *American Historical Review*, lxxx, 1244–76.

Larkin, E., 1978. *The Roman Catholic Church and the Plan of Campaign in Ireland 1886–1888*. Cork.

Larkin, E., 1979. *The Roman Catholic Church in Ireland and the Fall of Parnell 1888–1891*. Liverpool.

Larkin, E., 1980. *The Making of the Roman Catholic Church in Ireland, 1850–1860*. Chapel Hill.

Larkin, E., 1987. *The Consolidation of the Roman Catholic Church in Ireland, 1860–1870*. Dublin.

Law, C. M., 1967. 'The Growth of Urban Population in England and Wales, 1801–1911', *Transactions of the Institute of British Geographers*, No. 41, 125–43.

Lawlor, Sheila, 1983. *Britain and Ireland 1914–23*. Dublin.

Lee, J., 1968. 'Marriage and Population in pre-Famine Ireland', *Economic History Review*, 2nd Series, xxi, 283–95.

Lee, J., 1971. 'The Dual Economy in Ireland, 1800–50', *Historical Studies*, viii, 191–201.

Lee, J., 1973a. 'The Ribbonmen' in T. D. Williams (ed.), *Secret Societies in Ireland*, pp. 26–35. Dublin.

Lee, J., 1973b. *The Modernisation of Irish Society 1848–1918*. Dublin.

Lee, J., 1978. 'Women and the Church since the Famine' in Margaret MacCurtain and D. Ó Corráin (eds.), *Women in Irish Society: The Historical Dimension*, pp. 37–45. Dublin.

Lee, J., 1979a. 'Aspects of Corporatist Thought in Ireland: The Commission on Vocational Organisation, 1939–43' in A. Cosgrove and D. McCartney (eds.), *Studies in Irish History presented to R. Dudley Edwards*, pp. 324–46. Dublin.

Lee, J., 1979b. 'Continuity and Change in Ireland, 1945–70' in J. Lee (ed.), *Ireland 1945–70*, pp. 166–77. Dublin.

Lee, J., 1979c. 'Sean Lemass' in J. Lee (ed.), *Ireland 1945–70*, pp. 16–26. Dublin.

Lee, J., 1980. 'Patterns of Rural Unrest in Nineteenth-Century Ireland: A Preliminary Survey' in L. M. Cullen and F. Furet (eds.), *Ireland and France 17th–20th Centuries: Towards a Comparative Study of Rural History*, pp. 223–37. Paris.

Lee, J., 1984. 'The Social and Economic Ideas of O'Connell' in K. B. Nowlan and M. R. O'Connell (eds.), *Daniel O'Connell: Portrait of a Radical*, pp. 70–86. Belfast.

Lee, J., 1985a. 'Centralisation and Community' in J. Lee (ed.), *Ireland: Towards a Sense of Place*, pp. 84–101. Cork.

Lee, J., 1986. 'Whither Ireland? The Next Twenty-Five Years' in K. A. Kennedy (ed.), *Ireland in Transition: Economic and Social Change since 1960*, pp. 152–66. Cork.

Lee, R. M., 1985b. 'Intermarriage, Conflict and Social Control in Ireland: The Decree "Ne temere"', *Economic and Social Review*, xvii, 11–27.

Lewis, G. C., 1836. *On Local Disturbances in Ireland, and on the Irish Church Question*. London. Reprinted Cork 1977 – all references to the latter.

Longford, Earl of and O'Neill, T. P., 1970. *Eamon de Valera*. London.

Loughlin, J., 1986. *Home Rule and the Ulster Question 1882–93*. Dublin.

Lynch, P., 1966. 'The Social Revolution that Never Was' in T. D. Williams (ed.), *The Irish Struggle 1916–1926*, pp. 41–54. London.

Lynch, P., 1969. 'The Irish Economy since the War, 1946–51' in K. B. Nowlan and T. D. Williams (eds.), *Ireland in the War Years and After 1939–51*, pp. 185–200. Dublin.

Lynch, P. and Vaizey, J., 1960. *Guinness's Brewery in the Irish Economy 1759–1876*. Cambridge.

Lyons, F. S. L., 1951. *The Irish Parliamentary Party 1890–1910*. London.

Lyons, F. S. L., 1960. *The Fall of Parnell 1890–91*. London.

Lyons, F. S. L., 1968. *John Dillon: A Biography*. London.

Lyons, F. S. L., 1971. *Ireland since the Famine*. London.

Lyons, F. S. L., 1977. *Charles Stewart Parnell*. London.

Lyons, F. S. L., 1979. *Culture and Anarchy in Ireland 1890–1939*. Oxford.

McAleese, D., 1982. 'Political Independence, Economic Growth and the Role of Economic Policy' in P. J. Drudy (ed.), *Ireland: Land, Politics and People: Irish Studies 2*, pp. 271–95. Cambridge.

McAleese, D., 1986a. 'Ireland in the World Economy' in K. A. Kennedy (ed.), *Ireland in Transition: Economic and Social Change since 1960*, pp. 19–30. Cork.

McAleese, D., 1986b. 'Anglo-Irish Economic Interdependence: From Excessive Intimacy to a Wider Embrace' in P. J. Drudy (ed.), *Ireland and Britain since 1922: Irish Studies 5*, pp. 87–106. Cambridge.

Macardle, Dorothy, 1968. *The Irish Republic*. London (first published 1937).

MacArthur, W. P., 1956. 'Medical History of the Famine' in R. D. Edwards and T. D. Williams (eds.), *The Great Famine: Studies in Irish History 1845–52*, pp. 263–315. Dublin.

McCaffrey, L., 1962. 'Irish Federalism in the 1870s: A Study in Conservative Nationalism', *Transactions of the American Philosophical Society*, New Series, lii, part 6.

McCaffrey, L., 1966. *Daniel O'Connell and the Repeal Year*. Kentucky.

McCartney, D., 1957. 'The Writing of History in Ireland 1800–30', *Irish Historical Studies*, x, 347–62.

McCartney, D., 1987. *The Dawning of Democracy: Ireland 1800–1870*. Dublin.

McCashin, T., 1982. 'Social Policy: 1957–82' in F. Litton (ed.), *Unequal Achievement: The Irish Experience 1957–1982*, pp. 203–23. Dublin.

MacDonagh, O., 1970. *The Nineteenth Century Novel and Irish Social History: Some Aspects*. Dublin.

MacDonagh, O., 1975. 'The Politicization of the Irish Catholic Bishops, 1800–1850', *Historical Journal*, xviii, 37–53.

MacDonagh, O., 1983a. 'O'Connell and Repeal 1840–1845' in M. Bentley and J. Stevenson (eds.), *High and Low Politics in Modern Britain*, pp. 4–27. Oxford.

MacDonagh, O., 1983b. *States of Mind: A Study of Anglo-Irish Conflict 1780–1980*. London.

MacDonagh, O., 1988. *The Hereditary Bondsman: Daniel O'Connell 1775–1829*. London.

McDonald, W., 1925. *Reminiscences of a Maynooth Professor*, ed. D. Gwynn. London.

McDowell, M., 1982. 'A Generation of Public Expenditure Growth: Leviathan Unchained' in F. Litton (ed.), *Unequal Achievement: The Irish Experience 1957–1982*, pp. 183–200. Dublin.

McDowell, R. B., 1952. *Public Opinion and Government Policy in Ireland, 1801–1846*. London.

McDowell, R. B., 1964. *The Irish Administration 1801–1914*. London.

McGrath, F., 1971. 'The University Question' in P. J. Corish (ed.), *A History of Irish Catholicism*, V, Fascicule 6. Dublin.

McGrath, M. (ed.), 1936–7. *The Diary of Humphrey O'Sullivan*, 4 vols. Dublin. Volumes XXX to XXXIII in 'Publications of the Irish Texts Society.'

McGrath, T., 1982. 'Fairy Faith and Changelings: The Burning of Bridget Cleary in 1895', *Studies*, lxxi, 178–84.

Machin, G. I. T., 1977. *Politics and the Churches in Great Britain 1832 to 1868*. Oxford.

Macintyre, A., 1965. *The Liberator: Daniel O'Connell and the Irish Party 1830–1847*. London.

McKee, E., 1986. 'Church–State Relations and the Development of Irish Health Policy: The Mother-and-Child Scheme, 1944–53', *Irish Historical Studies*, xxv, 159–94.

McMahon, Deirdre, 1984. *Republicans and Imperialists: Anglo-Irish Relations in the 1930s*. New Haven.

McMinn, R., 1981. 'Presbyterianism and Politics in Ulster 1871–1906', *Studia Hibernica*, No. 21, 127–46.

MacNeice, L., 1965. *The Strings are False: An Unfinished Autobiography*. London.

MacNeill, Maire, 1962. *The Festival of Lughnasa: A Study of the Survival of the Celtic Festival of the Beginning of Harvest*. Oxford.

MacPhilpin, J., 1880. *The Apparitions and Miracles at Knock*. Dublin.

McQuaid, J. C., 1961. *Higher Education for Catholics* [A pastoral Letter]. Dublin.

MacSuibhne, P. (ed.), 1961-77. *Paul Cullen and His Contemporaries*, 5 vols. Naas.

Maguire, W. A., 1972. *The Downshire Estates in Ireland 1801–1845: The Management of Irish Landed Estates in the early Nineteenth Century*. Oxford.

Malcolm, Elizabeth, 1980. 'Temperance and Irish Nationalism' in F. S. L. Lyons and R. A. J. Hawkins (eds.), *Ireland under the*

279

Union: Varieties of Tension: Essays in Honour of T. W. Moody, pp. 69–114. Oxford.

Malcolm, Elizabeth, 1982. 'The Catholic Church and the Irish Temperance Movement, 1838–1901', *Irish Historical Studies*, xxiii, 1–16.

Malcolm, Elizabeth, 1986. *'Ireland Sober, Ireland Free': Drink and Temperance in Nineteenth-Century Ireland*. Dublin.

Mandle, W. F., 1977. 'The IRB and the Beginnings of the Gaelic Athletic Association', *Irish Historical Studies*, xx, 418–38.

Manning, M., 1970. *The Blueshirts*. Dublin.

Manning, M., 1979. 'The Farmers' in J. Lee (ed.), *Ireland 1945–70*, pp. 48–60. Dublin.

Marsh, M., 1981. 'Localism, Candidate Selection and Electoral Preferences in Ireland: The General Election of 1977', *Economic and Social Review*, xii, 267–86.

Martin, F. X., 1967a. '1916 – Myth, Fact, and Mystery', *Studia Hibernica*, No. 7, 7–126.

Martin, F. X. (ed.), 1967b. *Leaders and Men of the Easter Rising: Dublin 1916*. London.

Martin, F. X., 1968. 'The 1916 Rising – a *Coup d'Etat* or a "Bloody Protest"?', *Studia Hibernica*, No. 8, 106–37.

Matthews, A., 1982. 'The State and Irish Agriculture, 1950–1980' in P. J. Drudy (ed.), *Ireland: Land, Politics and People: Irish Studies 2*, pp. 241–69. Cambridge.

Mavrogordatos, G. Th., 1983. *Stillborn Republic: Social Coalitions and Party Strategies in Greece, 1922–1936*. Berkeley.

Meagher, W., 1853. *Notices of the Life and Character of His Grace Most Rev. Daniel Murray, late Archbishop of Dublin*. Dublin.

Meenan, J., 1967. 'From Free-Trade to Self-Sufficiency' in F. MacManus (ed.), *The Years of the Great Test*, pp. 69–79. Cork.

Meenan, J., 1970. *The Irish Economy since 1922*. Liverpool.

Meenan, J., 1971. 'Irish Agricultural Policies in the last Twenty Years' in I. F. Baillie and S. J. Sheehy (eds.), *Irish Agriculture in a Changing World*, pp. 44–55. Edinburgh.

Meenan, J., 1980. *George O'Brien: A Biographical Memoir*. Dublin.

Mescal, J., 1957. *Religion in the Irish System of Education*. Dublin.

Miller, D. W., 1968. 'The Roman Catholic Church in Ireland: 1898–1918', *Eire-Ireland*, iii, 75–91.

Miller, D. W., 1973. *Church, State and Nation in Ireland 1898–1921*. Dublin.

Miller, D. W., 1975. 'Irish Catholicism and the Great Famine', *Journal of Social History*, ix, 81–98.

Miller, D. W., 1978a. *Queen's Rebels: Ulster Loyalism in Historical Perspective*. Dublin.

Miller, D. W., 1978b. 'Presbyterianism and "Modernization" in Ulster', *Past & Present*, No. 80, 66–90.

Miller, D. W., 1983. 'The Armagh Troubles, 1784–95' in S. Clark and J. S. Donnelly, Jr. (eds.), *Irish Peasants: Violence and Political Unrest 1780–1914*, pp. 155–91. Manchester.

Miller, K. A., 1985. *Emigrants and Exiles: Ireland and the Irish Exodus to North America*. New York.

Mitchell, A., 1974. *Labour and Irish Politics 1890–1930: The Irish Labour Movement in an Age of Revolution*. Dublin.

Mitchell, B. R., 1981. *European Historical Statistics 1750–1975*, 2nd ed. London.

Mitchell, B. R. and Deane, Phyllis, 1971. *Abstract of British Historical Statistics*, revised ed. Cambridge.

Mogey, J. M., 1947. *Rural Life in Northern Ireland: Five Regional Studies*. London.

Mogey, J. M., 1948. 'The Community in Northern Ireland', *Man*, xlviii, 85–7.

Mokyr, J., 1981. 'Irish History with the Potato', *Irish Economic and Social History*, viii, 8–29.

Mokyr, J., 1983. *Why Ireland Starved: A Quantitative and Analytical History of the Irish Economy, 1800–1850*. London. There are some corrections in the paperback ed. 1985.

Mokyr, J. and Ó Gráda, C., 1984. 'New Developments in Irish Population History, 1700–1850', *Economic History Review*, 2nd Series, xxxvii, 473–88.

Mokyr, J. and Ó Gráda, C., 1986. 'From Poor to Poorer: Living Standards in Ireland before the Famine'. Centre for Economic Research (University College Dublin), Working Paper No. 33.

Montague, J., 1977. *Poisoned Lands*, new ed. Dublin.

Monypenny, W. F. and Buckle, G. E., 1910–20. *The Life of Benjamin Disraeli*, 6 vols. London.

Moody, T. W. (ed.), 1968. *The Fenian Movement*. Cork.

Moody, T. W., 1974. *The Ulster Question 1603–1973*. Dublin.

Moody, T. W., 1981. *Davitt and Irish Revolution 1846–82*. Oxford.

Munck, R., 1985. 'Class and Religion in Belfast – A Historical Perspective', *Journal of Contemporary History*, xx, 241–59.

Murphy, B., 1986. 'J. J. O'Kelly ("Sceilg") and the *Catholic Bulletin*: Cultural Considerations – Gaelic, Religious and National, c.1898–1926' (University College Dublin, Ph.D. Thesis).

Murphy, I. and Ó Súilleabháin S., 1971. 'Catholic Education' in

P. J. Corish (ed.), *A History of Irish Catholicism*, V, Fascicule 6. Dublin.

Murphy, J. A., 1965. 'The Support of the Catholic Clergy in Ireland, 1750–1850', *Historical Studies*, v, 103–21.

Murphy, J. A., 1975. *Ireland in the Twentieth Century*. Dublin.

Murphy, J. A., 1979b. '"Put Them Out!" Parties and Elections, 1948–69' in J. Lee (ed.), *Ireland 1945–70*, pp. 1–15. Dublin.

Murphy, Maura, 1976. 'Municipal Reform and the Repeal Movement in Cork, 1833–1844', *Journal of the Cork Historical and Archaeological Society*, lxxxi, 1–18.

Murphy, Maura, 1979a. 'The Ballad Singer and the Role of the Seditious Ballad in Nineteenth-Century Ireland: Dublin Castle's View', *Ulster Folklife*, xxv, 79–102.

Murphy, Maura, 1981. 'The Economic and Social Structure of Nineteenth Century Cork' in D. Harkness and Mary O'Dowd (eds.), *The Town in Ireland: Historical Studies XIII*, pp. 125–54. Belfast.

Murray, A. C., 1986a. 'Nationality and Local Politics in late Nineteenth-Century Ireland: The Case of County Westmeath', *Irish Historical Studies*, xxv, 144–58.

Murray, A. C., 1986b. 'Agrarian Violence and Nationalism in Nineteenth-Century Ireland: The Myth of Ribbonism', *Irish Economic and Social History*, xiii, 56–73.

Murray, D., 1985. *Worlds Apart: Segregated Schools in Northern Ireland*. Belfast.

Nelson, Sarah, 1984. *Ulster's Uncertain Defenders: Protestant Political, Paramilitary and Community Groups and the Northern Ireland Conflict*. Belfast.

Newman, J., 1962. 'The Priests of Ireland: A Socio-Religious Survey', *Irish Ecclesiastical Record*, xcviii, 1–27.

Newsinger, J., 1978. '"I Bring not Peace but a Sword": The Religious Motif in the Irish War of Independence', *Journal of Contemporary History*, xiii, 609–28.

Nolan, M., 1975. 'The Influence of Catholic Nationalism on the Legislature of the Irish Free State', *Irish Jurist*, New Series, x, 128–69.

Norman, E. R., 1965. *The Catholic Church and Ireland in the Age of Rebellion 1859–1873*. London.

Norman, E. R., 1967. 'The Maynooth Question of 1845', *Irish Historical Studies*, xv, 407–37.

Norman, E. R., 1969. *The Catholic Church and Irish Politics in the Eighteen Sixties*. Dundalk.

Nowlan, K. B., 1965. *The Politics of Repeal: A Study in the Relations between Great Britain and Ireland, 1841–50*. London.

Nowlan, K. B., 1967. 'President Cosgrave's last Administration' in F. MacManus (ed.), *The Years of the Great Test*, pp. 7–18. Cork.

Nowlan, K. B., (ed.), 1969. *The Making of 1916: Studies in the History of the Rising*. Dublin.

Nowlan, K. B., 1974. 'The Catholic Clergy and Irish Politics in the Eighteen Thirties and Forties', *Historical Studies*, ix, 119–35.

Nowlan, K. B. and Williams, T. D. (eds.), 1969. *Ireland in the War Years and After 1939–51*. Dublin.

O'Brien, C. C., 1964. *Parnell and His Party 1880–90*, corrected impression. Oxford.

O'Brien, George, 1921. *The Economic History of Ireland from the Union to the Famine*. London.

O'Brien, George, 1936. 'Patrick Hogan: Minister for Agriculture 1922–1932', *Studies*, xxv, 353–68.

O'Brien, Gerard, 1985. 'The New Poor Law in pre-Famine Ireland: A Case History', *Irish Economic and Social History*, xii, 33–49.

O'Brien, J. B., 1977. 'Agricultural Prices and Living Costs in pre-Famine Cork', *Journal of the Cork Historical and Archaeological Society*, lxxxii, 1–10.

O'Brien, J. B., 1979. *The Catholic Middle Classes in pre-Famine Cork*. Dublin.

O'Brien, J. V., 1976. *William O'Brien and the Course of Irish Politics 1881–1918*. Berkeley.

O'Brien, J. V., 1982. *'Dear Dirty Dublin': A City in Distress, 1899–1916*. Berkeley.

O'Brien, R. B., 1889. *Thomas Drummond Under-Secretary in Ireland 1835–40*. London.

O'Brien, R. B., 1912. *Dublin Castle and the Irish People*, 2nd ed. London.

Ó Broin, L., 1970. *Dublin Castle and the 1916 Rising*, revised ed. London.

Ó Broin, L., 1971. *Fenian Fever: An Anglo-American Dilemma*. London.

Ó Broin, L., 1976. *Revolutionary Underground: The Story of the Irish Republican Brotherhood 1858–1924*. Dublin.

O'Callaghan, Margaret, 1984. 'Language, Nationality and Cultural Identity in the Irish Free State, 1922–7: The *Irish Statesman* and the *Catholic Bulletin* Reappraised', *Irish Historical Studies*, xxiv, 226–45.

O'Clery, C., 1986. *Phrases Make History Here: A Century of Irish Political Quotations 1886–1986*. Dublin.

O'Connell, M. R. (ed.), 1972–80. *The Correspondence of Daniel O'Connell*, 8 vols. Dublin.

O'Connell, P. J., 1982. 'The Distribution and Redistribution of Income in the Republic of Ireland', *Economic and Social Review*, xiii, 251–78.

O'Connor, D., 1910. *St Patrick's Purgatory, Lough Derg. Its History, Traditions, Legends, Antiquities, Topography, and Scenic Surroundings*, enlarged ed. Dublin.

O'Connor, E., 1980. 'Agrarian Unrest and the Labour Movement in County Waterford 1917–1923', *Saothar: Journal of the Irish Labour History Society*, vi, 40–58.

O'Connor, T. P., 1886. *The Parnell Movement, with a Sketch of Irish Parties from 1843*. London.

Ó Cuív, B., 1966. 'Education and Language' in T. D. Williams (ed.), *The Irish Struggle 1916–1926*, pp. 153–66. London.

O'Day, A., 1986. *Parnell and the First Home Rule Episode 1884–87*. Dublin.

O'Donoghue, P., 1965. 'Causes of the Opposition to Tithes, 1830–38', *Studia Hibernica*, No. 5, 7–28.

O'Donoghue, P., 1966. 'Opposition to Tithe Payments in 1830–31', *Studia Hibernica*, No. 6, 69–98.

O'Donoghue, P., 1972. 'Opposition to Tithe Payment in 1832–3', *Studia Hibernica*, No. 12, 77–108.

O'Farrell, P., 1971. *Ireland's English Question: Anglo-Irish Relations 1534–1970*. London.

O'Farrell, P., 1975. *England and Ireland since 1800*. Oxford.

O'Farrell, P., 1982–3. 'Whose Reality? The Irish Famine in History and Literature', *Historical Studies* [Australia], xx, 1-13.

O'Ferrall, F., 1981a. *Daniel O'Connell*. Dublin.

O'Ferrall, F., 1981b. '"The Only Lever . . . "? The Catholic Priest in Irish Politics 1823–29', *Studies*, lxx, 308–24.

O'Ferrall, F., 1985. *Catholic Emancipation: Daniel O'Connell and the Birth of Irish Democracy 1820–30*. Dublin.

Ó Fiaich, T., 1968. 'The Clergy and Fenianism, 1860–70', *Irish Ecclesiastical Record*, cix, 81–103.

Ó Gráda, C., 1973. 'Seasonal Migration and post-Famine Adjustment in the West of Ireland', *Studia Hibernica*, No. 13, 48–76.

Ó Gráda, C., 1975a. 'Supply Responsiveness in Irish Agriculture during the Nineteenth Century', *Economic History Review*, 2nd Series, xxviii, 312–17.

Ó Gráda, C., 1975b. 'The Investment Behaviour of Irish Landlords 1850–75: Some Preliminary Findings', *Agricultural History Review*, xxiii, 139–55.

Ó Gráda, C., 1975c. 'A Note on Nineteenth-Century Irish Emigration Statistics', *Population Studies*, xxix, 143–9.

Ó Gráda, C., 1977. 'The Beginnings of the Irish Creamery System, 1880–1914', *Economic History Review*, 2nd Series, xxx, 284–305.

Ó Gráda, C., 1980. 'Demographic Adjustment and Seasonal Migration in Nineteenth-Century Ireland' in L. M. Cullen and F. Furet (eds.), *Ireland and France 17th–20th Centuries: Towards a Comparative Study of Rural History*, pp. 181–93. Paris.

Ó Gráda, C., 1983. 'Across the Briny Ocean: Some Thoughts on Irish Emigration to America, 1800–1850' in T. M. Devine and D. Dickson (eds.), *Ireland and Scotland 1600–1850: Parallels and Contrasts in Economic and Social Development*, pp. 118–30. Edinburgh.

Ó Gráda, C., 1984. 'Irish Agricultural Output before and after the Famine', *Journal of European Economic History*, xiii, 149–65.

Ó Gráda, C., 1988. *Ireland before and after the Famine: Explorations in Economic History, 1800–1925*. Manchester.

O'Hagan, J. W., 1980. 'An Analysis of the Relative Size of the Government Sector: Ireland 1926–52', *Economic and Social Review*, xii, 17–35.

O'Halloran, Clare, 1987. *Partition and the Limits of Irish Nationalism*. Dublin.

O'Halpin, E., 1987. *The Decline of the Union: British Government in Ireland 1892–1920*. Dublin.

O'Hegarty, P. S., 1952. *A History of Ireland under the Union 1801 to 1922*. London.

O'Leary, C., 1979. *Irish Elections 1918–77: Parties, Voters and Proportional Representation*. Dublin.

Ollerenshaw, P., 1985. 'Industry, 1820–1914' in L. Kennedy and P. Ollerenshaw (eds.), *An Economic History of Ulster, 1820–1940*, pp. 62–108. Manchester.

O'Malley, P., 1983. *The Uncivil Wars: Ireland Today*. Belfast.

O'Neill, K., 1984. *Family and Farm in pre-Famine Ireland: The Parish of Killashandra*. Madison (Wis.).

O'Neill, Thomas P., 1956. 'The Organisation and Administration of Relief, 1845–52' in R. D. Edwards and T. D. Williams (eds.), *The Great Famine: Studies in Irish History 1845–52*, pp. 209–59. Dublin.

O'Neill, Thomas P., 1976. 'In Search of a Political Path: Irish Republicanism, 1922 to 1927', *Historical Studies*, x, 147–71.

O'Neill, Timothy P., 1973. 'Poverty in Ireland 1815–45', *Folklife*, xi, 22–33.

Ó Raifeartaigh, T., 1955. 'Mixed Education and the Synod of Ulster, 1831–40', *Irish Historical Studies*, ix, 281–99.

Orridge, A. W., 1981. 'Who Supported the Land War? An Aggregate–Data Analysis of Irish Agrarian Discontent 1879–1882', *Economic and Social Review*, xii, 203–33.

O'Shea, J., 1983. *Priests, Politics and Society in post-Famine Ireland: A Study of County Tipperary 1850–1891*. Dublin.

Ó Tuathaigh, G., 1972. *Ireland before the Famine 1798–1848*. Dublin.

Ó Tuathaigh, G., 1975. 'Gaelic Ireland, Popular Politics and Daniel O'Connell', *Journal of the Galway Archaeological and Historical Society*, xxxiv, 21–34.

Ó Tuathaigh, G., 1977. *Thomas Drummond and the Government of Ireland 1835–41*. Dublin.

Ó Tuathaigh, G., 1982. 'The Land Question, Politics and Irish Society, 1922–1960' in P. J. Drudy (ed.), *Ireland: Land, Politics and People: Irish Studies 2*, pp. 167–89. Cambridge.

Pakenham, F. [Lord Longford], 1972. *Peace by Ordeal: An Account from first-hand Sources, of the Negotiations and Signature of the Anglo-Irish Treaty 1921*. London (first published 1935).

Palmer, N. D., 1940. *The Irish Land League Crisis*. New Haven.

Patterson, H., 1980. *Class Conflict and Sectarianism: The Protestant Working Class and the Belfast Labour Movement 1868–1920*. Belfast.

Patterson, H., 1985. 'Industrial Labour and the Labour Movement, 1820–1914' in L. Kennedy and P. Ollerenshaw (eds.), *An Economic History of Ulster, 1820–1940*, pp. 158–83. Manchester.

Pomfret, J. E., 1930. *The Struggle for Land in Ireland, 1800–1923*. Princeton.

Pope Hennessy, J., 1884. 'What do the Irish Read?', *The Nineteenth Century*, xv, 920–32.

Prager, J., 1986. *Building Democracy in Ireland: Political Order and Cultural Integration in a newly Independent Nation*. Cambridge.

Press, J. P., 1986. 'Protectionism and the Irish Footwear Industry, 1932–39', *Irish Economic and Social History*, xiii, 74–89.

Prest, J., 1972. *Lord John Russell*. London.

Prim, J. G. A., 1853. 'Olden Popular Pastimes in Kilkenny', *Journal of the Royal Society of Antiquaries of Ireland*, ii, 319–35.

Proudfoot, L., 1986. 'The Management of a Great Estate: Patronage,

Income and Expenditure on the Duke of Devonshire's Irish Property, c. 1816 to 1891', *Irish Economic and Social History*, xiii, 32–55.

Raymond, R. J., 1983. 'De Valera, Lemass and Irish Economic Development: 1933–1948' in J. P. O'Connell and J. A. Murphy (eds.), *De Valera and His Times*, pp. 113–33. Cork.

Raymond, R. J., 1984. 'The United States and Terrorism in Ireland 1969–1981' in Yonah Alexander and A. O'Day (eds.), *Terrorism in Ireland*, pp. 32–52. London.

Reynolds, J. A., 1954. *The Catholic Emancipation Crisis in Ireland, 1823–1829*. New Haven.

Roberts, P. E. W., 1983. 'Caravats and Shanavests: Whiteboyism and Faction Fighting in East Munster, 1802–11' in S. Clark and J. S. Donnelly, Jr. (eds.), *Irish Peasants: Violence and Political Unrest 1780–1914*, pp. 64–101. Manchester.

Robinson, Olive, 1962. 'The London Companies as progressive Landlords in Nineteenth-Century Ireland', *Economic History Review*, 2nd Series, xv, 103–18.

Rose, R., 1971. *Governing without Consensus: An Irish Perspective*. London.

Rose, R., 1976. *Northern Ireland: A Time of Choice*. London.

Rottman, D. B., 1986. 'Crime and the Criminal Justice System' in K. A. Kennedy (ed.), *Ireland in Transition: Economic and Social Change since 1960*, pp. 101–11. Cork.

Rottman, D. B. and O'Connell, P. J., 1982. 'The Changing Social Structure' in F. Litton (ed.), *Unequal Achievement: The Irish Experience 1957–1982*, pp. 63–88. Dublin.

Rumpf, E. and Hepburn, A. C., 1977. *Nationalism and Socialism in Twentieth-Century Ireland*. Liverpool.

Ryan, A. P., 1956. *Mutiny at the Curragh*. London.

Ryan, D., 1949. *The Rising: The Complete Story of Easter Week*. Dublin.

Ryan, D., 1967. *The Fenian Chief: A Biography of James Stephens*. Dublin.

Sacks, P. M., 1976. *The Donegal Mafia: An Irish Political Machine*. New Haven.

Savage, D. C., 1961. 'The Origins of the Ulster Unionist Party, 1885–6', *Irish Historical Studies*, xii, 185–208.

Scheper-Hughes, Nancy, 1979. *Saints, Scholars, and Schizophrenics: Mental Illness in Rural Ireland*. Berkeley.

Schrier, A., 1958. *Ireland and the American Emigration 1850–1900*. Minneapolis.

Senior, H., 1966. *Orangeism in Ireland and Britain 1795–1836*. London.

Sheehy, Jeanne, 1980. *The Rediscovery of Ireland's Past: The Celtic Revival 1830–1930*. London.

Sheehy, S. J., 1984. 'The Common Agricultural Policy and Ireland' in P. J. Drudy and D. McAleese (eds.), *Ireland and the European Community: Irish Studies 3*, pp. 79–105. Cambridge.

Solar, P. M., 1983. 'Agricultural Productivity and Economic Development in Ireland and Scotland in the early Nineteenth Century' in T. M. Devine and D. Dickson (eds.), *Ireland and Scotland 1600–1850: Parallels and Contrasts in Economic and Social Development*, pp. 70–88. Edinburgh.

Solar, P. M., 1984. 'Why Ireland Starved: A Critical Review of the Econometric Results', *Irish Economic and Social History*, xi, 107–15 (Critique of Mokyr 1983, with reply by Mokyr, pp. 116–21).

Solow, Barbara L., 1971. *The Land Question and the Irish Economy, 1870–1903*. Cambridge (Mass.).

South Meath Election Petition, 1892. *South Meath Election Petition. Tried at Trim, November, 1892*. Dublin.

Spencer, J. E. and Harrison, M. J., 1977. 'The Structure and Behaviour of Irish Economies (with an Illustrative Model)' in N. J. Gibson and J. E. Spencer (eds.), *Economic Activity in Ireland: A Study of two Open Economies*, pp. 1–39. Dublin.

Steele, E. D., 1974. *Irish Land and British Politics: Tenant-Right and Nationality 1865–1870*. Cambridge.

Steele, E. D., 1975. 'Cardinal Cullen and Irish Nationality', *Irish Historical Studies*, xix, 239–60.

Stewart, A. T. Q., 1967. *The Ulster Crisis*. London.

Stewart, A. T. Q., 1977. *The Narrow Ground: Aspects of Ulster 1609–1969*. London.

Sullivan, A. M., 1877. *New Ireland*, 2 vols. London.

Thackeray, W. M., 1879. *The Irish Sketch Book of 1842*. London.

Thompson, F., 1985. 'Attitudes to Reform: Political Parties in Ulster and the Irish Land Bill of 1881', *Irish Historical Studies*, xxiv, 327–40.

Thornley, D., 1964. *Isaac Butt and Home Rule*. London.

Thornley, D., 1967. 'The Blueshirts' in F. MacManus (ed.), *The Years of the Great Test*, pp. 42–54. Cork.

Tierney, M., 1976. *Croke of Cashel: The Life of Archbishop Thomas William Croke, 1823–1902*. Dublin.

Titley, E. B., 1983. *Church, State and the Control of Schooling in Ireland 1900–1944*. Dublin.

Tocqueville, A. de, 1958. *Journeys to England and Ireland*, ed. J. P. Mayer. London.

Towey, T., 1980. 'The Reaction of the British Government to the 1922 Collins–de Valera Pact', *Irish Historical Studies*, xxii, 65–76.

Townshend, C., 1975. *The British Campaign in Ireland 1919–1921: The Development of Political and Military Policies*. Oxford.

Townshend, C., 1983. *Political Violence in Ireland: Government and Resistance since 1848*. Oxford.

Townshend, C., 1987. Review of O'Halloran 1987 in *Irish Literary Supplement*, vi, No. 2, 12.

Turner, M., 1987. 'Towards an Agricultural Prices Index for Ireland 1850–1914', *Economic and Social Review*, xviii, 123–36.

Valiulis, Maryann G., 1983. 'The "Army Mutiny" of 1924 and the Assertion of Civilian Authority in Independent Ireland', *Irish Historical Review*, xxiii, 354–66.

Vaughan, W. E., 1977. 'Landlord and Tenant Relations in Ireland between the Famine and the Land War, 1850–1878' in L. M. Cullen and T. C. Smout (eds.), *Comparative Aspects of Scottish and Irish Economic and Social History 1600–1900*, pp. 216–26. Edinburgh.

Vaughan, W. E., 1980a. 'Agricultural Output, Rents and Wages in Ireland, 1850–1880' in L. M. Cullen and F. Furet (eds.), *Ireland and France 17th-20th Centuries: Towards a Comparative Study of Rural History*, pp. 85–97. Paris.

Vaughan, W. E., 1980b. 'An Assessment of the Economic Performance of Irish Landlords, 1851–81' in F. S. L. Lyons and R. A. J. Hawkins (eds.), *Ireland under the Union: Varieties of Tension: Essays in Honour of T. W. Moody*, pp. 173–99. Oxford.

Vaughan, W. E., 1984. *Landlords and Tenants in Ireland 1848–1904*. Dublin.

Vaughan, W. E. and Fitzpatrick, A. J. (eds.), 1978. *Irish Historical Statistics: Population, 1821–1971*. Dublin.

Vincent, J., 1966. *The Formation of the Liberal Party 1857–1868*. London.

Vincent, J., 1977. 'Gladstone and Ireland', *Proceedings of the British Academy*, lxiii, 193–238.

Walker, B. M. (ed.), 1978. *Parliamentary Election Results in Ireland, 1801–1922*. Dublin.

Wall, Maureen, 1961. *The Penal Laws, 1691–1760*. Dundalk.

Wall, Maureen, 1969. 'The Background to the Rising, from 1914 until the Issue of the Countermanding Order on Easter Saturday

1916' in K. B. Nowlan (ed.), *The Making of 1916: Studies in the History of the Rising*, pp. 157–97. Dublin.

Walsh, B. M., 1979. 'Economic Growth and Development, 1945–70' in J. Lee (ed.), *Ireland 1945–70*, pp. 27–37. Dublin.

Walsh, B. M., 1985. 'Marriage in Ireland in the Twentieth Century' in A. Cosgrove (ed.), *Marriage in Ireland*, pp. 132–50. Dublin.

Walsh, B. M., 1986. 'The Growth of Government' in K. A. Kennedy (ed.), *Ireland in Transition: Economic and Social Change since 1960*, pp. 62–70. Cork.

Weinz, W., 1986. 'Economic Development and Interest Groups' in B. Girvin and R. Sturm (eds.), *Politics and Society in Contemporary Ireland*, pp. 87–101. Aldershot.

West, T., 1986. *Horace Plunkett: Co-operation and Politics: An Irish Biography*. Gerrards Cross.

Whelan, C. T., 1986. 'Class and Social Mobility' in K. A. Kennedy (ed.), *Ireland in Transition: Economic and Social Change since 1960*, pp. 81–90. Cork.

White, J., 1975. *Minority Report: The Protestant Community in the Irish Republic*. Dublin.

Whyte, J. H., 1958. *The Independent Irish Party 1850–9*. Oxford.

Whyte, J. H., 1960. 'The Influence of the Catholic Clergy on Elections in Nineteenth-Century Ireland', *English Historical Review*, lxxv, 239–59.

Whyte, J. H., 1962. 'The Appointment of Catholic Bishops in Nineteenth-Century Ireland', *Catholic Historical Review*, xlviii, 12–32.

Whyte, J. H., 1966. *The Tenant League and Irish Politics in the Eighteen-Fifties*. Dundalk.

Whyte, J. H., 1967a. 'Political Problems 1850–1860' in P. J. Corish (ed.), *A History of Irish Catholicism*, V, Fascicule 2. Dublin.

Whyte, J. H., 1967b. '1916 – Revolution and Religion' in F. X. Martin (ed.), *Leaders and Men of the Easter Rising: Dublin 1916*, pp. 215–26. London.

Whyte, J. H., 1974. 'Ireland: Politics without Social Bases' in R. Rose (ed.), *Electoral Behavior: A Comparative Handbook*, pp. 619–51. New York.

Whyte, J. H., 1978. 'Interpretations of the Northern Ireland Problem: An Appraisal', *Economic and Social Review*, ix, 257–82.

Whyte, J. H., 1980. *Church and State in Modern Ireland 1923–1979*, 2nd ed. Dublin.

Whyte, J. H., 1983a. 'How much Discrimination was there under the Unionist Regime, 1921–68?' in T. Gallagher and J. O'Connell (eds.), *Contemporary Irish Studies*, pp. 1–35. Manchester.

Whyte, J. H., 1983b. Review of Carty 1983 in *Irish Historical Studies*, xxiii, 386–7.

Wilde, W. R., 1852. *Irish Popular Superstitions*. Dublin.

Williams, T. D., 1966. 'From the Treaty to the Civil War' in T. D. Williams (ed.), *The Irish Struggle 1916–1926*, pp. 117–28. London.

Wilson, B., 1961. *Sects and Society: A Sociological Study of three Religious Groups*. London.

Winstanley, M. J., 1984. *Ireland and the Land Question 1800–1922*. London.

Woodham-Smith, Cecil, 1962. *The Great Hunger: Ireland 1845–9*. London.

Wood-Martin, W. G., 1902. *Traces of the Elder Faiths of Ireland: A Folklore Sketch*, 2 vols. London.

Woods, C. J., 1980. 'The General Election of 1892: The Catholic Clergy and the Defeat of the Parnellites' in F. S. L. Lyons and R. A. J. Hawkins (eds.), *Ireland under the Union: Varieties of Tension: Essays in Honour of T. W. Moody*, pp. 289–319. Oxford.

Younger, C., 1970. *Ireland's Civil War*. London.

Younger, C., 1981. *Arthur Griffith*. Dublin.

Zimmermann, G.-D., 1967. *Songs of Irish Rebellion: Political Street Ballads and Rebel Songs 1780–1900*. Dublin.

Index